The Culture Industry Revisited

The Culture Industry Revisited

Theodor W. Adorno on Mass Culture

Deborah Cook

ROWMAN & LITTLEFIELD PUBLISHERS, INC.

ROWMAN & LITTLEFIELD PUBLISHERS, INC.

Published in the United States of America
by Rowman & Littlefield Publishers, Inc.
4720 Boston Way, Lanham, Maryland 20706

3 Henrietta Street
London WC2E 8LU, England

We gratefully acknowledge permission to reprint the following chapters.
Chapter 1, ''The Sundered Totality,'' was published in *The Journal for the Theory of Social Behaviour* 25, no. 2 (1995). An earlier version of Chapter 3, ''Psyche under Siege'' previously appeared as ''Domination and Enlightenment: The Limits of Manipulation'' in *The Journal for the British Society of Phenomenology* 26, no. 1 (January 1995).

British Cataloging in Publication Information Available

Library of Congress Cataloging-in-Publication Data

Cook, Deborah.
The culture industry revisited : Theodor W. Adorno on mass culture / by Deborah Cook.
p.   cm.
Includes bibliographical references and index.
1. Popular culture—History—20th century.   2. Popular culture--Economic aspects.   3. Adorno, Theodor W., 1903–1969.   4. Mass media—History—20th century.   5. Mass media—Economic aspects.
I. Title.
CB427.C626   1996   909.82—dc20   95-48151   CIP

ISBN 0-8476-8154-8 (cloth : alk. paper)
ISBN 0-8476-8155-6 (pbk. : alk. paper)

Printed in the United States of America

TM   The paper used in this publication meets the minimum requirements of American National Standard for Information Sciences—Permanence of Paper for Printed Library Materials, ANSI Z39.48—1984.

Contents

Acknowledgments

Like most books, this one is as much the product of discussion and dialogue as it is of research, writing and revision. When I began, the task of composing a monograph on an author as challenging as Theodor W. Adorno seemed virtually insurmountable. The faint gleam in my eye almost faded completely as I searched for, and failed to find, translations of some of Adorno's more important essays on the culture industry. Although Adorno's *Deutsch* is notoriously difficult, I decided to translate these essays myself. In this, I was aided occasionally by Paul Piccone at *Telos*. I should also express my indebtedness to his co-editor, Gary Ulmen, who taught me a great deal that I did not know about my own language.

During an interdisciplinary seminar on the public sphere at Cornell University, I benefited from the commentary and advice of our gracious host, Peter Hohendahl—it is unfortunate that his book on Adorno appeared while this one was in press. One of the participants in the Cornell seminar, Ruth Starkman, made an invaluable contribution with her comments on the prologue. Special thanks go to my reading-group partners at the University of Windsor, Ronald Aronson and Barry Adam. Their constructive criticism of earlier versions of chapters is greatly appreciated. Gratitude is also extended to Douglas Kellner, a more transient participant in our group readings, for his constant encouragement. Sean Kelly, Mark Letteri and Philip Merklinger read parts of the final manuscript, offering their advice and ideas. And, without the moral and emotional support of many other friends, I could not have brought this project to completion.

The University of Windsor has given me as much funding for research as current financial conditions within Canadian universities now permit. Its material support enabled me to travel to Frankfurt to buy books and consult libraries. On one such trip, I had the indescribable pleasure of sitting at Adorno's piano in the Adorno Archiv. I am also grateful to the Deutscher Akademischer Austausch Dienst for funding my five-week Odyssey to Ithaca. Lastly, despite federal cut-backs to the arts, the Social Sciences and Humanities Research Council of Canada did offer me assistance in the form of a modest Standard Research Grant.

Often overlooked, the anonymous reviewers of the work I submitted to scholarly journals and presses also merit recognition. Much of their criticism was useful. An early version of Chapter 3 appeared as "Domination and Enlightenment: The Limits of Manipulation" in *The Journal for the British Society of Phenomenology* 26, no. 1 (January 1995). One of the later drafts of Chapter 1, "The Sundered Totality," was published in *The Journal for the Theory of Social Behaviour* 25, no. 2 (1995). I gratefully acknowledge the permission granted by editors Wolfe Mays and Charles Smith to incorporate in the present work those parts of the drafts which are quoted verbatim.

Prologue

Am I to blame if hallucinations and visions are alive and have
names and permanent residences?

—*Karl Kraus*

Theodor W. Adorno's work on mass culture has had a significant impact
on research in the field, influencing such media analysts as Paul Lazarsfeld and Elihu Katz. During the late thirties, Adorno also worked with
Lazarsfeld on the Princeton Radio Research Project, which was funded
by the Rockefeller Foundation and involved a study of the psychological effects of radio on listeners. In the early fifties, Adorno was employed by the Hacker Foundation where he completed qualitative content analyses of the daily astrology column in the *Los Angeles Times*
and performed similar analyses of a number of television scripts. Yet
the importance of these few empirical studies of mass culture is no
match for the influence of Adorno's theoretical work—carried out at
the Institute for Social Research—on writers as diverse as Jürgen Habermas, Christopher Lasch, Stuart Ewen, and Guy Debord. Adorno pi-
oneered the exploration of many problems currently treated today in
theories of mass culture while undertaking a comprehensive appraisal
of mass societies under late capitalism.[1]

Adorno developed his theory of mass culture over a period that spans
nearly forty years. Although he also modified and revised his work,
Adorno's restatement and rephrasing of many of its key themes and
ideas are what most often strike a careful reader. Equally impressive are
the depth and breadth of Adorno's theory. Making use of philosophy,
psychology, sociology, and economic critique, Adorno succeeded in
grasping the more important features of the relatively new phenomenon

he called the "culture industry." Far from being a culture by and for the masses—as the older folk and popular cultures once were—the culture industry is geared to profit-making, controlled by centralized interlocking corporations, and staffed with marketing and financial experts, management and production teams, technicians, "star" reporters, writers, actors, musicians, and other creative talent. Since the nineteenth and early twentieth centuries, culture has gone into mass production. Owing to the mass production of culture, hundreds of millions of people now watch the same television programs and movies, listen to the same music in recordings and on radio, and read the same newspapers and magazines. The culture industry plays a powerful role in the daily life of the vast majority of individuals in the Western world.

In an analysis creatively informed by Karl Marx's critique of political economy and Sigmund Freud's instinct theory, Adorno attempted to account for the standardization and homogenization of contemporary culture; he also described how the culture industry promotes capitalism through its ideology, even as it undertakes to satisfy the needs and interests of individuals in late capitalist societies. This book begins with a discussion of Adorno's Freudo-Marxist paradigm and proceeds to treat the three issues central to Adorno's theory of the culture industry: the production of mass culture and its commodity form, its psychological techniques, functions and effects, and its positivist ideology. Challenging many interpretations of Adorno, I also show that Adorno's theory is not obsolete; it continues to open up promising avenues for both empirical and theoretical research in many disparate fields including cultural studies and communications, political economy, psychology, and sociology.

Unfortunately, it is extremely difficult to summarize Adorno's ideas about the culture industry in the limited space of a prologue. I only hope that you have a better understanding of them once you have read this book. I shall leave you to judge Adorno's work—especially since many critics have rejected it in spite of its initial impact and in apparent disregard of its prospects. Instead of summarizing Adorno's views, I would like to discuss the impetus behind my own work. So I shall ask you to indulge me for a moment while I tell you about a disturbing vision that first began to haunt me as I watched television one evening after a day spent in class explaining Plato's parable.[2]

I seem to be shut in a place much like the one the philosopher describes in his parable. It is a large, dark cave. I am there with many other people: women and men, boys and girls. We are literally riveted to our spots by an invisible but powerful electromagnetic field which surrounds our feet and hands and immobilizes our heads. But what really astounds me is that nearly everyone there appears to be quite happy. They are drinking and eating, and occasionally laugh or call out without showing the least concern for their condition; they seem to find it quite natural. In fact, when someone does not share in the fun, the others are incensed. They hurl abuse at their grumbling neighbors and segregate them as if they had a contagious disease. Whenever something bad happens in the cave, those who complain are the first to be blamed.

We all have our backs turned to the entrance of the cave and sit facing a giant screen. Behind us are the merchants of hope and fear. They promise us power, prosperity, eternal youth, and sex appeal even as they prey on our dread of rejection and death. The spectacle that unfolds is gilded by these artful dream weavers, and fuelled by greed. Controlling the whole show are many sober and thrifty captains of industry. Scattered among them are a few well-known politicians and some religious and military leaders. Each is furnished with a supply of tiny, colored transparencies which are so well made, so many and so varied, that they entertain us with all the dramatic, comic, and picturesque scenes of life.

As I later saw, these illusionists and their assistants were standing between us and the entrance to the cave. Using a big lamp which cast the shadows of their figures on the screen at the back, they created scenes which looked so realistic that almost everyone thought they were actually happening. Sometimes we would laugh until we thought our sides would split. Other times, we cried shamelessly. But, although the spectacle seemed real, there were still a few in the crowd who suspected it was only an illusion. They tried to free themselves so they could turn around but the charlatans behind us would shout: "Sit down and keep quiet." They called the malcontents trouble-making eggheads or bleeding-heart liberals. Some other time, I'll tell you what they did to those who persisted. Right now, I'd like to describe what I saw at different times on the screen.

At first, everything was disconnected; people laughed and wept, played, drank, gambled, killed and caressed each other. Just as someone was murdered, a woman would wash her hair; or a tragic love affair would end with people drinking coffee and buying a washing machine. But, eventually, everything seemed to flow and make sense. Here is a composite of the many things I saw. After being strobed in the dark by a series of fleeting images of healthy, smiling people in beautiful surroundings, a tall, ruggedly attractive man, dressed in black and carrying some kind of weapon, rides a motorcycle right through a plate glass window in hot pursuit of another man. Bystanders scream and scatter to get out of his way. Then, as if by magic, his bike vanishes and we see him next in his luxurious apartment. He is in bed with a ravenously thin, but perfectly coiffed blonde. The vivid and sexually explicit scene that follows is shot in close-ups and accompanied by panting and moaning. A popular song also plays in the background but no one watching pays much attention. Afterwards, the man turns on a TV set where his earlier escapade just happens to be shown on the news. Somewhat annoyed, he throws a T-shirt and a tight pair of Levi's over his muscular frame, grabs his partner, and insists that she come with him. They are seen leaving his apartment in a shiny new Ford, heading straight for the dingy tenement building where the woman's former boyfriend lives.

Many women in the cave try to get a closer look at the heroine and most of the men have sucked in their stomachs. When the woman's boyfriend—a slender, unassuming man wearing wire-rimmed glasses—returns home, the couple threatens him until he fearfully agrees to let them hide out in his dilapidated studio. Once the danger has passed, they shoot him. Some of the cave-dwellers snicker at this. In the next scene, a sinister grey-haired figure, who seems to wield a mysterious power over the leading man, angrily demands that he leave the country with his girlfriend. Traveling to Europe with a suitcase full of money and weapons provided by the older character, the handsome couple enjoys a day of unbridled love-making at an expensive hotel until Interpol appears with warrants for their arrest. Our dashing hero shoots the agent in the face and the couple speeds away in a sleek Ferrari. A chase ensues but they make a daring, even miraculous, escape.

After buying new clothing to conceal their identity, the couple stops in a small village where they are soon visited by the shadowy figure seen earlier. Everyone in the village seems to know and respect him. Many of the cave-dwellers also think they recognize him. They prattle smugly to themselves, teasing others who are still scratching their heads. More images of good-looking, smiling people doing housework and eating cereal scroll across the screen. What follows is a scene where the three main characters in the drama are deciding what they should do while drinking Coke at a café. As often happens, the people in the cave begin to drink too. But now the drama is coming to an end and everyone is on the edge of their seats. In the fast-paced finale, the old patriarch is revealed to be a major underworld figure. His enemies discover his hide-out and riddle him with machine-gun fire. The hero confesses his involvement with the man and is acquitted after agreeing to name his accomplices. He and his fashionably dressed companion drive away on his motorcycle to start a new life.

People in the cave chatter excitedly about what they have seen. The women wonder where they can find clothing like the heroine's and talk about dying their hair. The men compare the cars they have driven and boast of their sexual exploits. Almost everyone thinks the drama is very life-like—even though their entire lives have been spent in front of a screen. What really frightens me is that most of my fellow cave-dwellers see life as the demagogues portray it, acting out their counter-feit fantasies while remaining paralyzed in their seats. Like a recurring nightmare, this vision has troubled me for several years. But I was more astonished than disturbed when I realized recently that the same vision often animates Adorno's work on mass culture. Adorno was plagued by the same nightmare. Perhaps readers of this book will also discover that this troubling vision speaks powerfully to their own experience as they see how Adorno transformed, in broad but clear strokes, the ancient allegory of the cave into an explosive critique of the culture industry.

The chapters that follow will describe this critique. The first chapter deals with the theoretical framework for Adorno's discussion of mass culture. In it, I profile Adorno's debts to Marx's economic analyses of capitalist societies and to Freud's work on narcissism and group psy-chology. The second chapter treats Adorno's claims about the produc-tion of mass culture; it describes Adorno's attempt to develop one of the first critiques of the political economy of the culture industry using Marx's ideas about capitalist modes of production and the commodity form. In the third chapter, I take a closer look at both the "psychotech-nics" of mass culture and the reception of cultural commodities; I also examine Adorno's views about the potential for resistance. The indus-try's growing importance as a mode of mass production is matched only by its increasing influence over the psychology of those it has helped to turn into masses.

Adorno's ideology critique of the culture industry is discussed in the fourth chapter. To the abstract identity promoted in the positivist ideol-ogy of mass culture as it falls under the sway of the exchange principle, Adorno critically opposed the speculative identity offered by ideals de-rived from enlightened thought. Basing my last chapter on these views about the culture industry's ideology, and on Adorno's ideas about its psychological techniques and political economy, I proceed with a reas-sessment of the industry and of the likelihood for resistance to it. If prospects for resistance do not appear to be very good today—

especially given the persuasiveness of the culture industry's irrational appeals to the instincts and emotions—Adorno did find a number of cracks in the homogenous surface of mass societies under late capitalism. These cracks permit an admittedly waning light to seep into the darkness of the cave.

Chapter 1

The Sundered Totality: Adorno's Freudo-Marxist Paradigm

Theodor W. Adorno frequently borrowed ideas from Sigmund Freud and Karl Marx which were useful for understanding the production, ideology, content, and reception of cultural commodities; and he did so without adopting orthodox Marxist and Freudian positions. Modifying and adapting Freud's metapsychology and Marx's critique of the political economy of capitalism, Adorno produced an elaborate theoretical framework for his work on the culture industry. However, unlike his co-worker Herbert Marcuse, who endeavored to integrate psychoanalysis and Marxism, Adorno made no systematic attempt to reconcile the two theories. According to Adorno, psychoanalysis and Marxism are incompatible because the individual and the socio-economic order of late capitalism have been "torn apart."[1] The task of a critical theory is to understand the nature of this antagonistic relationship rather than to conceal or occlude it. Martin Jay emphasizes this point when he writes: "Adorno insisted on the ideological dangers of overcoming in thought what was still split in reality, the antagonism between universal and particular."[2]

Critical of the revisionists, including Karen Horney and the later Erich Fromm, Adorno sought a material basis for his work on the culture industry. Freud's instinct (*Trieb*) psychology provided him with one such basis. Inasmuch as they are biological, the instincts or drives are distinct material forces which both shape history and are shaped by it. In *Civilization and Its Discontents*, Freud had shown that individuals often oppose, on an instinctual level, repressive social demands and obligations. Aggression and self-destructive behavior have been the his-

1

torical result. Adorno borrowed from Freud this idea of a fundamental conflict between the socio-economic and psychological realms. He also employed Freud's psychoanalytic theory to explain many of the psychological techniques, functions, and effects of nazism and cultural commodities. Using similar techniques, such as the reanimation of superego introjects, Nazi leaders and the culture industry both solicit and repress the instincts, encouraging them to conform to and harmonize with the goals and interests of the existing socio-economic order.

Adorno speculated that both nazism and the culture industry work on a depth-psychological level, reinforcing the narcissism he claimed was symptomatic of individuals under late capitalism. Lacking sufficient ego autonomy, narcissistic individuals are virtually defenseless against the culture industry's libidinally charged techniques. As the historian Alan Bullock has observed with respect to nazism, demagogues like Hitler "aimed to appeal not to the rational but to the emotional faculties, those 'affective interests,' against which (as Freud pointed out) students of human nature and philosophers had long recognized that logical arguments were impotent."[3] Like these demagogues, the culture industry also calls into play not only emotions but also irrational and often self-destructive instincts, undermining rational thought and rational self-interest. Although they are not the direct cause of the weak narcissistic ego, nazism and cultural commodities do exploit it, thwarting the capacity to resist repression by offering satisfactions which are often enough to placate individuals under late capitalism.

If Freud's theory of drives provided Adorno with one material basis for his theory of the culture industry, the economic relations which Marx criticized in his work on capitalism offered him another. The individual psyche targeted by the culture industry invariably reveals the scars inflicted by the demands and obligations of late capitalist societies. Moreover, Adorno argued that "not only the individual, but even the category of individuality, is a product of society."[4] A social and historical construct, this category now often serves only to underscore the weakness of the isolated human being in relation to society; the concept has become increasingly vacuous, a nearly empty place-holder for a potentially resistive force. Individual psychology has been affected by developments within capitalism—including the growth of the culture industry—to such an extent that the individual has regressed "to the state of a mere social object."[5]

Marx's analysis of the modes and relations of capitalist production, his theory of class society, and his work on the commodity form provided Adorno with the conceptual tools he needed to grasp the "extra-

psychic'' connections between the individual and the totally administered world of capitalism. Although he believed that capitalism had
reached a new stage in the twentieth century, especially as the exchange
principle began to extend into areas of life that had formerly been immune from or resistant to it, Adorno adopted many of Marx's critical
insights about the nature of capitalist societies. As social facts, both
individual psychology and the culture industry must be framed within
this larger socio-economic context. Where the individual psyche had
been weakened by reification and the loss of economic autonomy, the
''culture industry sprang from the profit-making tendency of capital.''
Today the industry continues to churn out standardized products for
distribution and exchange on the market. Packaging culture as a commodity for narcissistic consumption, the culture industry has attempted
to prevent individuals ''from coming to consciousness of themselves as
subjects.''[6]

Adorno's critique of the culture industry begins in 1932 with one of
his early essays, ''On the Social Situation of Music,'' and ends with his
1969 essay ''Free Time.'' Although it was developed and modified,
Adorno's work on mass culture demonstrates a remarkable degree of
consistency. On the psychological level, the culture industry's impact
on consciousness is often mediated by the superego; the superego's
introjects are reanimated by a number of images, themes, and ideas in
cultural commodities. However, since the regressive traits and object
cathexes that are called into play in response to the culture industry
also have a history within capitalism, the narcissistic tendencies Adorno
diagnosed must themselves be viewed in light of the larger historical
context of social and economic exploitation and oppression. It is to the
latter that I shall now turn.

Late Capitalist Societies

If, as Marx held, the individual is conditioned (or ''determined'') by
economic factors—or the totality of the relations of production—then
the first task of a critical theory of culture is to understand this larger
''extra-psychic'' socio-economic state of affairs. Adorno hoped that social psychology itself would ultimately ''uncover the decisive social
forces at work in the innermost mechanisms of the individual'' (RP,
27). Although its approach is one-sided, Adorno wrote: ''The truth of
the whole sides with one-sidedness. . . : a psychology that turns its back
on society and idiosyncratically concentrates on the individual and his

archaic heritage says more about the hapless state of society than one which seeks by its 'wholistic approach' or an inclusion of social 'factors' to join the ranks of a no longer existent *universitas literarum*'' (SP1, 70). Social psychology can show how the culture industry has been able to play an increasingly important role in individual psychology by rooting out the socio-economic forces which have already penetrated and shaped consciousness. Understanding these forces also helps to explain how nazism became so powerful in Germany.

Many commentators have misunderstood Adorno's discussion of the extra-psychic connection between the individual and society. So, for example, Jürgen Habermas argues that the "Freudo-Marxism of the earlier Frankfurt School could conceptually integrate psychology and sociology only through the mechanism of internalization.''[7] By contrast, Adorno maintained that the integration of the individual through a process like internalization was possible only because individual psychology is already partially shaped by the capitalist system. If the individual were not, from the beginning, an integral part of this system, he or she would be far less amenable to its offers of satisfaction. The individual is antagonistic to capitalism because of its ungratified biological instincts which have a potentially resistive force. Yet, it is also, in some measure, a social, political, and economic construct. The uneasy integration of the individual into society has a history in the vicissitudes of socio-economic domination (through exploitation and repression) which explain why resistance has so often failed to take place.

In *Eros and Civilization*, Herbert Marcuse attempted to trace the phylogenetic and extra-psychic roots of domination in his reading of Freud's speculative hypothesis of the murder of the primal father. However, Adorno could not accept Marcuse's reading of *Totem and Taboo*.[8] Marcuse failed to see that, in his "leap from psychological images to historical reality," Freud forgot "that all reality undergoes modification upon entering the unconscious." He ended up turning purely psychological events into factual or objective ones.[9] Still, although he rejected the claim that the murder of the primal father was a factual, extra-psychic event, Adorno did discover extra-psychic bases for the repression of instincts. In late capitalist societies, it is the economic impotence of the father and reification which partially explain the current state of individual psychology.

Critical theorists discussed the first of these economic factors shaping individual psychology in their well-known thesis of the fatherless society. In the heyday of bourgeois liberalism, socio-economic domination was mediated through the father whose values and norms, reflecting his individual economic interests, were introjected or internalized by his children. The father *could* play the role of a purveyor of norms because he had a certain degree of autonomy with respect to the capitalist system. However, with changes in the market economy—its increasing centralization in monopolies and its growing collaboration with the state—the place of the bourgeois entrepreneur within the system was undermined. Russell Jacoby explains that "the individual of 'classic' psychoanalysis managed to eke an existence out of the relatively undeveloped market. . . . With the centralization and synchronization of the market, the individual lost its relatively independent and private sources of sustenance."[10] As wage-laborers or salaried employees who are increasingly dependent on the often fickle largesse of the state and corporations for the means of their subsistence, individuals are now largely in thrall to a new ruling class. Today, domination is exercised through new and different conduits.

Before proceeding to examine more closely Adorno's description of the economic changes which contributed to the erosion of the family in late capitalism, I should parenthetically address an objection which is sometimes leveled against his views: his alleged "nostalgia for the family." On this critical view, Adorno turned the bourgeois, patriarchal family into an ideal or norm. However, the problem with this criticism is that it mistakenly characterizes Adorno's ideas about the patriarchal family as *pre*scriptive. In fact, Adorno was *de*scribing a state of affairs which he claimed had existed for roughly two and a half centuries. He was by no means advocating a return to this state of affairs—an impossibility in any case—but he wanted it to be seen in both its positive and negative features. Viewed positively, Adorno contended that the bourgeois patriarchal family fostered a certain degree of independent decision-making and rational self-control. He valued this ego-autonomy because it offered the potential for resistance. Such autonomy can now be realized, not by reverting or regressing to a former state, but by progressing to a new one. Adorno would claim that what has happened to the family today is the historical consequence of the existence of that same bourgeois patriarchal family which had allowed for a certain degree of autonomy in the first place.[11]

Socialization agencies other than the family began to play an increasingly pivotal role in individual development at the end of the nineteenth and beginning of the twentieth centuries. In their chapter on anti-Semitism in *Dialectic of Enlightenment*, Horkheimer and Adorno described some of the changing economic factors which led to this situation in Germany:

When the big industrial interests incessantly eliminate the economic basis for moral decision, partly by eliminating the independent economic subject, partly by taking over the self-employed tradesmen, and partly by transforming the works [*sic*: workers] into objects in trade unions, reflective thought must also die out. . . . There is no object left for the conscience because the responsibility of the individual for himself and his family is replaced by his contribution to the apparatus, even if the old moral assumptions are retained.[12]

Adorno and Horkheimer argued that similar changes had also occurred in non-totalitarian societies.

These economic changes in both totalitarian and non-totalitarian states led to a different type of socio-economic stratification which Adorno discussed in his 1942 essay "Reflexionen zur Klassentheorie."[13] In Adorno's version of the "new world order," a new ruling group or élite, combining the interests of industrial and business monopolies with those of the state, emerged over and against the mass of individuals which now included both the bourgeoisie and the proletariat. This more developed stage of the class society originally analyzed by Marx is "dominated by monopolies; it presses towards fascism, to the form of political organization it deserves." It represents a much more polarized form of domination; the latest form of socio-economic stratification "vindicates the theory of class struggle with monopolization and centralization, directly placing in complete opposition to each other the most extreme power against the most extreme powerlessness" (RK, 376).

In his discussion of this more recent form of class society, Adorno described the "dictatorship of the self-appointed élite" as that of an "anonymous class." In much of his work, Adorno also used the adjective "abstract" to qualify the forms of domination he discovered in the United States and Western Europe. The ruling class has "disappeared behind the concentration of capital." Monopoly capital now appears as an "institution" which subsumes the individual by abstracting from its distinctive qualities (RK, 380). The resulting reification exacerbates the problem of seeing through class relations. In fact, one of the things that has changed in relation to Marx's analysis of class society is that the exploited are no longer able "to experience themselves as a class" (RK 377). Given the proletariat's de facto amalgamation with the bourgeoisie and the more generalized lack of class consciousness, those who profit most from the impersonal rule of the exchange principle are left free to pursue their own interests.

It is in part the "abstract" character of domination which signals the transition from the earlier stage of capitalism described by Marx to what Adorno described as late capitalist and industrial society.[14] Today, more contemporary writers claim to have discerned a further transition within capitalism from manufacturing or industrial to service and information-based economies. However, it would be difficult to maintain that this shift toward "techno-capitalism" marks a qualitatively new stage in capitalism because, as Douglas Kellner writes: "many systematic features of the phenomena of 'organized capitalism' analyzed by Hilferding and the environment of capitalism analyzed by Critical Theory . . . remain the same."[15] Like its predecessor, techno-capitalism represents the interests of "corporate domination and profitability, and thus continues to follow the imperatives of capitalist logic."[16] In techno-capitalism, capital follows its earlier trend toward increasing concentration and centralization; mass society obdurately conceals class relations; and the balance of power characteristic of late capitalism persists. Domination is perpetrated by an abstract "them" concealed behind the corporate and monopoly capital that is undergirded by the welfare state.

The impact which these changes have had on the family is profound. The economic power which parents once wielded in the high liberal era commanded respect from their children. It also motivated rebellion against the reality principle they represented. Parents were figures who were both emulated and resisted. By contrast, in late capitalist societies, the father has become a simple functionary and no longer serves as an authority figure. His children neither introject his values nor measure their strength against him by resisting him. For Adorno, the real problem in the new "fatherless" society is that the "forces of opposition" within it have become paralyzed (*MM*, 23). The rise of nazism can largely be explained by this paralysis in the forces of opposition resulting from economic changes in capitalist societies. But, as Martin Jay observes, even after the collapse of nazism, "the psychological impediments to emancipation could no longer be ignored by radical analysts of the manipulated society of mass consumption that seemed to follow in its wake."[17]

Adorno was among the first theorists to point out the parallels between the socio-economic situation in Nazi Germany and that in less totalitarian countries. This situation, characterized as it is by new forms and modalities of domination, has made the techniques of mass psychology more effective in both parts of the Western world. Nazi leaders and the culture industry play on the emotions, on irrational impulses and drives, undermining critical and rational thought, and they do so on a mass scale. There is a "regression to illogical judgment" as "stereotypes replace individual categories" (*DE*, 201), and individuals identify with "stereotyped value scales" (*DE*, 198). The fatherless society is one in which conformity to these external and stereotypical figures is more easily fostered.

Adorno's work on the problems facing the family under late capitalism approaches these problems from a perspective which should not be conflated with the liberal one found in many works of sociology and history. Adorno—and critical theorists in general—frequently reiterated the claim that the socio-economic realm (often in the form of socialization agencies) increasingly intervened in family life, making a mockery of the family's former independence. The picture of society which emerges from this difference in perspective can, of course, be corroborated empirically—as David Riesman, for example, has done in *The Lonely Crowd*.[18] But to adopt this perspective also obliges one to reconsider the liberal values implicit in the other view. Christopher Lasch writes that, for critical theorists, the "sanctity of the home is a sham in a world dominated by giant corporations and the apparatus of mass production."[19] Assailed by powerful social and economic forces beyond its control, the family's ability to foster ego autonomy and spontaneity has collapsed.

The second extra-psychic factor which helps to explain the individual's uneasy "integration" into the socio-economic order is found in its virtually complete subsumption under the exchange principle. Individuals have become as fungible as any of the commodities they produce or purchase. Their relations both to themselves and to others now fall under the sway of the abstract identity of the exchange principle. If Adorno adopted Marx's analysis of the commodity form, he also followed Georg Lukács who extended this analysis, applying it to areas of social and cultural life formerly resistant to capitalist modes of production where "abstract labor" is sold on the market as a commodity. Individuals now measure their own self-worth in terms of both the commodities they buy and their place within the economic system. Interpersonal relations have also been affected. In their capacity as "economic subjects," individuals "do not relate to one another at all immediately but act according to the dictates of exchange-value" (SP1, 74). Human relations become increasingly reified as individuals are reduced to the "agents and bearers of exchange value" (S, 148–49).

What results from this abstract identity are individuals who are no longer really "individuated" but who appear as interchangeable social objects. For Adorno, as I have already indicated, both the concept and the reality of individuality have become a sham. Adorno put his own spin on this Lukácsian idea concerning the effects of reification on consciousness in the following bleak passage from *Minima Moralia*:

> Only when the process that begins with the metamorphosis of labour-power into a commodity has permeated men through and through and objectified each of their impulses as formally commensurable variations of the exchange relationship, is it possible for life to reproduce itself under the prevailing relations of production. Its consummate organization demands the coordination of people that are dead. (*MM*, 229)

Of course, Adorno did not share Lukács's view that increased reification would serve as the precondition for revolutionary praxis. Owing to its inability to penetrate the reality of domination, the proletariat offered little hope for radical change.

Unlike Habermas, who contends that the economic realm has a logic of its own which cannot ultimately corrupt the "lifeworld," Adorno continued to affirm Marx's views about the primacy of the economic, instrumental sphere within Western societies. In Adorno's work, the primacy of the economy compromises the independent status of the interpersonal lifeworld which Habermas maintains has structurally differentiated itself from the system and its steering media of money and power. Reification, which grows as the exchange principle becomes increasingly pervasive, results in the degradation of relations between people into relations between things. Under late capitalism, "people are really atomized and separated from each other by an unbridgeable chasm" (RP, 35). As Freud implicitly saw, interpersonal relations "issue neither from their [individuals'] free will nor from their instincts but from social and economic laws which prevail over their heads" (RP, 36).

Adorno located the "sociological root" of narcissism in the individual's compulsion "to direct his unutilized instinctual energy against himself because virtually insurmountable difficulties lie in the way of any spontaneous and direct relationship between people today" (RP, 33). Although Habermas recognizes that the lifeworld has been colonized, that "the subsystems of the economy and state have become more and more complex as a consequence of capitalist growth, and penetrate ever deeper into the symbolic reproduction of the lifeworld," [20] he understates the damage such colonization has inflicted on the sphere of interpersonal relations and does not examine it in any detail. Once he has redefined reification, Habermas does admit that it can and does have pathological consequences in the lifeworld but he neither specifies with any rigor or depth what such consequences might be nor is his recommendation that these pathologies be explained by object-relations theory and ego psychology unproblematic. Habermas lacks the theoretical framework necessary to explain the specific and widely documented pathologies (especially narcissism) suffered by individuals in industrial societies—pathologies which Adorno first diagnosed.[21]

The continued primacy of the economy in Adorno's critical theory calls into question the integrity of the intersubjective realm—a realm which holds out as much promise for Habermas as it once did for Lukács. Communicative rationality, which presupposes a thriving lifeworld, is therefore equally compromised. In an article published in 1975, Pietro Bellasi contends that, whereas the everyday lifeworld once had an autonomy which meant that reification was experienced in the residues of unhappy consciousness, at present this lifeworld has been reduced to a pure abstraction: "As the last remains of unhappy consciousness dissolve. . . , individuality itself seeks its own definitive dissolution in the abstract pseudo-totality of the everyday. . . ; eaten away by reification, individuality is only an encrustation of object worlds."[22] Having theoretically uncoupled system from lifeworld, Habermas is obliged to claim: "Systematic imperatives do not so much insinuate themselves into the family, establish themselves in systematically distorted communication, and inconspicuously intervene in the formation of the self as, rather, openly come at the family from the outside."[23] By contrast, for Adorno, what Habermas calls lifeworld has not been uncoupled from system. It has been robbed of the little autonomy it may once have had by the often insidious incursions of the newly allied economic and political systems.

A number of influential commentators have maintained that some critical theorists, including Adorno, did not share Marx's emphasis on the primacy of the economic sphere. Instead, critical theorists are alleged to have given equal, or sometimes greater, stress to the "superstructural" realm. Along with Friedrich Pollock, Adorno and Horkheimer supposedly believed that "The replacement of the economic means by political means . . . signifies the transition from a predominantly economic to an essentially political era."[24] Although this trend could be observed more easily in the Third Reich, Pollock claimed that it was also visible in non-totalitarian states. According to Helmut Dubiel, in their *Dialectic of Enlightenment*, Adorno and Horkheimer adapted Pollock's argument to their own theory, arguing that "domination in highly developed, industrial societies no longer assumes an economic form, as in liberalism, but rather an immediately political form, as in the pre-bourgeois era.''[25]

Pollock's analysis was directly challenged by Franz Neumann in his *Behemoth*. Based on his detailed critique of economic structures and operations in the Third Reich, Neumann concluded that ''the antagonisms of capitalism are operating in Germany on a higher and, therefore, a more dangerous level, even if these antagonisms are covered up by a bureaucratic apparatus and by the ideology of the people's community.''[26] Dubiel's claim that Adorno adopted Pollock's belief in the primacy of political over economic factors is based solely on Dubiel's somewhat questionable reading of *Dialectic of Enlightenment*. That Adorno does not entirely share Pollock's view is evident in essays like ''Late Capitalism or Industrial Society.'' In this late work, Adorno did argue that ''the dynamics of the system as a whole'' reveal that ''the control of economic processes is increasingly becoming a function of political power.'' On a general level then, and in terms of very general tendencies, there is a move toward political domination. Nonetheless, ''there are compelling facts which cannot, in their turn, be adequately interpreted *without* invoking the key concept of 'capitalism.' Human beings are, as much as ever, ruled and dominated by the economic process.''[27]

In the realm of human behavior, domination often assumes the psychological form of repression because it is partially bound up with instincts. But, although the instincts form part of the individual psyche, they are also thoroughly affected by economic factors. As Adorno wrote in ''Sociology and Psychology,'' there is an ''undeniable priority of economic over psychological moments in the sphere of human behaviour'' (SP1, 72). On this point, Martin Jay remarks: ''however much he [Adorno] may have moved away from the orthodox Marxist primacy of the economy, he would frequently remind his readers of its continued importance in a still essentially capitalist world.''[28] In the ''final analysis,'' the psychological reality of repression finds its basis in the reality of economic exploitation and the domination of the exchange principle. Furthermore, Adorno did not wait until 1968 and his essay on late capitalism to make this point. As early as 1951, in *Minima Moralia*, Adorno had claimed that the primacy of the economy in decision-making could be demonstrated everywhere (*MM*, 112–13). This means that the critique of political economy remains in principle as essential a feature in Adorno's analysis as it was in Marx's. Unfortunately, it was this very critique which remained underdeveloped in Adorno's own work.

The lasting importance of economic factors in Adorno's analysis is matched by his insistence on the survival of a society stratified into classes despite the lack of class consciousness and the "massification" of society. For Adorno, mass society is simply the latest manifestation of the class society Marx first investigated; it brings Marx's class society to fruition. With the new socio-economic order, "the division of society into exploiters and exploited not only continues to exist but gains in force and strength" (RK, 377). As an amalgamation of the bourgeoisie and the proletariat, the new "mass class" confronts a political and economic élite which "oppresses both those who support it and the worker with the same police threat, imposes on them the same function and the same need, and thus makes it virtually impossible for workers to see through the class relation" (RK, 380).

In his *Mass Society*, Salvador Giner accused Adorno (and Critical theory in general) of adopting a conservative mass society theory in which the term "mass" serves as an abusive epithet for the lower class.[29] This lower class is supposedly characterized in part by its appetite for the vulgar and mediocre products of the culture industry. Adorno and his co-workers are alleged to have held an élitist view of a high and a low culture; as members of the privileged upper-middle class, they viewed themselves as capable of appreciating the former, while the "masses," or lower-class "rabble," were capable only of understanding the latter. In general, according to Giner, the "intellectual left" has succumbed to an aristocratic and anti-populist mass culture vision; its "often unrecognized debt to the conservative critique of modern popular culture, from Arnold to Eliot, is immense."[30]

It is, however, clear from his discussion in "Reflexionen zur Klassentheorie" that Adorno included both workers and the bourgeoisie among those he occasionally labeled the "masses." In addition, although the masses are an amalgamation of both classes, Adorno does not use the concept to refer to a homogeneous group, nor does it replace the Marxist notion of class. It is still possible to speak of classes because of the continued existence of economic exploitation. Adorno wrote: "Screened from subjectivity, the difference between the classes grows objectively with the increasing concentration of capital" (S, 150). Nonetheless, owing to the bourgeoisie's loss of economic autonomy, to the veil screening economic exploitation, and the effects of reification, two different socio-economic strata have become a "mass," confronting anonymous political and economic powers which impose the same laws on both. Mass society is the historical outgrowth and continuation of class society. In it, economic exploitation and domination by "abstract'' political and economic forces have become far more ubiquitous than they were in Marx's time.

As for the charge that Adorno is a cultural élitist and has a conservative view of the lower class, a few words will suffice to show that this accusation must be carefully qualified. Pseudo-culture—the historical successor to what was once ''high'' culture—is, in Adorno's words, ''spirit overcome by fetishism of commodities.''[31] No one and nothing are immune from commodity fetishism. The commodification and reification of culture has affected even those who once belonged to the privileged and ''happy few'' (as the extensive marketing and commodified consumption of works of ''high culture'' decisively shows). Adorno calls the belief that ''anyone—and by this one always means oneself—might be exempt from the tendency to socialized pseudo-culture'' a conceited illusion (PC, 37). Just as ''mass society'' is the historical outgrowth of class society, so too ''mass culture'' is the historical consequence of ''class culture.'' There is no escape from either.

Furthermore, according to Adorno, it is ''the stratum of middle class white-collar workers'' which provides ''the model of pseudo-culture'' (PC, 22). With the increase in their standard of living, these workers want to be considered part of the upper class and ''pretend to have a culture which in fact they do not'' (PC, 29). Far from impugning the lower classes exclusively, then, Adorno also targeted the bourgeoisie. He described this class as suffering from the narcissism he attributed to the erosion of the bourgeois patriarchal family. Members of the middle class attempt to compensate for the loss of their power in the economic realm by ''turning themselves either in fact or imagination into members of something higher and more encompassing to which they attribute qualities which they themselves lack and from which they profit by vicarious participation'' (PC, 33). Commodified culture offers the economically disempowered middle class the narcissistic illusion that it still has power and prestige.[32]

The Narcissistic Individual

Economic changes in industrial societies, accompanied by the father's loss of authority and reification, prepared the way for the mass psychology of nazism and the culture industry. Adorno claimed that Freud had anticipated important aspects of this new mass psychology in his 1921 essay, ''Group Psychology and the Analysis of the Ego.'' Adorno wrote: ''According to Freud, the problem of mass psychology is closely

related to the new type of psychological affliction so characteristic of
the era which for socio-economic reasons witnesses the decline of the
individual and his subsequent weakness."[33] This new psychological affliction is, of course, that of narcissism. With the decline of the father's
authority, the Oedipus complex—that psychosexual stage in which the
superego is formed and object cathexes more firmly established—
remains unresolved "and the satisfaction of the instincts is partially or
totally withdrawn from other people."[34]

Although Adorno's work is short on empirical detail, Christopher
Lasch has supplemented Adorno's theory in many important respects.
For example, Lasch pointed to more recent clinical evidence which indicates that narcissistic tendencies arise *after* the child has succeeded
in distinguishing or separating itself from objects; ego formation has
therefore already been initiated. If the child experiences its separation
from objects as intensely painful, it will attempt to recover its sense of
omnipotence and of symbiotic fusion with the mother characteristic of
the stage of primary narcissism in which there are two sexual objects—
the mother and the ego—and the boundaries between them are not
fixed.[35] According to Lasch, in this regression to primary narcissism,
children of both sexes reject "the Oedipal solution to the problem of
separation, in which the child renounces the fantasy of an immediate
reunion with the mother in the hope of growing up into adult roles that
promise something of the same potency once associated with the infantile illusion of self-sufficiency."[36]

Pathological narcissism thus presupposes the development of an ego
but it is an ego which is constantly regressing to the more undifferentiated state of primary narcissism. Furthermore, although the Oedipal
solution is rejected, Lasch observes that a superego also develops in
narcissistic individuals:

> The decline of parental authority and of external sanctions in general,
> while in many ways it weakens the superego, paradoxically reinforces the
> aggressive, dictatorial elements in the superego and thus makes it more
> difficult than ever for instinctual desires to find acceptable outlets. The
> "decline of the superego" in a permissive society is better understood as
> the creation of a new kind of superego in which archaic elements predomi-
> nate.[37]

Lasch maintains that the archaic content of what is introjected into the
narcissistic superego consists in "images of the parents," or "parental
introjects instead of identifications" which are fused with "grandiose

self-images.''[38] These introjected and archaic representations of the parents are ''unmitigated by reality'' and so include images of an ''all-powerful father'' and a ''primitive mother.''[39]

Adorno's explanation for the psychological attraction of Nazi leaders in ''Freudian Theory and the Pattern of Fascist Propaganda'' relied on a similar view of superego introjects. The Nazi follower had formed in his or her superego the image of ''an omnipotent and unbridled father figure, by far transcending the individual father and therewith apt to be enlarged into a 'group ego' '' (FT, 124). The follower's libido is completely invested in this image which the Nazi leader reanimates and uses to generate both positive and negative emotions. Generating negative emotions toward out-groups results in a narcissistic gain which suggests ''that the follower, simply through belonging to the in-group, is better, higher and purer than those who are excluded'' (FT, 130). This narcissistic gain can also be seen in the pseudo-cultured who derive from the culture industry the sense of being part of an elect group: ''The pseudo-cultured person counts himself among the saved; among the damned is everything which might call his reign—and everything connected with it—into question'' (PC, 35).

Unfortunately, Adorno's discussion of narcissism provided only a bare sketch of this pathology. Furthermore, unlike Adorno, contemporary psychoanalysts often distinguish between identification and introjection (or internalization), as well as between the superego and the ego ideal. In postulating the independent existence of an ego ideal, analysts—such as Janine Chasseguet-Smirgel in her *The Ego Ideal*—have focused on Freud's 1914 essay ''On Narcissism.'' In this essay, Freud claimed that the ego ideal represents the image of early narcissistic perfection and self-sufficiency. Contemporary theorists contrast the generally positive content of this ideal to the negative and punitive content of the superego which they view as the outgrowth of the later Oedipal stage. According to C. Fred Alford, Béla Grunberger also distinguishes between identification with the ego ideal and the introjection of moral commands in the superego. Identification is a less mature psychological mechanism which involves '' 'borrowing' the goodness of another rather than making it one's own.''[40]

In the view of these more contemporary Freudian theorists, the concept of the ego ideal is indispensable. They believe that the early infantile desire for omnipotence and self-sufficiency can become transformed into ''a loving exploration of the world through art, playful scientific curiosity, and the activities of nurture and cultivation.''[41] The newer theories of narcissism therefore deny that narcissism is solely a regressive and pathological phenomenon; it may also take a progressive form. Alford argues that in the more mature form of narcissism, the ego can reconcile itself with its ego ideal, achieving psychic wholeness. The "progressive" form of narcissism "reminds us that even modern lives have the potential (generally unrealized) for narrative unity, understood as a lifelong quest for self- perfection via the pursuit of ideal values."[42] However, Alford makes clear that the mature solution to narcissism will become possible for the majority of individuals only when social and economic conditions change.

The newer theories contend that a mature reconciliation of the ego with its ideal can occur. They also indirectly point to the fact that Adorno's views about the more regressive form of narcissism need to be supplemented and revised, though not abandoned. Adorno was satisfied with a very general analysis of the pathology of narcissism, seeing it as an impediment to resistance against the totally administered world. The successful resolution of the Oedipal complex in the bourgeois patriarchal family meant that the child gained a certain amount of ego autonomy which allowed it to resist authority. Once the family's central role as an agent of socialization had been undermined, ego autonomy was compromised and individual resistance to external forces diminished. In recent history, these external forces have appeared in various forms of demagoguery which exploit the narcissistic ego by targeting the positive and negative contents of its superego introjects. As Freud had shown, narcissists are particularly inclined to distinguish themselves from out-groups. This symptom of narcissism underscores the weakness of the ego which, by focusing "hostility upon the out-group, does away with intolerance in one's own group to which one's relation would otherwise be highly ambivalent" (FT, 130).

A much more influential critique of Adorno's analysis of individual psychology within late capitalism can be found in Jessica Benjamin's work. In her well-known essay "The End of Internalization," Benjamin claims that, for Adorno, "narcissism is a weakness of the ego, a diminution of its conscious cognitive side which replaces internalization as the cause of compliance."[43] On Benjamin's reading, Adorno maintained that domination had become direct or unmediated owing to the weakness of the narcissistic ego. However, this so-called "direct domination"—a phrase Adorno did in fact use[44]—resulting from the loss of the mediating influence of the father as the object of internalization, continues to be mediated by the image of the ferocious, all-consuming parent which is drawn from infantile experiences of frustration resulting from the child's separation from the objects of its desires. It is this image which Nazi leaders and many products of the culture industry reanimate and with which the masses identify. Often undifferentiated from grandiose images of the self in the narcissistic superego, the image of the primal father is externalized in the Nazi leader or in the "sinister father images"[45] of television and film. In these cases, then, domination is mediated by the superego. For Adorno, "society extends repressively into all psychology in the form of censorship and superego" (SP2, 79).

In her later essay, "Authority and the Family Revisited," Benjamin also rejects the view that the internalization of the father's values during the resolution of the Oedipus complex leads to ego autonomy. She cites empirical studies which show that such internalization is still widespread among the middle classes. Moreover, internalization has been found to make children *more* dependent on authority rather than less. In contrast to Adorno, Benjamin maintains that what accounts for the current diminution in ego autonomy is the "breakup of kin-group ties and other networks, especially among women." Closer affective relationships "would provide personal solidarity rather than impersonally mediated expertise."[46] As women have become "more isolated and lonely in their mothering activity," they have often demanded from their children "the appearance of self-reliance with a lack of true independence: internalization of individuality as an ideal rather than a reality."[47]

The role mothers play in the development of ego autonomy was only indirectly acknowledged in such works as *The Authoritarian Personality*.[48] However, Adorno does make passing reference to the importance for ego autonomy of the pre-Oedipal stage of psycho-sexual development. Citing Freud in "Group Psychology and the Analysis of the Ego," Adorno wrote that a pre-Oedipal identification with an archaic father image might explain the attraction of the Nazi leader: "Since the child's identification with his father as an answer to the Oedipus complex is only a secondary phenomenon, infantile regression may go beyond this father image and through an 'anaclitic' process reach a more archaic one" (FT 125). Adorno thought that this hypothesis called for further clarification which he himself did not provide. Had he explored this hypothesis, he might have realized that there were other factors in pre-Oedipal development which are responsible for ego autonomy or the lack thereof. Adorno's view that ego autonomy results from the internalization of the father's moral commands does need to be reassessed.

If accepted, Benjamin's thesis in "Authority and the Family Revisited" would not require a complete revision of Adorno's theory—

especially if her claim that Adorno replaced internalization with direct domination is rejected. Both she and Adorno believe that the family is crucial for the development of ego autonomy. For both, essentially the same social and economic conditions are responsible for changes in the family and these changes have similar psychological consequences. At issue is which factor mediates between socio-economic conditions and the loss of ego autonomy: is it the instrumentalization of mother love in a "patriarchy without the father,"[49] or is it the father's loss of authority? As a third alternative, one might also suggest that the diminution in ego autonomy results from a combination of both factors. Whatever answer is given to this question, the real problem, for both Benjamin and Adorno, is the lack of ego autonomy with its roots in transformations in the family, especially in parental roles and functions.

According to Adorno, the narcissistic ego that results from these transformations does not adequately distinguish between itself and its objects and regresses to an infantile state in which it is more vulnerable to the demands of both the id and the superego. This vulnerability can be glimpsed indirectly in the narcissist's ambivalence toward authority figures. He or she identifies with them and resents them at one and the same time. Else Frenkel-Brunswik described the consequences of this ambivalence in *The Authoritarian Personality*:

> A person possessed by such ambivalence may easily be kept in check and may even behave in an exemplary fashion in following those external authorities who take over the function of the superego—and partly even those of the ego. On the other hand, if permitted to do so by outside authority, the same person may be induced very easily to uncontrolled release of his instinctual tendencies, especially those of destructiveness.[50]

Ego weakness, exploited by external agencies and forces, allows the superego and the id to play a far greater role in individual psychology than they did in the past.

Although the ego still carries out repression on the orders of the superego, Adorno thought it had regressed so much toward "what Freud called ego-libido" that its role as the agent of repression had been undermined (SP2, 87). Owing to this ego weakness, an alliance between the superego and id is formed, and the superego "arbitrarily breaks off the process of psychoanalytic enlightenment" (SP2, 85). Since the work of making conscious to the ego the unconscious processes in the id is obstructed, the individual's "crude, undifferentiated unconscious happily co-operates with the organized standardization without" (SP1,

79–80). The gratification of drives becomes subject to the approval of a superego whose introjects are targeted by extra-familial agents and forces. Political leaders, demagogues, and the culture industry take advantage of the weakness of the narcissistic ego, harnessing the instincts and reinforcing superego introjects. They need not resort to overt manipulation and control but simply exploit an already existing psychological pathology.

The superego not only contains images of father and mother figures; it is also the locus of moral commands and norms. Although Christopher Lasch contests the view that the superego is the "representative of established morality" for the rather weak reason that parental introjects in the superego "bear little resemblance to the actual figures of the parents,"[51] Adorno (following Freud) clearly believed that the superego consists in introjected norms and values. Lasch recognizes that child-rearing functions have been assumed more and more "by surrogate parents responsible not to the family but to the state, to private industry, or to their own codes of professional ethics." This means that "the advertising industry, the mass media, the health and welfare services, and other agencies of mass tuition took over many of the socializing functions of the home."[52] But, for Lasch, the increasingly important role of these socialization agencies does not imply that their moral codes serve as introjects in the superego. By contrast, Adorno believed that because fascist leaders and the culture industry reanimate the image of the primal father, their values and norms play a role in the superego owing to the ego's mediated identification with them.[53] Such identification undermines the individual's ability to make decisions which are in his or her own self-interest.

Adorno's study of narcissism had a controversial counterpart in the series of studies which culminated in *The Authoritarian Personality*. Like the narcissist, the authoritarian personality, targeted by Nazi leaders and the culture industry, is characterized by ambivalence. He or she both submits to authority out of fear and wants to dominate out-groups because of its resentment toward authority. An important question raised by some critics concerns the genesis of this character type. Is the authoritarian personality the outgrowth of authoritarian families or is it the product of weak family relations? In the work Adorno did on narcissism, it is clear that weak families are responsible for this pathology. However, there is an ambiguity in *The Authoritarian Personality* itself which might lead to the conclusion that strong families produce authoritarian character types in late capitalist societies.

This ambiguity has been convincingly described and documented.

In their methodological critique of *The Authoritarian Personality*, for example, Herbert Hyman and Paul Sheatsley point out that Adorno and his co-workers "implicitly" regard the authoritarian personality "as a product of *actual familial experience*." Basing their work on the subjective reports of the people they interviewed, research team members "oscillate between the view that these reports have only a *psychological* reality in conveying the subject's personality, and the view that they have *objective* reality as an accurate description of the subject's actual family life."[54] Hyman and Sheatsley do not think it is possible to derive any information about the genesis of the authoritarian personality from the subjective reports of the interviewees. The question of the type of family which produces this personality structure remains unanswered.

In *Haven in a Heartless World*, Christopher Lasch often appeared to believe that Adorno and his co-workers simply assumed the authoritarian personality was the product of strong authoritarian families. While it is clear that Lasch was wrong here—the ambiguity in the research team's description of the genesis of the authoritarian personality has been well documented—he makes an interesting point when he remarks that Max Horkheimer and Erich Fromm had both shown in work written before *The Authoritarian Personality*[55] that "bourgeois society had moved steadily away from authoritarian family systems."[56] For Lasch, neither totalitarian nor non-totalitarian societies need the authoritarian family. In non-totalitarian societies: "the individual's emancipation from the family makes it impossible but also unnecessary to appeal to his guilty conscience; instead, society appeals to shame, self-interest, and his duty to enjoy himself."[57]

Lasch's description of the erosion of the authoritarian family and its replacement by social and cultural (or pseudo-cultural) agencies reiterates points which Adorno had already made in such essays as "Sociology and Psychology," "Revised Psychoanalysis," and "Freudian Theory and the Pattern of Fascist Propaganda." There is, moreover, no need to dwell on the subject of the problematic genesis of the authoritarian personality type in *The Authoritarian Personality*. As early as *Minima Moralia*, Adorno had already put forward the view that the patriarchal authoritarian family was coming to an end.[58] But if the older generation was no longer authoritarian, could the younger generation be described in this way?[59]

The hypothesis of an authoritarian personality is controversial for a number of reasons. One of these can be found in Adorno's own criticism of character typology. In his 1946 paper, "Die Revidierte Psychoanalyse," Adorno strongly condemned the use of such typology by revisionists like Erich Fromm. On Martin Jay's reading of this criticism, Adorno rejected the revisionists' use of "integrated character types" because it amounted to "abandoning that insistence on nonidentity that was one of the central tenets of Critical Theory."[60] In Adorno's own words: "The totality of the character, which the revisionists presuppose as given, is an ideal which could be realized only in a non-traumatic society" (RP, 24). When he spoke entirely in his own voice in books like *Minima Moralia* (which he was writing at the same time as he collaborated in *The Authoritarian Personality*), Adorno only rarely referred to personality or character types, preferring instead to speak in terms of pathologies like paranoia and narcissism.

Despite the fact that authoritarianism is a personality type and narcissism a psychological pathology, they share a number of important features. Once again, these include an ambivalent compliance to authority based on fear and resentment, hostility toward out-groups, stereotypical thinking, and ego weakness. However, unlike the hypothesis of authoritarianism, narcissism does not presuppose a unified character structure; it can be explained by instinct psychology rather than by the ego psychology the revisionists formulated. Furthermore, Adorno's hypothesis concerning the prevalence of pathological narcissism allowed him to focus on the antagonistic relationship between the individual and socioeconomic structures and institutions. The narcissist thus appears as

> a system of scars integrated only through suffering—though never completely. The inflicting of these scars is actually the form which the infiltration of society into the individual takes, not that illusory continuity in whose name revisionists disregard the shock-filled structure of individual experience. (RP, 24)

For Adorno, it was narcissism—rather than the authoritarian personality—which was the psychological key to understanding the damage that had been done to individuals by social and economic factors. The speculative hypothesis of narcissism explained both how individuals were more easily integrated into the system and why they were fundamentally antagonistic to that system.

Although there are both theoretical and empirical difficulties inherent in explaining the success of nazism and the culture industry with reference to certain personality types, or to pathologies like narcissism, Adorno's life-long attempt to find an explanation is laudable and remains timely. Quoting Freud's remarks—in "Thoughts for the Times on War and Death"—about the debilitating effects of uninhibited emotional impulses on the intellect, Alan Bullock claims that Hitler was "well aware" of these effects. According to Bullock, Hitler's "most original achievement was to create a movement that was deliberately designed to highlight by every manipulative device—symbols, language, ritual, hierarchy, parades, rallies, culminating in the Führer myth—the supremacy of the dynamic, irrational factors in politics: struggle, will, force, the sinking of individual identity in the collective emotions of the group, sacrifice, discipline."[61] This makes Adorno's view that psychological types or pathologies are responsible for nazism appear plausible at the very least. Adorno believed that "the masses would hardly succumb to the brazen wink of untrue propaganda if something within them did not respond to the rhetoric of sacrifice and the dangerous life" (SP1, 68). However, owing to the nature of his diagnosis, Adorno's theory can easily give rise to misinterpretation and misplaced criticism.

Adorno often described his own work as speculative. It is characteristic of speculative theories to "venture out too far"; they do not entirely agree with the results of empirical research and "tend towards false generalizations."[62] Speculative theory attempts to "give shape to a tendency, to sketch the physiognomy of a spirit which also determines the signature of an age even if its validity is still very limited both quantitatively and qualitatively" (PC, 22). Adorno based much of his work concerning the culture industry on Freud's metapsychology which he considered to be just as speculative as his own theory. In its defense, Adorno claimed that Freud's theory had proved to be enormously productive for understanding social behavior: "Freud's theory which, for reasons of a complex nature, prompted established science to shrug its shoulders . . . provided intra-scientifically practicable hypotheses for the explanation of what otherwise cannot be explained; namely that the overwhelming majority of human beings tolerate relations of domination, identify themselves with them and are motivated towards irrational attitudes by them—attitudes whose contradiction with the simplest interests of their self-preservation is obvious."[63]

In an apparently paradoxical way, Freud's much maligned theory of drives or instincts was useful, not only for understanding why people accept domination, but also for explaining why domination can never become total. Without Freud's material psychology of the instincts, it would be extremely difficult to account for the fact that people *suffer* from the effects of domination and that totalitarian forms of domination have never succeeded completely. Yet one should also realize that Adorno's application of Freud's instinct theory to phenomena like nazism and the culture industry was heuristic and critical in character. In fact, in *Minima Moralia*, Adorno summarized his assessment of psychoanalysis in the following aphorism: "In psycho-analysis nothing is true except the exaggerations" (*MM*, 49). The validity of Freudian theory was demonstrated by its ability to explain, in a general and speculative way, such phenomena as the techniques used by the culture industry as well as their effects on consciousness. However, as speculative, Freudian theory suffered from the same tendencies toward over-generalization as Adorno's own.

What is remarkable is not Adorno's sanguine admission that both Freud's theory and his own tend toward "false generalizations," but the fact that his speculative and Freudian characterization of the Zeitgeist should have found empirical confirmation so often—as in his discussion of narcissism. That narcissism has become a prevalent pathology has been confirmed by numerous psychologists.[64] For example, Joel Whitebook writes that patients currently seen by analysts increasingly suffer "from disorders of . . . [the] very sense of self" because they have not "sufficiently traversed the requirements of the pre-Oedipal period." These individuals frequently mask their suffering with "grandiose, narcissistic fantasies, which in many instances prove socially adaptive."[65] Whitebook also cites the American psychoanalyst Heinz Kohut for whom "narcissism is to our time as hysteria was to Freud's. Just as the investigation of the hysteric led Freud to a critique of the sexual repressiveness of Victorian society, so the study of narcissism leads to the pathogenic core of ours."[66] One may concede that the authoritarian personality type is too false a generalization. However, it would appear as if the prevalence of narcissism, which Adorno was one of the first theorists to diagnose and explore, has found empirical confirmation.

Concluding Remarks

The individual psyche and the social totality intersect in the "pre-social" libido. Adorno wrote: "if radical psychoanalysis focuses on the libido as something pre-social, it reaches that point where the social principle of domination coincides with the psychological one of the repression of drives both ontogenetically and phylogenetically" (RP, 27). The modification and integration of "pre-social" drives is reinforced by the various psychological techniques specific to nazism and the culture industry; these techniques include the reanimation of superego introjects and the use of stereotypes. It is not simply introjection or internalization but also these techniques which account for the interaction between society and the individual and explain the individual's integration. Integration must also be explained with reference to the changes within capitalism which have led to increased reification as well as to the erosion of the bourgeois patriarchal family.

Of course, Adorno did not claim that integration was, or could ever be, complete. Given the conflicts between the economic imperatives of late capitalism and the individual's instincts and rational self-interest, integration has limits. On this point, Habermas accuses Adorno of setting up a "false antagonism between the domain of the organism, which is described in biological terms, and the domain of the social apparatus, which invades the individual from the outside."[67] For Habermas, it would "make more sense to attempt to integrate both disciplines from the beginning within the *same* conceptual framework."[68] Yet, as Martin Jay points out in the passage I cited at the beginning of this chapter, Adorno did not believe that what was sundered in reality should be reconciled or integrated—even in thought. There is a very real antagonism between the individual's unsatisfied instincts and the demands of the social totality—an antagonism which one should not occlude in order to make theorizing easier. Adorno cautioned that the "resolution of the antinomy of universal and particular remains mere ideology as long as the instinctual renunciation society expects of the individual neither can be objectively justified as true and necessary nor later provides him with the delayed gratification" (SP2, 85).

Even if it is limited, integration is bought at a price which the individual should not have to pay. Within late capitalist societies, individuals are forced to renounce the satisfaction of many instincts in order to fulfill socio-economic goals and interests. They defend their renunciation with ostensibly rational arguments, but it remains largely irrational. It is ultimately fear, hammered in by capitalism and reinforced by the culture industry, which promotes conformity. The apparent rationality of the economy conceals its true basis in "physical coercion, . . . bodily torment, a material moment that transcends both immanently economic 'material incentives' and the intrapsychic instinctual economy" (SP1, 71–72). It is the fear of physical annihilation, the loss of the means of subsistence, which makes people cling in desperation "to the now highly problematic and largely absurd quest for material goods of civilization which economically rational behaviour is supposed to guarantee them . . . ; and the communications media play their part in keeping them in line" (SP1, 71).[69]

In spite of this fear, the individual's capacity to resist has not been compromised completely. Most commentators fail to acknowledge this. For example, Joel Whitebook claims that while Adorno's use of Freud's id psychology allowed him to "dramatize the conflict between the individual and society, and demonstrate the depth psychological consequences of social oppression in a way that was unique in Marxism," it also had the consequence of preventing him "from conceiving the condition of the possibility of a free society."[70] Along with Herbert Marcuse, who took up and developed many of the ideas contained in "Die Revidierte Psychoanalyse" in his *Eros and Civilization*,[71] Adorno supposedly maintained that domination in industrial societies was so overwhelming that only an "eschatological rupture" could break with prevailing modes of repression and exploitation. Although Whitebook's views about the prospects for emancipation in Adorno's theory are not entirely correct, Adorno was certainly more skeptical than not about these prospects.

Nonetheless, a theory cannot be rejected on the grounds that it is bleak and pessimistic since, though pessimistic, the theory may also help to explain a really existing state of affairs. Moreover, for all its pessimism, Adorno's theory is not without its elements of hope. In a very early essay, "Thesen über Bedürfnis," Adorno pointed out that the culture industry encourages a false reconciliation with the social order by preparing individuals for the reproduction of labor power and by forcing "their needs to harmonize with their employers' interests in profit and domination." At the same time, however, Adorno also speculated that the culture industry would cease to exist in a society which satisfied needs that had not been hammered in and accepted out of fear. A more rationally and instinctually robust individual would not need the satisfactions provided by cultural commodities. Yet, even here and now: if "*production were forthwith unconditionally and unrestrainedly reorganized for the satisfaction of needs—even and especially for those needs produced by capitalism—needs themselves would be transformed decisively.*"[72] Given the irreconcilable conflicts between the socioeconomic system and the individual's drives, the latter represent a potentially explosive force. Once detonated, this force could lead to the creation of a qualitatively different social and economic order.

However empty it had become, Adorno wanted to retain the concept of the individual. It functions as the place-holder for a resistive force, revealing the fundamental antagonisms between ungratified drives and the socio-economic order of late capitalism. As a product of the historical stage of liberalism with its allegedly free-market economy, this con-

cept also preserves the ideas of autonomy and spontaneity—the emancipatory goals of Adorno's theory. Furthermore, although Adorno often
described individual psychology as a fiction, he also believed that in
some special cases, more psychologically robust individuals do exist
in late capitalism—albeit in an abnormal but still essential form. As
maladjusted as these individuals are, they are among the few people
Adorno thought capable of conceiving of a more pliable socio-economic order in which their suffering would be redeemed.

Adorno's idea of utopia is a curious blend of rational and instinctual
elements. On the one hand, Adorno discovers utopia in "blind somatic
pleasure" (*MM*, 61). On the other, he recommends the development of
the enlightened use of reason as a means to achieve this utopian end.
An Adornian utopia would engage both the rational faculties and the
instincts. Pleasure in such a society could well take the form of non-
purposive enjoyment: " 'being, nothing else, without any further definition and fulfilment,' might take the place of process, act, satisfaction." According to Adorno: "None of the abstract concepts comes
closer to fulfilled utopia than the idea of eternal peace" (*MM*, 157). If
this utopian society is to be realized, it will be necessary to cast off the
forms of domination perpetrated under late capitalism and to open a
space for non-instrumental forms of human fulfillment.

Chapter 2

Toward a Political Economy of the Culture Industry

The discussion offered in Chapter 1 of the broader theoretical framework for Adorno's work on the culture industry demonstrated his intellectual debts to Freud and Marx. Adorno viewed society as an antagonistic whole in which material biological forces confront equally material economic forces. Like Marx, Adorno also believed that one of the keys to understanding these economic forces lay in solving the riddle of the commodity form. But Adorno went further than Marx when he contended that the commodity form had permeated and transformed areas of life outside of the economic sphere proper. The ubiquity of the exchange principle has become one of the principal features of late capitalism. Cultural life itself has not been immune; it too suffers from the effects of commodification and reification. Nowhere is this more apparent than in the culture industry.

In his *Kulturindustrie und Populärkultur*, Michael Kausch paraphrases Adorno's well-known remark about the salient distinction between art and the culture industry. For Adorno, "the former was certainly always *also* a commodity, but the latter is *only* a commodity through and through."[1] Adorno argued that the high modern art he championed could provide "the negative knowledge of the actual world"[2] only insofar as it exhibited a measure of autonomy or independence from the effects of commodification and reification. By contrast, he believed that products of the culture industry were enmeshed inextricably in capitalist modes of production, distribution, and exchange. The success of television, radio, and newspapers is predicated entirely on the ability of these media to attract an audience—itself a commodity sold to advertisers—to whom other commodities, like cars and dish-

27

washing detergent, can be sold. Popular music and film are marketed even more directly to target audiences as commodities; they become "hits" when a critical mass of consumers buys a quantity of tickets or recordings sufficient to generate a profit. Although some critics have charged that Adorno's discussion of commodified culture is far too superficial and vague, Adorno did offer a striking, if general, description of the capitalist basis of contemporary culture.[3]

Adorno's discussion of the commodification of culture is grounded in Marx's analysis of the commodity form. According to Marx:

> The commodity is, first of all, an external object, a thing which through its qualities satisfies human needs of whatever kind. The nature of these needs, whether they arise, for example, from the stomach, or the imagination, makes no difference. Nor does it matter here how the thing satisfies man's need, whether directly as a means of subsistence, i.e. an object of consumption, or indirectly as a means of production.[4]

An object has a use-value when it satisfies human needs by means of certain properties which are either intrinsic to it or which it acquires as the product of human labor. But as a commodity, whose sole value lies in exchange, the object "changes into a thing which transcends sensuousness" because all of its physical properties are depreciated.[5] In the process of exchange, both the use-value of the commodity and the concrete human labor involved in its production are transformed from qualities into quantitative determinations. It is precisely this transformation of quality into quantity which makes the commodity so mysterious.

Adorno borrowed from Marx the concepts of use and exchange-value, pressing them into service in his own analysis of commodified culture. In so doing, however, he also modified them. If—as Marx remarked in a footnote to his *Critique of Political Economy*—Aristotle had criticized exchange-value as an improper or secondary use of objects,[6] Adorno claimed that this secondary value now actually supersedes the object's "proper and primary" use-value. The exchange-value of commodities has become a primary value in its own right, often displacing use-value "proper." Having once described culture as a "paradoxical commodity,"[7] Adorno devoted some of his later work on the culture industry to an analysis of the incongruous exchange-cum-use value of its products. This analysis will be discussed in the first section of this chapter. Brief reference will also be made here to Adorno's discussion of the needs satisfied by cultural commodities—however "illusory" such satisfaction might be.

Adorno's analysis of the fetish character of cultural commodities complements his account of production processes in different sectors of the culture industry. Together, they provide the theoretical background for a study of the effects of commodification on culture. According to Adorno, cultural goods have become standardized and pseudo-individuated; their portrayal of empirical reality is schematized and stereotypical. These effects of commodification, along with Adorno's early sketch of the culture industry's material basis in capitalist economies, will be examined in the second section of this chapter. At the same time, I shall show that Adorno's political economy of the culture industry lacks detail and depth. It is also incomplete—especially in its treatment of advertising. In the final section of this chapter, I shall review some of the missing elements in Adorno's analysis.

Mass Culture and the Commodity Form

As commodities, products of the culture industry obey the dictates of the laws of exchange. The dominance of the exchange principle is what is truly new in culture. It seriously compromises culture's autonomy which was always fragile, even and especially in the heyday of liberal capital. The primacy of the exchange principle within culture reflects the fact that cultural production plays an increasingly important role in the economic system. But it also demonstrates the pervasiveness of the exchange principle in society as a whole. In all realms of human activity, exchange-value inexorably "destroys use-values for human beings," disguising itself "as the object of enjoyment."[8] Failing to avert such destruction, cultural goods are now primarily "governed . . . by the principle of their realization as value." In the culture industry in particular, "the profit motive" is transferred "naked onto cultural forms."[9] The industry does not attempt to conceal this; it openly acknowledges that its commodities are produced with the sole aim of making a profit.

Adorno reiterated these ideas throughout his work. In 1959, he complained: "the venerable profit motives of culture have overgrown the whole culture like a fungus."[10] The culture industry unapologetically transforms the "secondary or improper" value of its own products into their primary value. In cultural commodities, exchange-value has become a substitute for use-value, serving as a kind of ersatz or counterfeit use-value, the object of enjoyment. It is no longer the case, as Marx once maintained, that commodities are obliged to "stand the test as use-values before they can be realized as values.''[11] Cultural goods now demonstrate their usefulness primarily as exchange-values. For Adorno: "pure use-value, whose illusion the cultural goods must preserve in completely capitalist society, must be replaced by pure exchange-value, which precisely in its capacity as exchange-value deceptively takes over the function of use-value" (FC, 279).

This substitution of exchange-value for use-value has also had a profound impact on consumption: "The woman who has money with which to buy is intoxicated by the act of buying. . . . The auto religion makes all men brothers in the sacramental moment with the words: 'That is a Rolls Royce' " (FC, 279). It is not only the producers and purveyors of commodities who derive "enjoyment" from exchange-value; consumers enjoy the commodity's exchange-value as well. Wolfgang Haug indirectly refers to this more recent function of exchange-value when he discusses the role of brand names or trademarks in consumption. Owing to the effects of advertising, the brand names of industrial commodities are often associated with images. The consumer may be less interested in the actual use to be derived from a product's physical properties than in the ownership of a product with a particular name connoting "all the aesthetic, visual and verbal communications contained in the styling of a commodity."[12] This name-buying trend has become prevalent today as many products, especially articles of clothing, display their company logos prominently; those who buy them literally wear a label. The label serves as an advertisement for both the consumer's income level and his or her "discerning" sense of what is in fashion and what is not; it is intended to signal the consumer's social, economic, and cultural status.

If, as Haug indicates, the use-value of many industrial commodities has virtually become an illusory appearance, the use-value of cultural commodities has met a similar fate. It has succumbed to the instrumentality characteristic of exchange-value to such an extent that it cancels itself out. Like all other goods, cultural commodities have become fetishes. Although consumers believe that these commodities have a value independent of the process of exchange, Adorno declared that, in the final analysis

> The consumer is really worshipping the money that he himself has paid for the ticket to the Toscanini concert. He has literally "made" the success which he reifies and accepts as an objective criterion, without recognizing himself in it. But he has not "made" it by liking the concert, but rather by buying the ticket. (FC, 278–79)

Consumers do not acknowledge the part they have played in producing the ostensibly objective value of cultural commodities; they attribute the value of the products they buy to the products themselves. So, in his essay on pseudo-culture, Adorno defined it as "spirit overcome by fetishism of commodities" (PC, 28).

In their *Dialectic of Enlightenment*, Adorno and Horkheimer reiterated the claim that Adorno had made earlier in his 1938 essay "On the Fetish Character of Music and the Regression of Listening":

> What might be called use value in the reception of cultural commodities is replaced by exchange value; in place of enjoyment, there are gallery-visiting and factual knowledge: the prestige seeker replaces the connoisseur. The consumer becomes the ideology of the pleasure industry, whose institutions he cannot escape. One simply "has to" have seen *Mrs. Miniver*, just as one "has to" subscribe to *Life* and *Time*. Everything is looked at from only one aspect: that it can be used for something else, however vague the notion of this use may be. No object has an inherent value; it is valuable only to the extent that it can be exchanged.

Adorno and Horkheimer went on to describe the exchange-cum-use-value of cultural commodities as their "social rating [*Schätzung*] (misinterpreted as . . . artistic status)" (*DE*, 158). Cultural commodities serve as exchangeable information or status symbols. If, as Wolfgang Haug has shown, Marx's concept of exchange-value represents "the intangible social character of the economic determinant of form,"[13] consumers now trade the intangible social markers of gallery-attendance or film-going for the prestige these markers confer on them in the socio-economic marketplace.

Adorno returned to this idea when he wrote that "culture is reduced to the identifying marks of social immanence and integration; it becomes something exchangeable, something useable" (PC, 33). Although he puts a different spin on the exchange-cum-use value of cultural commodities, Jean Baudrillard also argues that consumers use them as social markers:

> The apparent passivity of long hours of viewing . . . prefers . . . to present itself as pleasure, interest, "free" distraction, spontaneous choice. But this alleged pleasure is a challenge to the profound charge of cultural inferiority which doubtless will never be formulated (or only secretly in ritual recriminations: "They bore us with their stuff!" or "It's always the same!"—simulacra revealing by default superior cultural processes: judgement, selection, etc.).[14]

Consumers of cultural commodities go so far as to present their very boredom as a sign of superior taste and discernment. Yet, these attempts at demonstrating cultural superiority mask the consumer's reluctance or inability to engage in more demanding cultural activities.

Adorno was one of the first theorists to analyze the commodity character of products of the culture industry. Nevertheless, his application of Marx's concepts of use and exchange-value to cultural commodities should be scrutinized more closely. Marx had claimed that objects have a use-value by virtue of satisfying certain human needs—regardless of whether these were needs of stomach or of the imagination. However, Marx restricted his own discussion of use-value to those objects which primarily satisfy physical or sensuous needs; no sustained attempt was made to differentiate between the use-values of commodities of different kinds. Furthermore, while asserting that it was the physical or sensuous body of a commodity which housed its use-value,[15] Marx never fully developed this idea. Applying the concept of use-value to cultural commodities poses certain problems. For Terry Lovell, the major problem "stems ultimately from the lack of intrinsic connection between the usefulness to the consumer of a particular type of cultural artefact, and the physical form of commodity under which it is sold."[16]

As Baudrillard would later do, Adorno rejected the idea that commodities like television programs have the use-value of entertainment and relaxation. In *Dialectic of Enlightenment*, Adorno and Horkheimer wrote: "Pure amusement, with its result of relaxed self-surrender to all kinds of association and happy nonsense, is cut short by entertainment on the market . . . " (*DE*, 142: translation altered). The culture industry "ruins the fun" which cultural goods might have supplied by allowing "business considerations to involve it in the ideological clichés of a culture in the process of self-liquidation" (*DE*, 142–43). Nonetheless, even if one agrees with the view of these authors that the industry does not provide its consumers with entertainment, but rather with social prestige, the latter is probably only one among other use-values (or even among other exchange-cum-use-values) of cultural commodities. As theoretically unsophisticated as it often is, contemporary work on the reception of cultural commodities does promise to remedy the largely undeveloped analysis of their use-value for consumers.

Wolfgang Haug insists that industrial commodities have not entirely lost their use-values even though the ideal of marketing experts is to "deliver the absolute minimum of use-value, disguised and staged by a maximum of seductive illusion, a highly effective strategy because it is attuned to the yearnings, and desires, of the people."[17] Similarly, despite the fact that cultural commodities are entangled inextricably in the mechanisms of exchange, some writers contend that these goods continue to preserve a measure of "proper and primary" use-value. For example, in his seminal *Making Capital from Culture*, Bill Ryan follows Adorno and Baudrillard when he applies the concepts of use and exchange-value to cultural commodities. Like these authors, Ryan acknowledges that the exchange-value of cultural commodities has undermined their use-value. At the same time, however, he insists that such commodities do retain a use-value.

Ryan claims that the use-value of products of the culture industry lies in their ostensible originality. A cultural good "must appear to audiences as a novel object which promises to satisfy their needs for knowledge, meaning and pleasure by virtue of the new meanings it bears and which it alone possesses."[18] Ryan bases his ideas about the use-value of cultural goods on his reconstruction of the history of the culture industry. He contends that the culture industry originated in pre-industrial artistic practices and that it continues to reflect its origin in early-modern conceptions of art and artistic creativity: "The status of the artist as talented, creative genius, and the work of art as unique and original expression, were the essential elements of artistic practice as instituted in the early period of the modern epoch, notions which, to a significant extent, remain embedded in modern cultural practice."[19] Conceding that traditional arts like theater, music, and dance are generally considered to be more artistic and creative than the products of the culture industry, Ryan asserts that the latter have retained many of the features or characteristics of art—including its primary use-value of originality.

For Ryan, there is no substantial rupture between traditional and more industrialized cultural practices even though capital has played an increasingly central role in cultural production over time. However, Adorno would strongly contest this view. According to Martin Jay: "Adorno contended that the products of the culture industry were not works of art that were then turned into commodities, but were rather produced *from the very beginning* as fungible items for sale in the market place."[20] Partial confirmation for Jay's interpretation can be found in "Culture Industry Reconsidered." After making the remark quoted above about the thoroughly commodified character of the industry's products, Adorno added: "This quantitative shift is so great that it calls forth entirely new phenomena" (CIR, 13).[21] By contrast, Ryan's views about the use-value of cultural commodities are based on his supposition of a continuous, "linear," and unbroken history of art. Ryan argues that since mass culture is just the latest historical version of art, its use-value must be the same as that of art. However, this argument will not withstand scrutiny.

Not only is Ryan's argument invalid (genetic fallacy) —because he derives his ideas about the use-value of commodified culture from its alleged origins in early modern artistic practice—but there are other problems with his reasoning as well. The first concerns the needs which originality is supposed to satisfy. Can one really speak, as Ryan does, of *needs* for knowledge, meaning and pleasure? What kinds of needs are these? Adorno himself maintained that the culture industry attempts to sell its products by vaunting their originality or novelty. The industry does not do so in order to satisfy consumers' needs but only in order "to hide the increase of standardization" in cultural commodities.[22] Apart from concealing standardization, cultural commodities must also manifest a certain degree of originality simply because consumers will not buy multiple copies of the same (or similar) hit song, video, or newspaper. Ryan should have looked more closely at the nature of con-sumers' needs for cultural commodities. The second problem with Ryan's analysis is one he shares with Adorno, Horkheimer, and Bau-drillard: it is just as reductive as theirs.

The application of Marx's concept of use-value to cultural commodi-ties runs into further difficulties with the question of need. What are needs "of the imagination," and how does the culture industry satisfy them, if indeed it does? In his "Theses on Need," Adorno refused to distinguish between social and natural, primary and secondary, true and false, deep and superficial needs.[23] He thus circumvented Marx's dis-tinction between needs of the stomach and needs of the imagination. For Adorno, all needs are socially mediated and administered by monopoly capital: "in their current form, existing needs are themselves the prod-uct of class society" (TB, 393). Referring to the needs met by film and radio, Adorno wrote that these media "probably already satisfy hardly any need now" (TB, 394). At the same time, however, he implied that cultural commodities do satisfy at least some of the needs of those who buy them.

In later work, such as his essay "Theory of Pseudo-Culture," Adorno speculated that cultural commodities primarily satisfy the narcissistic need consumers have to prove themselves cultivated—a need which arises from their experience of their own socio-economic powerless-ness.[24] Here again, Adorno insisted that cultural goods provide consum-ers with a sense of social prestige which compensates for their impo-tence in relation to "the totally administered world." Even in Adorno's more mature work, then, he maintained that it is the exchange-cum-use-value of commodities, their fetish character, which continues to mediate between narcissistic needs and their satisfaction. This implies that cultural commodities offer no uncorrupted or primary use-values for the satisfaction of need. The need to offset socio-economic powerlessness—itself a by-product of late industrial societies—is met with a simulacrum of use-value. In Chapter 3, I shall discuss Adorno's theory of needs in greater detail.

If the commodity form is the riddle whose solution will reveal both the nature and the problems of capitalism, an analysis of cultural commodities shows that this form is far more complex and difficult to "crack" than Marx himself had realized. Adorno's analysis of the use-value of cultural commodities must be developed more fully. Since cultural commodities can be reproduced or used again, not only by one person but by many different people, their use-value may be different in each case. As contemporary theorists of culture, like John Fiske, have tried to show, the use-value of cultural commodities may take as many forms as there are people who consume them. While Fiske's claim is somewhat exaggerated in light of Adorno's discussion of the conformist tendencies and narcissistic pathologies common to large groups of people, it does indicate that much more work needs to be done in this area.[25] More work is also required to flesh out Adorno's description of the economic basis of the culture industry and of the production processes involved in its different sectors. It is to this rudimentary description that I shall now turn.

Commodified Culture

In *Dialectic of Enlightenment*, Adorno and Horkheimer briefly referred to the economic entanglement of cultural production in other sectors of capitalist industry. They wrote: "The dependence of the most powerful broadcasting company on the electrical industry, or of the motion picture industry on the banks, is characteristic of the whole sphere, whose individual branches are themselves economically interwoven" (*DE*, 123). Although the authors also recognized that the companies and industries producing cultural goods had become monopolies, their analysis of the culture industry's economic base in monopoly capital ends with these cursory remarks.

Fortunately, other writers have taken up these issues where Adorno and Horkheimer left off. For example, Graham Murdock and Peter Golding call for and initiate a political economy of the mass media. They conduct a brief investigation into both the concentrated ownership of culture industries and their dependence on other economic sectors "through reciprocal investments and shareholdings and interlocking directorships . . . , and secondly through advertising."[26] Following in their wake, Nicholas Garnham devised a political economy of mass communication which resembles Murdock and Golding's in its extensive use of Marxist theory.[27] In his influential book, *The Media Monopoly*,[28] Ben Bagdikian also documents the consolidation of media ownership in the hands of a decreasing number of corporations in the United States. At the same time, he provides illuminating examples of the ways in which culture industries have been forced to accede to the demands and interests of other industrial sectors.

It is interesting to note that Murdock, Golding, and Garnham all make reference to the work of the Frankfurt School and, more particularly, to Adorno's work on the political economy of the media. Moreover, unlike many contemporary commentators—who wrongly believe Adorno's interest in culture implies the privileging of superstructural elements over those in the economic base—Garnham recognizes that critical theorists were actually claiming the cultural superstructure had collapsed into the economic base. Garnham writes: "under monopoly capitalism the superstructure becomes precisely industrialized; it is invaded by the base and the base/superstructure distinction breaks down but via a collapse into the base rather than . . . via the transformation of the base into another autonomous superstructural discourse."[29] However, Garnham also criticizes Critical theory, insisting that "the real weakness of the Frankfurt School's original position was not their failure to realize the importance of the base or the economic, but insufficiently to take account of the economically contradictory nature of the process they observed and thus to see the industrialization of culture as unproblematic and irresistible."[30] Bill Ryan will take up this critique in his examination of the contradictions in the art/capital relationship within the culture industry. As I have already indicated, Ryan's analysis of this contradiction is not without its problems—owing to its supposition of an unbroken history leading from early modern artistic practice to the practices of the culture industry—but Ryan nonetheless endeavors to correct the weaknesses Garnham has pinpointed in Adorno's theory.

For Murdock and Golding, Adorno's description of the basic features of capitalism "is correct as far as it goes but does not go nearly far enough towards explaining how the American 'culture industry' actually works." What is required, according to these writers, is "the concrete analysis of material production advocated by Marx."[31] However, in addition to this analysis of the increasingly concentrated ownership of the means of cultural production, and of the culture industry's dependence on other sectors of the economy, a political economy of the culture industry should also focus on the material processes involved in the production of cultural commodities. Murdock and Golding's work has been supplemented in many important ways by Ryan's analysis of what he calls the "corporate form of cultural production."[32] Ryan's work will serve here to complement and extend Adorno's own description of cultural production.

However, before examining the processes Adorno believed were involved in the production of cultural commodities, I should briefly discuss the phrase "culture industry" itself. Although it refers to something singular, the phrase is not intended to imply that all sectors of cultural production share the same production processes. Instead, it refers to "the standardization of the thing itself—such as that of the Western, familiar to every movie-goer—and to the rationalization of distribution techniques" (CIR, 14). By using the phrase "culture industry" to refer to distribution and standardization, Adorno securely linked the industry to profit interests. As Nicholas Garnham has shown, it is cultural distribution, not production, which "*is the key locus of power and profit*" within the culture industry.[33] In fact, it is important to note that very few cultural commodities actually make a profit. Only a small number of the commodities produced become "hits." This makes capital investment in cultural production extremely risky. Garnham contends that producers of cultural commodities attempt to reduce investment risks by creating "a relationship with an audience or public to whom they offer not a simple cultural good, but a cultural repertoire across which the risks can be spread."[34] In addition, as Ryan observes, culture industries also compensate for investment risks by engaging in the constant production of "new," though thoroughly standardized, products.[35]

The culture industry satisfies the ever-greater demand for its products by resorting to increasingly advanced techniques of production, reproduction, promotion, and distribution. Despite their cursory nature, Adorno's few remarks about the processes involved in the production of cultural commodities are noteworthy. As one might expect, different production processes are used in different sectors of the industry. In the production of popular music, for example, Adorno noted that

> the act of producing a song-hit still remains in the handicraft stage. The production of popular music is highly centralized in its economic organi-

zation, but still "individualistic" in its social mode of production. The division of labor among the composer, harmonizer, and arranger is not industrial but rather pretends industrialization, in order to look more up-to-date.[36]

By contrast, in "Culture Industry Reconsidered," Adorno wrote that film production "resembles technical modes of operation in the extensive division of labor, the employment of machines and the separation of the laborers from the means of production—expressed in the perennial conflict between artists active in the culture industry and those who control it" (CIR, 14).

Yet, however much the production of film and popular music may differ, Adorno also insisted that, even in film, "individual forms of production are . . . maintained" (CIR, 14). The production of cultural commodities begins with composers and musicians, script-writers and actors, investigative reporters and journalists. In addition to providing empirical confirmation for Adorno's view that cultural production has retained an individual and craft-like stage, Bill Ryan supplements it when he criticizes Marx for glossing over the cooperative model of the capitalist workshop in his description of the transition from feudal to capitalist modes of production. The capitalist workshop "reflects a *transformation* of the relations of and in production, but evidences *identifiable connections to craft forms of work and their division of labour.*"[37] According to Ryan, this organizational model characterizes one of the earlier stages in the production of cultural commodities. Although it is increasingly incorporated into the more advanced stages, this early stage also retains, at least in principle, its creative or artistic status linked to individual achievement.

In order to encourage the creation of "original" products, the owners of the means of cultural production grant a certain degree of autonomy to cultural workers. Even though a stratum of creative management now regulates the early stages of production, its intervention is generally benign and cooperative. Nevertheless, "despite the relative autonomy of the collective artist in the project team, there *is* a tendency towards formula and cliché in creation and . . . it flows from *the formatting of the creative stage of production.*"[38] With "formatting," or the imposition by creative management of a policy (format) on creative labor, a further step has been taken to control production in some sectors of the culture industry. In his discussion of formatting, Ryan attempts to confirm empirically the tendency toward standardization in the culture industry which Adorno was one of the first to identify and criticize.

While acknowledging in some passages of his work that early stages in the production of many cultural goods are actually pre-industrial in character,[39] in other passages, Adorno sometimes stressed the predominately industrial character of all aspects of cultural production, contradicting his analysis in "On Popular Music." Since he did not believe that a continuous history linked traditional forms of cultural labor to more industrialized forms, Adorno occasionally resolved what Ryan describes as the contradiction between art and capital in favor of the latter. As Ryan himself points out,[40] in *Dialectic of Enlightenment* Adorno and Horkheimer primarily emphasized the assembly-line character of the culture industry with its "synthetic, planned method of turning out its products (factory-like not only in the studio but, more or less, in the compilation of cheap biographies, pseudodocumentary novels, and hit songs)" (*DE*, 163). In this passage, Adorno and Horkheimer appear to ignore the pre-industrial stages of cultural production.

These few and contradictory remarks on the production of cultural commodities are Adorno's only contribution to a political economy of this rapidly growing sector of capitalist industry. As far as the reproductive techniques used in cultural production are concerned, Adorno's remarks are scattered and undeveloped.[41] Other aspects of capitalist production, such as distribution and circulation, marketing and advertising, and the corporate organization of the industry, are also given short shrift. Instead of discussing these, Adorno tended to focus on the dominant characteristics of commodified culture. These characteristics are diverse but, throughout his work, Adorno repeatedly stressed four distinct features of cultural goods which accompany their commodification: standardization, pseudo-individualism, schematization, and stereotypes. Each of these features has its own distinctive logic. In what follows, I shall examine them separately.

The industrialization of cultural production allows cultural commodities to be mass produced. Nevertheless, what Adorno described as the standardization of cultural commodities is not rooted in the industrial or assembly-line character of the labor process. In other sectors of capitalist industry, where commodities like automobiles and breakfast cereals are manufactured, the costs of production would increase greatly if these products were not churned out on an assembly line. In these other sectors, "all industrial mass production necessarily eventuates in standardization" (PM, 23). But, in the case of popular music, whose production retains pre-industrial features, this explanation for standardization will not suffice. According to Adorno: "It would not increase the costs of production if the various composers of hit tunes did not follow certain standard patterns'' (PM, 23). It costs the culture industry no more to produce an original work than to produce a standardized one. Adorno therefore attempted to find other explanations for the standardization of commodities like popular music.

In his essay ''Theodor Adorno Meets the Cadillacs,'' Bernard Gendron criticizes Adorno because he allegedly claimed that ''techniques of mass production or the economics of market concentration'' account for standardization.[42] However, for Adorno, it is actually imitation—not mass production techniques—which partially accounts for the fact that cultural goods have become standardized. Different companies competing in the same cultural sector imitate successful products, and standards begin to crystallize. Furthermore: ''Under centralized conditions such as exist today these standards have become 'frozen' '' and they are ''rigidly enforced upon material to be promoted'' (PM, 23). Of course, Adorno should have acknowledged that imitation also serves as a partial explanation for the standardization of other types of commodities, but he is correct to point out that it is the exigencies of industrial mass production and reproduction, and the lower costs associated with them, which primarily explain why a Ford product is no different from one produced by Chrysler.

Adorno's explanation for standardization in popular music may also hold for those more industrialized sectors of cultural production—including the motion picture industry—which have preserved an early ''handicraft'' stage. As Bill Ryan points out, however, there are probably additional explanations for the sameness and repetitiveness of cultural commodities. Ryan cites two writers who attribute the standardized character of cultural goods to the growing monopoly in cultural capital.[43] Observing that Adorno and Horkheimer themselves seem to offer a similar explanation for standardization in some passages of *Dialectic of Enlightenment*, Ryan assembles a few key phrases from this book:

> 'Films, radio and magazines make up a system which is uniform as a whole and in every part'; 'Under monopoly all mass culture is identical . . .'; '. . . the achievement of standardisation and mass production . . .'; 'The ruthless unity in the culture industry . . .', and so on.[44]

In these passages, the growing concentration in ownership of the means of cultural production is suggested as another explanation for standardization. Although it is not the only explanation, Gendron is correct when he writes that Adorno claimed "the economics of market concentration" account for standardization.

Regressive tendencies in the reception of cultural commodities also play a role in standardization. In the case of popular music, for example, Adorno argued that people now listen "according to formula" (FC, 285); their listening has been "arrested at the infantile stage" (FC, 286). The consumer wants what Adorno described as "natural" music—a music which stems from "his earliest musical experiences, the nursery rhymes, the hymns he sings in Sunday school, the little tunes he whistles on his way home from school" (PM, 24). Owing largely to the enervating nature of their work in offices and factories, consumers demand products which have been pre-digested and made easier to swallow. For Adorno, these demands reveal the "deconcentration" of perception. Consumers "cannot stand the strain of concentrated listening and surrender themselves resignedly to what befalls them, with which they can come to terms only if they do not listen to it too closely" (FC, 288). They prefer what is already familiar to them.[45]

Adorno would claim that the psychological dispositions which give rise to the demand for standardized products are themselves the result of a socialization process which tends to eliminate autonomy, spontaneity, and individuality in consumers. However, Gendron offers an alternative explanation for consumers' listening habits: "In both its traditional and its industrial forms, standardization is such an important feature in folk, elite, and popular music . . . that it must be connected somehow to deep and entrenched psychological dispositions."[46] Gendron appears to believe that the human ear is inherently conservative. Adorno would disagree. He maintained that in late industrial societies, consumers lack "any residues of free will with relation to popular music and tend to produce passive reactions to what is given them and to become mere centers of socially conditioned reflexes" (PM, 45). The conservative traits associated with regressive listening appear "as soon as nothing is left for the consciousness [*sic*] but to capitulate before the superior power of the advertised stuff and purchase spiritual peace by making the imposed goods literally its own thing" (FC, 287).

The roots of standardization thus lie in imitation, the increasingly concentrated ownership of culture industries, and regressive reception. As standardized, cultural commodities are produced in accordance with formulas, or, as Ryan explains, in conformity with the creative policies of the management stratum of the culture industry. Although Ryan lends a great deal of support to some of Adorno's claims about the culture industry and its products, his primary concern in *Making Capi-*

tal from Culture is to highlight the contradictory relation between creative labor and industrial production. If, in spite of the significant inroads it has made, capital has not colonized entirely the creative labor process, this is because "capital is unable to make the artist completely subservient to its drive for accumulation,"[47] and formats "can never be more than loosely-connected parameters, pointing to preferred outcomes."[48] Yet one could object here that Ryan seems to presuppose the existence of a sphere of creative and artistic freedom which is virtually unaffected by capital. Ryan himself falls victim to the romantic ideology which he claims has made the art-capital contradiction possible. Adorno would certainly reply that creative labor itself has been subsumed by capital: the "freedom" of cultural workers is almost as illusory as the freedom of those who consume their products (though Adorno did say that resistance to the "socio-psychological norms of production" was generally "greater the closer one gets to the writers, directors and actors").[49] On this point, of course, Adorno could be accused of being too pessimistic but Ryan's romantic optimism is equally unacceptable.

Cultural commodities like popular music must satisfy a paradoxical demand: they have to be "fundamentally the same as all the other current hits and simultaneously fundamentally different from them" (PM, 27). Standardization satisfies the first demand; pseudo-individualism the second. Both features of cultural goods are meant to ensure their commercial success in the capitalist marketplace. Consumers will not buy identical products. The function of pseudo-individualism is to create the illusion that there are real differences between the standardized products offered by the culture industry. It provides a "handle" which allows the consumer to remember each product as something unique and distinct. Pseudo-individualism offers consumers the appearance of choice: "The consumer is unwilling to recognize that he is totally dependent, and he likes to preserve the illusion of private initiative and free choice. Thus standardization . . . produces the veil of pseudo-individualism."[50]

Adorno further illustrated this point about pseudo-individualism in one of his controversial discussions of jazz:

> [W]hile it must constantly promise its listeners something different, excite their attention and keep itself from becoming run-of-the-mill, it is not allowed to leave the beaten path; it must be always new and always the same. Hence, the deviations are just as standardized as the standards and in effect revoke themselves the instant they appear. Jazz, like everything

else in the culture industry, gratifies desires only to frustrate them at the same time.[51]

The pseudo-individuation of cultural commodities conceals the fact that they are actually identical in most or many respects. The illusion of originality or novelty is created by using different labels for cultural goods, or by promoting superficial differences between them.

Bernard Gendron concedes that, viewed synchronically, the recordings produced by the music industry are often substantially identical. But he also contends that popular music undergoes significant stylistic changes over the course of time. Gendron supports his claim with an inventory of the various styles of popular music which have succeeded one other historically. They include "ragtime, dixieland, swing, crooning, be-bop, and rhythm and blues." Within rock and roll, the following styles have come and gone: "doo-wop, rockabilly, the girl group sound, surf music, the British invasion, psychedelic rock, folk rock, heavy metal, and punk."[52] These rapid stylistic changes reflect an essential feature of modernity itself—all that is solid melts into air—and are reinforced by the vicissitudes of musical production in the capitalist marketplace. For Gendron, the fact that musical styles change abruptly contradicts Adorno's criticism of popular music as never-changing and always the same, revealing that Adorno has an "essentialist conception of the musical text."[53]

Although Gendron cannot account for the rapid turnover in styles, Bill Ryan explains that it is a consequence of the erosion of use-value by exchange-value. The commodification of cultural goods "undermines the utility upon which their circulation depends" because it subverts whatever aesthetic qualities they may have. Furthermore, "by appearing as equivalents of other commodities, cultural commodities lose something of their uniqueness whereby they exist as individual artistic objects."[54] This loss of uniqueness and utility leads to the production of new styles to replace the outmoded ones. Nonetheless, whatever explanation is given for the rapid turnover in musical styles, Gendron's criticism of Adorno's "essentialism" may have a certain degree of validity. At any given point in time, cultural commodities will resemble each other but their life cycle is short and companies are obliged constantly to replace them with something stylistically new.

What is moot, however, is whether such stylistic novelty marks a genuine change in quality. Stylistic changes certainly do not mitigate the commodity character of popular music. Gendron may be correct when he objects that Adorno's criticism of the culture industry is élitist and essentialist because Adorno did in fact champion certain traditions in culture. However, one must add that there is enough empirical documentation to show that style in cultural commodities is intimately connected with the formulas that producers impose on their products. This means that what is really ''new'' in the industry's products first appears in the form of certain corporate directives which loosely define the style of the desired product. The corporation's choice of a style is influenced by the success of other products in the same cultural sector. So, although Gendron strongly criticizes Adorno for failing to respect the conventions specific to different musical traditions, Gendron himself fails to appreciate fully the fact that, for Adorno, the conventions essential to style in popular music are dictated from the board-rooms of corporate capital in the form of formulas or formats.

Adorno primarily spoke of pseudo-individualism in connection with commodified music. However, he did refer briefly to the effects of pseudo-individuation on commodities in other sectors of the culture industry. Along with Horkheimer, Adorno wrote: ''Pseudo-individuality is rife: from the standardized jazz improvization to the exceptional film star whose hair curls over her eye to demonstrate her originality'' (*DE*, 154). The culture industry's products reveal the ''predominance of the effect, the obvious touch, and the technical detail over the work itself'' (*DE*, 125). But in addition to masking standardization, the industry's quasi-individuated effects, tricks, and technical details also conceal a third feature of cultural goods: their schematization. According to Adorno and Horkheimer, the schematization of cultural commodities serves to obviate the consumer's need to think for himself or herself. If Kant still expected individuals to perform the independent task of relating concepts to objects, the culture industry's ''prime service to the consumer is to do his schematizing for him'' (*DE*, 124).

Adorno's analysis of the culture industry's schemata is briefer and more truncated than his other forays into the effects of commodification on cultural goods. This analysis is found in ''The Schema of Mass Culture''—an addendum to the incomplete and fragmentary chapter on the culture industry in *Dialectic of Enlightenment*—as well as in such essays as ''Fernsehen als Ideologie.'' In the former essay, Adorno and Horkheimer linked the schemata of mass culture to those found in advertising, business and sports. Commenting on the schemata which the culture industry borrows from advertising, the authors observed that cultural commodities derive their ''poetic mystery'' from the fact that they participate ''in the infinite nature of production and the reverential awe inspired by objectivity fits in smoothly with the schema of advertising.''[55] Unfortunately, apart from their earlier and equally brief discussion of a related topic in *Dialectic of Enlightenment*—the idiom shared by advertising and cultural commodities—Adorno and Horkheimer never developed these ideas and their treatment of them is rather obscure. Moreover, the authors' analysis of the schemata appropriated from the business world is just as sketchy. As "objective," mass culture merely reflects "an objective style of life and perception," but in its "non-objective" character, the culture industry "does not declare war on the world of business but merely exploits its worn out expressive schemata—the myth of personification and platitudes about 'humanity' as a crude material resource" (SMC, 70).

The final reference to schemata in "The Schema of Mass Culture" reads: "The sporting events from which the schema [*sic*] of mass culture borrows so many of its features and which represent one of its favourite themes have divested themselves of all meaning" (SMC, 77). Earlier in the essay, Adorno and Horkheimer had written that cultural commodities begin to exhibit sport-like characteristics. They explained:

> The task of the screen actor breaks down into a set of precisely defined obligatory exercises each of which is compared with the corresponding one in the work of all the other competitors in the same group. And then in the end we have the final spurt, the ultimate exertion which has been kept in reserve all along, the culmination without antecedent intensification isolated from the previous action, the opposite of the dramatic climax. The film is articulated into so many sequences but its total duration, like that of the hit song, is regulated as if by stopwatch. In a space of one and a half hours the film should have knocked out its audience as planned. (SMC, 74–75)

Consumers themselves are also encouraged to compete, "whether by virtue of the way in which goods are offered to them or through the techniques of advertising" (SMC, 74).

In "The Schema of Mass Culture," Adorno and Horkheimer never analyzed with any rigor the specific provenance and functions of the schemata of advertising, business, and sports.[56] However, in "Fernsehen als Ideologie," Adorno explicitly ascribed to the culture industry's schemata the same Kantian function he had given them in *Dialectic of Enlightenment*. Moreover, the origin of the schemata appears to have changed. In the earlier version of this essay, "How to Look at Television," Adorno chose the English word "pattern" to refer to what he later called "*Schema*" in the German essay. Patterns or schemata can be found in such genres as the T. V. crime show. They alert the viewer to expect certain events to unfold during the program. For example, viewers will anticipate violence and murder when, in the opening scene of a television sketch (with the implausible and somewhat comical name "Dante's Inferno"), they see a man sitting in a bar at some distance from a rather dissolute young woman who orders another double cocktail (FI, 521–22). In this and similar cases, patterns or schemata can be understood as standardized frames of reference. Adorno claimed that these frames of reference were drawn from early modern novels and adhered "to the almost unchanged ideology of early middle-class society."[57]

The main effect that schemata have on viewers is to condition or encourage them to understand their own experiences unreflectively in a way similar to that found in the media. This effect is bolstered by the pseudo-realism of cultural commodities; the schemata or patterns found in television and film have an even greater impact on viewers because these media reproduce everyday life in such "realistic" detail. In his discussion of stereotypes—a fourth feature of cultural goods, closely related to schemata—Adorno expressed a similar concern about the effects of cultural commodities on individuals under late capitalism. Like schemata, stereotypes promote conformity to prevailing behavioral standards. As Miriam Hansen notes, the stereotypical characters of mass culture "spell out norms of social behavior—ways of being, smiling, and mating."[58] In so doing, they also rehearse "the compulsive assimilation of human beings to the commodity."[59] Stereotypes and schemata help to standardize behavior, ensuring that individuals do not deviate from what is socially acceptable. Adorno warned: "The repetitiveness, the selfsameness, and the ubiquity of mass culture tend to make for automatized reactions and to weaken the forces of individual opposition" (HLT, 138).

At the same time, however, Adorno did recognize that stereotypes are "an indispensable element of the organization and anticipation of experience, preventing us from falling into mental disorganization and chaos." As such, they are necessary in the realm of art. Nevertheless, in the hands of the culture industry, stereotypes have been turned into rigid and reified clichés. The industry may defend these clichés on the grounds that it needs to take into account "an infantile or adolescent public" (FI, 519), or with reference to the technological necessity of "having to produce an enormous amount of material in the shortest amount of time" (PF, 515). But this latter claim is suspicious. Adorno argued that the stereotypes found in products of the culture industry are qualitatively different from those in art. They are "cunningly calculated

psychological models'' which ''aim to pattern people after mass production.'' With its stereotypes the culture industry ensures that people
remain what they are anyway and reduces them ''even further to unconscious modes of behaviour'' (PF, 515).

Both stereotypes and schemata serve to reinforce certain types of
behavior and, as Adorno pointed out in other work, the behavior they
reinforce is largely narcissistic in character.[60] Pseudo-individualism attempts to conceal the repetitive sameness of stereotypes and schemata
as well as the standardization of cultural commodities. For its part, standardization ultimately represents the triumph of the general over the
particular. And, on Martin Jay's reading, this is how Adorno defines
reification. When Adorno used the term ''reification'' in a ''pejorative
sense,'' he meant ''the suppression of heterogeneity in the name of
identity.''[61] Insisting that some works of high modern art advanced ''the
perennial claim of the particular over the general, as long as the latter
remains unreconciled to the former,''[62] Adorno criticized products of
the culture industry for failing to honor this claim. Cultural commodities sacrifice ''whatever involved a distinction between the logic of the
work [the particular] and that of the social system [the general]'' (*DE*,
121).

Formulas for writing bestsellers, hit songs and blockbuster movies
have replaced the ''specific demands of the subject matter'' with which
artists were once concerned (*DE*, 130). This formulaic production of
cultural commodities has also become a cipher for the fate of particulars
in late capitalist societies. In their subsumption of particular objects and
subjects under standardized formulas, stereotypes, and schemata, the
culture industry's reified products reflect the more widespread damage
that late capitalism inflicts upon individuals. Glossing over whatever
conflicts may still exist between particular individuals and the general
socio-economic order of late capitalism, the culture industry now ''discloses the fictitious character of the 'individual' in the bourgeois era.''
While Adorno believed that bourgeois society did at one time develop
the individual through its technology (and against ''the will of its leaders''), he also argued that ''every advance in individuation . . . took
place at the expense of the individuality in whose name it occurred''
(*DE*, 155).

What the culture industry offers is always the same (*das Immer-
gleiche*): thoroughly planned, controlled, predictable, and calculable
commodities. By contrast, Adorno maintained that some instances of
high modern art successfully resist reification, evoking the conflicts between the individual and the socio-economic order of late capitalism.

Yet high modern art has never been completely independent of the
socio-economic sphere; its autonomy has always been relative. Moreover, Adorno sometimes expressed the fear that even the more successful forms of cultural production would end up forfeiting the autonomy
they once had. All culture would ultimately become as reified as mass
culture. As I have tried to show, there is empirical evidence to support
some of Adorno's views about the increasing standardization of many
cultural commodities. Yet his analysis of commodification is too superficial to provide justification for more extensive claims. In the final section of this chapter, I shall examine some of the lacunae in Adorno's
analysis.

Concluding Remarks

Stereotypes and schemata accompany the growing standardization of
cultural commodities. Pseudo-individualism attempts to mask standardization, responding to the demands of the cultural marketplace and regressive perception. As commodities entangled in mechanisms of exchange, products of the culture industry are scarcely able to supply
consumers with anything more valuable than social prestige—a fungible item in late capitalist societies. Although Adorno's analysis has
many flaws, it does serve as an important attempt to specify both the
use-value of the products of the culture industry and the consumer's
need for them. It is unfortunate, however, that Adorno barely touched
on the processes involved in cultural production. Indeed, what he says
about these processes is sometimes implicitly contradictory. Adorno
should also have examined far more closely the culture industry's economic dependence on other industrial and non-industrial sectors. The
connections which the industry has to the broader economy are mentioned only in passing in *Dialectic of Enlightenment*.

Another area of cultural production which the often prescient Adorno
virtually ignored is marketing and advertising. Bill Ryan shows how
marketing and advertising "increase or conserve use-value" by vaunting the commodity's utility.[63] (Wolfgang Haug makes a similar point
about the role of advertising in his book on commodity aesthetics.) In
Making Capital from Culture, Ryan provides examples of how the culture industry both directly and indirectly advertises and markets its
products. Films are sometimes promoted directly by being broadcast on
television, for example. Such promotion has become even more important with the growth in sales of video recordings. In radio, the air-time

given to a particular piece of music serves as a direct advertisement or "plug" for it. More indirect forms of advertising can be found in the use of "press, radio and television news, and reviews dealing with newly released books and recordings, publication of best-seller lists, interviews with artists. . . ."[64]

Despite their failure to examine the complex relationship between advertising and cultural commodities, Adorno and Horkheimer did recognize that both commodified culture and advertising merge technically in terms of their mode of production and economically in terms of their motives. In the forties, it might have been difficult to perceive all the mechanisms underlying the exchange of commodified culture because, although already a booming business, advertising would really come into its own only with the advent of television.[65] Adorno and Horkheimer were satisfied with a discussion of some of the similarities between commodified culture and advertising. They observed that the style of advertising had "permeated the idiom" of cultural commodities (*DE*, 162) and that "the mechanical repetition of the same culture product has come to be the same as that of the propaganda slogan" (*DE*, 163). It is entirely unfortunate that Adorno never followed up these remarks in later work. They should be explored in greater detail especially since it is becoming standard practice for corporations to pay the producers of movies and television programs to show their products being used by actors. This practice reveals that the culture industry indirectly promotes industrial commodities as well. It is therefore not surprising that cultural commodities should share the same idiom as advertising.

Cultural commodities indirectly promote industrial commodities in a second way. Adorno described this phenomenon on a very general level as early as 1938 in his article "On the Fetish Character in Music and the Regression of Listening." The music played during a radio program, for example, acts as a form of advertising: "Music, with all the attributes of the ethereal and sublime which are generously accorded it, serves in America today as an advertisement for commodities which one must acquire in order to be able to hear music" (FC, 278). More particularly, in order to finance production costs and generate a profit, cultural producers use their commodities to capture a stable audience with the highest possible income level which they can then market or sell to the advertisers of industrial (or other cultural) commodities. This aspect of cultural production deserves to be explored in much greater detail.[66] Nicholas Garnham claims that it allows the culture industry to circumvent some of the "economic contradictions that arise from the nature of cultural commodities.''[67] Indeed, these ''contradictions'' themselves should have been explored. As I mentioned earlier, one of Garnham's more interesting criticisms of Adorno can be found in his charge that Adorno did not take sufficient account of the conflict-ridden nature of the commodification of culture.

A number of other commentators have also criticized Adorno for overestimating the degree to which culture has become reified. For example, Andreas Huyssen writes: ''Even though Adorno recognizes quite frequently that there are limits to the reification of the human subject, he never asks himself whether perhaps there are also limits to the reification of cultural commodities themselves.''[68] Huyssen's criticism should be taken seriously. If there are conflicts in the relationship between culture and capital, then there may well be limits, not only to commodification, but also to the reification or fetish character of the culture industry's products. Similarly, Adorno could also be criticized for failing to explore in any depth the circulation and distribution of cultural commodities. If, as Garnham points out, distribution is really the locus of profit for the culture industry, then it is incumbent on anyone attempting to analyze the industry to study in more detail this aspect of exchange.

However, despite these lacunae in Adorno's political economy of the culture industry, it is no coincidence that his theory should continue to serve as the basis for a number of contemporary ''Marxian'' studies of the media. Garnham, Golding and Murdock, and Ryan all make use of Adorno's critique in their own work on the commodification of culture. Although he may often have done so only implicitly or summarily, Adorno obviously sketched out some of the major problems and questions that should inform this work. In advance of other theorists, Adorno identified the more important economically motivated tendencies and traits of both the culture industry and its products. Although his work on the political economy of the burgeoning industry was generally cursory and often superficial, Adorno can at least be credited with having charted waters for which maps had not yet been drawn.

Chapter 3

Psyche under Siege: The Psychology of Domination and Resistance

As they undertake their theoretical constructions of the socio-cultural realm, many social theorists mistakenly take as their foil Adorno's critical theory. For Adorno's allegedly "top-down" model of domination, they often substitute a model of resistance "from below," based in the social and cultural sphere of interpersonal and group relationships. In contemporary social theory, Adorno's views about the influence the culture industry exercises over individuals are frequently described as excessively pessimistic.[1] However, in spite of the undeniably pessimistic cast of many of his views,[2] Adorno did acknowledge that domination within the "totally administered world" has limits. In his work on the culture industry, Adorno not only pointed out that its ideology is transparent and weak, he also claimed that the industry plies its wares to consumers who are not entirely duped by them.

Owing to the narcissism Adorno believed was widespread in late capitalist societies, and to the equally debilitating effects of reification, the integrity of interpersonal relations has been undermined radically. The prevalence of narcissistic tendencies has made close involvement with and emotional attachment to others much more difficult. Reification compounds these problems. Individuals are "determined only through the abstract, thing-like act of exchange."[3] They are monads without windows, fated to remain socially isolated. Adorno therefore paid somewhat less attention to interpersonal relationships and the experiences of social groups than he did to individual psychology (although he certainly did explore some of the dimensions of class or group appurtenances).[4] On the few occasions when he spoke of resistance to the reified socio-economic order, Adorno appeared to locate it solely in the Promethean struggle of the isolated marginal against the social totality.

The instincts or drives potentially provide one of the material bases for resistance. Although society expects individuals to renounce many of their instincts, such renunciation cannot "be objectified as true and necessary" and is often not compensated even by delayed gratification.[5] This antagonistic situation sets the framework for resistance. Economic rationality is fundamentally "irrational"; so too is the reality principle which supports and sustains it. In the face of this irrationality of the real, neuroses themselves evince a kind of resistance. Adorno once wrote: "narcissism in its current form is nothing but the individual's desperate attempt to compensate at least partially for the injustice that no one ever gets his money's worth in the society of universal exchange."[6] Conversely, a thoroughgoing and critical psychoanalysis would ultimately "show the sickness proper to the time to consist precisely in normality." Although it is not healthy to be sick or neurotic, current standards of psychological health have had pathological consequences: "The libidinal achievements demanded of an individual behaving as healthy in body and mind, are such as can be performed only at the cost of the profoundest mutilation, of internalized castration in extroverts, beside which the old renunciation of identification with the father is the child's play as which it was first rehearsed."[7]

If the neurotic individual can be said to offer unconscious resistance to the social order, it is also the case that resistance may take a more conscious and rational form. Adorno did not believe that individuals were the passive objects of an overwhelming system of socio-economic domination and control. In fact, he saw quite clearly that in late capitalist societies, individuals were deceiving *themselves* about both the social order and the culture industry which reproduces and reinforces it. This self-deception can be made conscious. Since the ideology purveyed by the culture industry has become threadbare, only a "thin veil" prevents individuals from recognizing how flimsy this ideology has actually become. Moreover, Adorno also contended that individuals in late capitalist societies were the beneficiaries of enlightenment. If educators, psychologists, and sociologists were to lift the veil which screens the truth about cultural commodities from consciousness, consumers would be able to see how the culture industry perpetuates psychological repression and conformity to the status quo.

Domination and resistance are entwined dialectically in Adorno's work. Yet it is certainly also the case that, throughout his many essays and books, Adorno appeared to be far more interested in describing the nature of domination than in assessing the potential for resistance to it. Adorno's discussion of the social and psychological dimensions of domination in the ''totally administered world'' will be the topic of the first section of this chapter where Axel Honneth's interpretation and critique of Adorno will act as a counterpoint to Adorno's own views. The second section is devoted to Adorno's claims about the potential for resistance. In particular, the potential for conscious and enlightened resistance to the social totality will be explored. Although Adorno often seemed to attribute such resistive potential only to the non-heroic and marginal figures of the artist, the criminal, and the philosopher, he never abandoned completely the idea that narcissistic and reified individuals might succeed in opposing the culture industry's psychological techniques and effects. It is this dimension of Adorno's work which is more deserving of commentary since it has been occulted so often by his critics.

The Psychology of Domination

Axel Honneth criticizes Adorno for portraying the consumer of cultural commodities as ''a helpless victim of an all-pervasive media reality.''[8] According to Honneth, Adorno maintained that the ideology of the culture industry ''is sufficient for securing the required measure of social consensus formation in late-capitalist societies.''[9] Social integration takes three forms: ''political-economic reproduction, administrative manipulation, and psychic integration.''[10] In Adorno's work, political and economic reproduction are supposedly safeguarded by state capitalism. The economy and politics are centralized within bureaucratic state institutions which ensure their co-ordination; all social behavior is subordinated to these institutions. In conjunction with this political and economic reproduction, the culture industry practises what Honneth calls ''administrative manipulation.'' Such manipulation allegedly allows the industry to control completely the consciousness of its consumers.

For Honneth, Adorno's belief that the culture industry can ''control individual consciousness at the level of motivations''[11] has as its corollary his equally bleak view of the psychological constitution of individuals in industrial societies. Psychic integration is possible in late capitalist societies because the ego has become weak; children fail to internalize paternal authority during the Oedipal stage. Honneth correctly claims that Adorno ascribed the failure of internalization to the father's loss of economic independence. The liberal, laissez-faire market once "institutionalized a space for individual economic responsibility and freedom of discretion."[12] However, with the transformation of liberal capitalism into state capitalism, individual autonomy had eroded and children lacked "the personal counterpart required for internalizing the norms of prohibition that form the conscience." Enter the culture industry, which "is able to assume as a surrogate the task of regulating the instincts."[13] As a result of the weakness of the narcissistic ego, the culture industry encounters no resistance and can successfully integrate individuals, achieving social consensus.

On Honneth's reading, then, Adorno claimed that "The loss of paternal authority, which is the inner-familial result of that political restriction of economic independence and human control of dispositions, allows for a direct socialization of the child through administrative power."[14] In his discussion of the culture industry, Adorno supposedly heralded the "end of mediation." This thesis of the end of mediation (or of indirect manipulation) allegedly "arises out of the context of the *Dialectic of Enlightenment*, and . . . dominates the sociological writings of the 1960s as a guiding motif."[15] Social integration has been assumed effectively by extra-familial agencies which have a "direct" or immediate influence on human behavior. Although he does not offer any textual support for this interpretation of Adorno, Honneth turns to Jessica Benjamin's end of internalization thesis for substantiation.

Benjamin's thesis is a curious one. On Benjamin's reading, what results from the failure of the internalization of paternal authority is the "direct" and unmediated domination of individuals by extra-familial agencies and institutions. Benjamin states that Adorno believed the culture industry itself had become the object of immediate identification for children in late capitalist societies. The culture industry presumably plays the role of surrogate parent with the failure of internalization. Nevertheless, Freud—whose work Adorno followed closely—did not adequately distinguish between internalization and identification (or between these and introjection, for that matter),[16] although he did eventually make a distinction between the different activities of the superego which result from internalization or identification: "self-observation, conscience, and the holding up of ideals."[17] Like Freud, Adorno generally used the terms "internalization" and "identification" synonymously. Identification with the norms and values of the culture industry engages the same psychic processes that are involved in internalization. If identification persists, then internalization has not ended.

Another reason why Benjamin's end of internalization thesis is questionable is because Adorno believed that both the internalization of parental authority and identification with the culture industry are mediated by the superego. Identification is not direct or unmediated. The only textual support Benjamin provides for her thesis is one sentence in *Dialectic of Enlightenment*: "Instead of the internalization of the social command . . . , there is an immediate and direct identification with stereotyped value scales."[18] Benjamin treats this ambiguous passage as evidence for her claim that Adorno asserted that "fascism, like mass culture in advanced capitalism, results from a failure of internalization."[19] But, even if one concedes that Benjamin's reading of this sentence in the *Dialectic of Enlightenment* is correct, and Adorno and Horkheimer did intend to say that the end of the internalization of paternal authority resulted in direct domination, Adorno himself clearly presented a different view in other work.

To add insult to injury, Benjamin proceeds to accuse Adorno of contradicting himself. According to Benjamin, Adorno held two incompatible positions; he failed to choose between "the end of internalization, or the reaction of a weak ego to a strong ego-ideal."[20] In fact, however, there is no contradiction in Adorno's work. The narcissistic individual in late capitalist societies does have a powerful superego (or ego-ideal) formed from primitive introjects. Owing to the content of these introjects, it is possible that some activities of the superego (such as conscience and self-observation) have declined. But Adorno did not speak of a decline. In an article liberally cited by Benjamin, Adorno emphasized the strength of the narcissistic superego: "What takes place is that merger between id and superego that psychoanalytic theory already focused on, and it is precisely where the masses act instinctively that they have been preformed by censorship and enjoy the blessing of the powers that be" (SP1, 80). Against both Benjamin and Honneth, then, Adorno maintained that the culture industry exercises indirect domination via the superego.

Even when the Oedipus complex is more or less successfully negotiated, the superego remains closely allied to the id. In late capitalist societies, this alliance has become far more powerful. The merger of the superego and the id in narcissism effectively means that a superego formed in the image of a ferocious, voracious, omnipotent, and unbridled parent either refuses or permits the release of instinctual energy. Nazi leaders and American demagogues reanimate these primal and archaic superego introjects, exacting compliance by reinforcing conformity to the status quo. Moreover, this reanimation of introjects in the superego is also one of the principal psychological techniques used by the culture industry in its own "indirect" domination of consciousness. If, as Freud had shown throughout his work, "it is power which the individual internalizes" (RP, 32), the internalization of social domination is now mediated by the repressive and narcissistic superego.

Despite his assertion about the merger between the id and the superego, Adorno accused those he called "revisionists"[21] of oversimplifying the role played by the ego in individual psychology. As he explained in "Sociology and Psychology": "it is another aspect of the 'totalitarian' nature of present society that, perhaps more completely than in the past, people . . . reinforce with the energy of their ego the assimilation society imposes on them; and that they blindly pursue their self-alienation to the point of an illusory identity between what they are in themselves and what they are for themselves" (SP2, 86). The narcissistic ego plays an active role in promoting the values and ideology purveyed by cultural commodities. Since it is weak, however, the ego promotes these values at the behest of its stronger libidinal drives which are channeled through both the id and the superego.

In "Sociology and Psychology," Adorno briefly examined some of the theoretical problems connected with Freud's concept of the ego. These problems are only exacerbated with narcissism. Although he did not scrutinize it in any detail, Freud implicitly recognized that the ego has a dialectical structure. According to Adorno, Freud described the ego as both "psychic and extrapsychic, a quantum of libido and the representative of outside reality" (SP2, 86). This dual character of the ego as both unrepressed and conscious and unconscious and repressive makes it inherently weak, points to the fragility of all ego formations, and explains why the ego would regress. Under late capitalism, the already fragile ego encounters virtually insurmountable difficulties: it has to "understand reality and operate consciously" within an irrational world and, at the same time, "set up unconscious prohibitions and . . . remain largely confined to the unconscious" in order to carry out the renunciations expected of it (SP2, 87).

In narcissistic individuals, the claims of a largely unconscious and repressive ego-libido triumph over those of self-preservation and reality-testing. Adorno described the self-preservative interests of individuals in late capitalist societies as "split off" from consciousness and thereby "lost to rationality" (SP2, 88). When it regresses, the ego sacrifices consciousness itself; the ego's regression simultaneously negates and rigidifies it. Targeted by mass movements and the culture industry, the narcissistic individual "invariably combines the ruthlessly partial rationality of self-interest with a destructive, self-destructive, misshapen irrationality'' (SP2, 88). Since the interests associated with self-preservation have been relegated to the unconscious, it is easier for demagogues and the media ''to win the support of millions of people for aims largely incompatible with their own rational self-interest'' (FT, 121).

Individuals now often lack the capacity for rational self-control and independent decision-making. This loss of autonomy, accompanying both the ''ubiquity of modern mass culture'' and the decline of the family's role as the primary agent of socialization, has resulted in ''automatized reactions'' and the weakening of ''the forces of individual resistance,''[22] providing fertile ground for the culture industry's appeals to the emotions and its ersatz-gratification of human needs. The narcissistic ego has become so weak that its defenses against the id are also weak and infantile. In narcissism, what ''actually wanted to get beyond the unconscious . . . re-enters the service of the unconscious and may thus even strengthen its force'' (SP2, 87). The defenses of the formerly autonomous ego are now largely instinctually—not rationally—motivated. As a result, the prospects for resistance to the blandishments of the culture industry appear to be seriously compromised.

In a phrase he borrowed from Leo Löwenthal, Adorno characterized the domination exercised by the culture industry and Nazi leaders as ''psychoanalysis in reverse.'' The industry is instrumental in preventing the unconscious from becoming conscious—thus subverting the Freudian goal of making conscious to the ego the unconscious processes of the id. Like nazism, the culture industry expropriates ''the unconscious by social control instead of making the subjects conscious of their unconscious'' (FT, 136). Yet it is also the case that individuals foster their own integration into society by defending themselves against their drives through repression or by satisfying these drives following the orders of their superego. Since the culture industry and Nazi leaders reanimate introjects already internalized in the superego, they ''merely process the raw material supplied to them by the psychodynamics of those they weld into masses'' (SP2, 89). They ensure that individuals remain what they are anyway.

Adorno discussed the psychological mechanisms at work in propaganda in ''Freudian Theory and the Pattern of Fascist Propaganda'' and ''The Psychological Technique of Martin Luther Thomas' Radio Addresses.'' In these essays, he focused specifically on the reanimation of the ''idea of the all-powerful and threatening primal father'' (FT, 124). However, Adorno provided no comparable study of the reanimation of this primal father figure by the culture industry. Fortunately, in

Haven in a Heartless World, Christopher Lasch not only adopted Adorno's claim that the culture industry reanimates superego introjects, he also illustrated it. In television, comic strips, and film:

> The melodrama of crime brings to quasi-consciousness a sinister father-image, buried but not forgotten, in the disguise of a criminal, a "lord of the underworld," or a law-enforcement officer who commits crimes in the name of justice. In *The Godfather*, the identification of the father with the master-criminal becomes unmistakable, but in a more tenuous form it has always provided the excitement on which the popular thriller depends for its appeal to a mass audience.[23]

Lasch proceeds to examine another stock situation in which superego introjects are reanimated. In this situation, where a son is wrongly accused of his father's crimes, the superego is externalized in the form of the falsely accusing authorities. However, more work needs to be done, especially on phenomena like "mass idols" (Madonna or Michael Jackson, for example), but Lasch's analysis is quite convincing as far as it goes.

Apart from its reanimation of superego introjects, Adorno also described other psychological techniques used by the culture industry. All these techniques serve the function of making it difficult for individuals to transcend the social totality either in thought or imagination. According to Miriam Hansen, the "ideological effect" of mass culture "is not so much a matter of administering positive (or negative) models but, rather, of preventing human beings from changing, from being different, from distinguishing their own wishes and needs from those imposed upon them by distribution from above."[24] With their unstinting reproduction of the real, cultural commodities make the ideological claim that the way things are is the way they should be; they turn facts into values. Using the various psychological techniques at its disposal, the culture industry also realizes this ideology by reinforcing the psychological mechanisms and processes already present in narcissistic individuals. So, Adorno wrote: "The culture industry smirks: become what you are, and its lie consists in just this repetitive confirmation and reinforcement of the pure essence of that into which the course of the world has changed people."[25] These reinforcement techniques are discussed in a number of different essays to which I shall now turn.

In "Sociology and Psychology," Adorno contended that the culture industry induces individuals to mobilize those infantile defense mechanisms which "best dovetail into the pattern of the ego's social conflicts'' (SP2, 89). Since the translation of the passage in which Adorno described this reinforcement of the infantile defense mechanisms characteristic of narcissism is problematic, I shall quote the original:

> In Wahrheit werden selektiv diejenigen infantilen Abwehrmechanismen mobilisiert, welche in das Schema der sozialen Konflikte des Ichs je nach der geschichtlichen Lage am besten hineinpassen. Erst das, nicht die vielzitierte Wunscherfüllung, erklärt die Gewalt der Massenkultur über die Menschen.[26]

I am translating the second sentence as follows: ''It is primarily this [i.e., the selective mobilization of infantile defence mechanisms], not the much-touted wish-fulfillment, which explains mass culture's power over people.''

Owing to the individual's regression to the stage of primary narcissism—or toward ego-libido, the work of defense is carried out by ''a hybrid, ego-oriented and yet unsublimated, undifferentiated form of ego'' (SP2, 88). In this regressive state, the ego's only remaining line of defense is ''infantile'' in character and, given its libidinal form, its mobilization of these ''infantile'' defense mechanisms is increasingly instinctual. Once again, this situation gives much greater power to the id and the superego. Id psychology can now be ''mobilized by ego psychology with the help of demagogy and mass culture'' (SP2, 89). The same idea is repeated in another essay, ''Prolog zum Fernsehen,'' where Adorno wrote that ''the culture industry, with television at the forefront, reduces people even further to unconscious modes of behaviour instead of paying tribute to the unconscious, raising it to a conscious level, and thus both complying with its urges and satisfying its destructive power'' (PF, 515).

Nevertheless, Adorno's discussion of the way in which the culture industry aids and abets the ego's mobilization of infantile defense mechanisms is problematic because Adorno neither specified what these ''infantile'' defense mechanisms might be nor did he provide any examples of them. In ''Inhibitions, Symptoms and Anxiety,'' Freud speculates that before the ego separates from the id and the superego is formed, it is possible that ''the mental apparatus makes use of different methods of defence from those which it employs after it has reached these stages of development.''[27] Anna Freud, whose *The Ego and the Mechanisms of Defense* was criticized by Adorno in ''Sociology and Psychology,'' cited the above passage from her father's work, pointing out how difficult it is to link the different defense mechanisms to partic-

ular stages in psycho-sexual development. According to the younger
Freud: the "chronology of psychic processes is still one of the most
obscure fields in analytic theory."[28] However, she also noted that some
analysts believe introjection and projection are at work before the ego
develops. Since he did not specify precisely which defenses he considered to be infantile, Adorno's account of their mobilization is incomplete and unclear.

123   Apart from its reanimation of superego introjects and mobilization
of infantile defense mechanisms, the culture industry also uses wish-
fulfillment as a reinforcement technique. Having virtually dismissed it
in "Sociology and Psychology," Adorno did make more detailed reference to wish-fulfillment in other essays, such as "Prolog zum Fernsehen," where he described television as "the boldest form of wish-
fulfilment." However, in the same sentence, Adorno appears to contradict himself when he claims that television has also revoked "the very
principle of wish-fulfilment." Adorno's paradoxical view of the wish-
fulfillment offered by the culture industry reflects his belief that our
capacity to identify and formulate our desires or wishes has become
problematic:

> The hollow phrase about the fulfilment of fairy-tale fantasies by modern
> technology ceases to be hollow only if one adds to it the fairy-tale wisdom
> that the fulfilment of wishes seldom redounds to the benefit of those who
> wish. The most difficult art of all is to wish correctly and we are cured of
> it in childhood. (PF, 516)

In other words, the images of television serve to fulfill our wishes, just
as dream images do but we no longer know how to wish or what we
should wish for. The wishes television fulfills have been colonized and
corrupted.

In an earlier article, "On Popular Music," published in 1941, Adorno
discussed the wish-fulfillment at work in "sentimental" film and popular music. Both media evoke the "possibility of happiness," allowing
audience members to "dare to confess to themselves what the whole
order of contemporary life ordinarily forbids them to admit, namely,
that they actually have no part in happiness." Despite its implicitly
emancipatory function, however, the alleged wish-fulfillment at work
in Hollywood and Tin Pan Alley really only amounts to "the scant
liberation that occurs with the realization that at last one need not deny
oneself the happiness of knowing that one is unhappy and that one
could be happy."[29] Adorno maintained that the experience of liberation

provided by wish-fulfillment is always frustrated. Happiness is both evoked and refused at the same time. Wish-fulfillment provides "katharsis for the masses" and, as Aristotle already implied, catharsis only serves to keep people "all the more firmly in line." The woman who weeps for happiness in the darkened movie theater "does not resist any more than one who marches" (PM, 42).

A fourth technique employed by the culture industry can be found in its widespread use of stereotypes and schemata. Like the other techniques, stereotypical images and schematized themes prevent individuals from thinking beyond the given. They fix and rigidify experience. As a result, "people may not only lose true insight into reality, but ultimately their very capacity for life experience may be dulled by the constant wearing of blue and pink spectacles" (HLT, 147). Adorno argued that the culture industry "assiduously concerns itself with the production of those archetypes in whose survival fascistic psychology perceives the most reliable means of perpetuating the modern conditions of domination."[30] The industry's employment of stereotypes finds its counterpart in nazism's use of endlessly repeated standard psychological and rhetorical devices. The speeches and rituals of the National Socialists had a mechanically rigid pattern. It is partially through their stereotypes and clichés that nazism and the culture industry foster contemporary forms of domination, reinforcing the status quo.

Stereotypes and schemata serve to reinforce the status quo in a second way: by providing a narcissistic gain. They thereby successfully process the raw material—the narcissistic tendencies—supplied to them by individuals within late capitalist societies. In an article dealing in part with Adorno's views on mass culture, Miriam Hansen referred indirectly to this function when she wrote that, for Adorno, stereotypes solicit viewers "as experts, as active readers." Hansen explains that "identification *with* the stereotype is advanced by the appeal to a particular type of knowledge or skill predicated on repetition: the identification *of* a familiar face, gesture or narrative convention takes the place of genuine cognition."[31] Individuals derive a narcissistic gain from the successful recognition of constantly repeated stereotypes and schemata. In addition to this narcissistic gain, both Nazi propaganda and cultural commodities offer yet another which results from the constant and sometimes devious suggestion that those who belong to the in-group are "better, higher and purer" than those in other groups (FT, 130). The reinforcement of narcissistic tendencies through flattery is one of the central techniques of both nazism and the culture industry.

Adorno identified a number of different stereotypes at work in television programs. For example, in one of his content analyses of television scripts, Adorno described the portrayal of a woman who behaved "with indescribable cruelty and inhumanity towards her father" but whose behavior was "rationalized as an amusing prank."[32] Since she was never punished, the audience would consider the woman's actions to be socially acceptable, reinforcing the stereotypical idea that "the pretty young woman is always right." Another particularly widespread stereotype, which Adorno examined in many essays, is that of the artist or intellectual as "an abnormal, and somewhat ridiculous weakling or emotional cripple who does not know how to live." Popular culture "glorifies the strong man—its image of the man of action—and intimates that artists are really homosexuals." Stereotypes like these curry favor "with the international climate of anti-intellectualism" (FI, 524).

What underlies the identification with stereotypes, wish-fulfillment, the mobilization of infantile defense mechanisms, and the reanimation of superego introjects are human needs. The culture industry deals with these needs in a variety of ways. Having first discussed the problem of needs in his 1942 essay, "Thesen über Bedürfnis" (where, once again, Adorno refused to distinguish between "social and natural, primary and secondary, true and false" needs),[33] Adorno reiterated his ideas in "Sociology and Psychology" where he wrote that "the manifest or repressed instinctual moment finds expression only in the form of needs, which have today become wholly a function of profit interests" (SP1, 77). However, an interpretation of Adorno on this issue is complicated by a later statement made in "Late Capitalism or Industrial Society?": "It is quite definitely possible to distinguish between objectively 'true' and 'false' human needs."[34]

In "Late Capitalism," however, Adorno did not himself distinguish between true and false needs. He merely maintained that this distinction was possible in principle.[35] In order to determine which needs are false and which true, one would have to acquire knowledge of "the structure of society as a whole . . . , together with all of its mediations" (LC, 242). In the absence of such an analysis, it can safely be said that even allegedly genuine or authentic human needs are socially mediated:

Human needs have become a function of the machinery of production. . . . They are thoroughly manipulated [gesteuert]. It is of course true enough that in this transformation, in being thus molded and shaped to the requirements of the social apparatus, human needs are to some degree met— needs which the social apparatus can then effectively mobilize in its own defense. But the use-value aspect of commodities has, in the interim, lost whatever immediate self-evidence it may once have possessed. It is not only that human needs are met indirectly, by way of exchange value; in some sectors of the economy these needs are in fact directly created by the profit-interests themselves, to the detriment of objective consumer needs—adequate housing, for instance, and especially the need for education and for information about general events which most directly concern the consumer. (LC, 238–39)

In this passage, Adorno also qualifies the remark made in "Sociology and Psychology" that *all* needs are created by profit interests.

Honneth objects to what he claims is Adorno's description of the relationship between the needs expressing human instincts and their gratification under late capitalism. He complains that, in Adorno's work, "the organic substrate of human instincts is so designed that it fits without any remainder into the model of the offers for satisfaction borne by the system."[36] However, Honneth's interpretation cannot be substantiated; Adorno did acknowledge that the system often demands "instinctual renunciation" and sometimes refuses to give the individual even delayed gratification (SP2, 85). In his "Late Capitalism" essay, Adorno also spoke about the "illusory and distortive aspects of satisfaction of needs." The disparity between the demands of the instincts and their gratification by institutions or agencies like the culture industry is "today undoubtedly registered at the subconscious level, and this contributes to the discontent with civilization" (LC, 242).

There is no easy fit between human needs and the gratification of those needs by the culture industry. Some needs are simply repressed. Others are deflected "with the help of well-tried psychological techniques that have long been in use in totalitarian and non-totalitarian countries alike." These needs are diverted into "a few chosen channels" (SP1, 79) with the aid of techniques which probably include the condensation and displacement that are at work in dream images. Still other needs, which are socially engineered, may be satisfied by the culture industry. Furthermore, one may also speculate that cultural commodities do satisfy some "true" human needs. In his "Prologue to Television," Adorno wrote that the culture industry is connected to "the instinctual urges of the masses—be they repressed or simply unsatisfied—which cultural goods accommodate directly or in a mediated fashion; mostly the latter. . . ." He then proceeded to describe how sexual needs are indirectly satisfied by the depiction of violence on television, citing the work of the psychologist George Legman who claimed that, in mass culture, "sexual drives are replaced by the repre-

sentation of desexualized brutality and acts of violence'' (PF, 513).[37] It
should be clear from these remarks that Adorno realized the culture
industry deals with needs in a variety of ways: from repression to gratification.

It is entirely unfortunate that Adorno never fully developed his analysis of the culture industry's gratification of needs. In fact, in ''Thesen
über Bedürfnis,'' Adorno went so far as to say that contemporary film
and radio ''probably already satisfy hardly any need'' (TB, 394). Yet
Adorno did identify and briefly discuss one instinctually based need
which cultural commodities attempt to meet. In *Dialectic of Enlightenment*, Adorno and Horkheimer had claimed that the use-value of the
culture industry was that of social esteem or prestige. Adorno later ex-
panded on this idea concerning the culture industry's use-value when
he wrote that the need it satisfies is expressed in the desire to compensate for social powerlessness.[38] The fact that individuals actually do
experience this powerlessness is explained by their conscious or latent
recognition of the discrepancy between the normative truth of liberal
ideology and its empirical falsity. In the face of this discrepancy between their actual state of unfreedom and dependence and the ideology
of freedom and autonomy, individuals attempt to compensate for their
inability to bridge the gap by cultivating themselves using the cultural
commodities at their disposal. Cultivation—or pseudo-cultivation
(*Halbbildung*)—allows individuals to turn themselves, ''either in fact
or imagination,'' into aspects ''of something higher and more encompassing to which they attribute qualities which they themselves lack
and from which they profit by vicarious participation'' (PC, 32–33).

This need that individuals have to prove themselves cultivated manifests narcissistic tendencies: ''The attitude which links pseudo-culture
and collective narcissism is that of being in charge, of having a say, of
conducting oneself and considering oneself as an expert.'' People derive a sense of ''empowerment'' from their pseudo-cultivation; they
flatter themselves with the social prestige they believe they gain from
it. To become cultivated now requires little; ''enrollment in a better
school, sometimes even the pretention of being from a good family,
are already sufficient'' (PC, 33). In return, cultivation provides ''the
narcissistic gratification of leading a secret life and belonging to a select
group.'' This narcissistic gain exempts individuals ''from reality-
testing'' and allows them to live in the ''delusional systems'' supplied
by the schemata of the culture industry (PC, 34–35).

Adorno himself conceded that much more work needed to be done
on the problem of needs. He insisted that what the culture industry

really offers people by way of the gratification of their needs could be ascertained only by undertaking depth-psychological analyses. These studies would also uncover the industry's psychotechnical expertise in attracting and sustaining its audience's attention. Adorno recognized early on how crucial to the culture industry "mind management" had become. In Herbert Schiller's words, the "managers of cultural industries are acutely sensitive to the moods and feelings of the nation's many publics." Although they may frequently be wrong, they are certainly very well paid to make "day-by-day, if not hour-by-hour, assessments of these feelings." Schiller also points out that culture industries have invested heavily in the marketing of their products: "the industries have at their disposal a very elaborate, expensive, and sophisticated technology—polling and surveying—to ascertain popular preferences, likes and dislikes, expectations, etc."[39] Yet, along with a detailed discussion of why the masses want what the industry produces, Adorno's work lacks a study of the industry's marketing strategies and techniques.

Psychological studies of both the culture industry's techniques and individual reception would probably also serve to corroborate some of the views of contemporary social theorists, especially their idea that "manipulation" has limits. Moreover, social theorists like Honneth should not ignore Adorno's own claims about the limits to reinforcement and the possibility for resistance from below. Having considered some of the reinforcement techniques used by the culture industry in its indirect domination of consumers, I would like to go on to examine these limits as well as the prospects for emancipation in Adorno's work. Contra Honneth, Adorno did not believe that "the human instinctual potential can become directly tied by the administrative power to the tasks of social reproduction through the utilization of narcissistic energies."[40] The question of how the instincts or drives might provide one of the bases for resistance will be one of the problems considered in the next section of this chapter.

The Psychology of Resistance

The failure of the socio-economic order to satisfy drives or instincts is often "stifled by consciousness" by means of rationalizations (SP2, 85). However, these rationalizations do not succeed in eliminating the antagonisms between the individual's instinctual drives and the socio-economic system's demands and offers of gratification. Moreover, these very antagonisms are responsible for what Adorno diagnosed as "the general unease" experienced by individuals in late capitalism (LC, 242). Instinctual dissatisfaction serves as a potentially resistive force that may be translated into action. During the sixties, for example, "traces of a counter movement . . . [had] become visible, primarily among the most diverse sections of the youth, namely resistance to blind conformism, freedom to opt for rationally chosen goals, disgust with the condition of the world as the hoax and illusion it is and an awareness of the possibility of change" (LC, 245). Radical protests had occurred despite the loss of those personality traits which had once facilitated resistance.

In his refusal to integrate sociology and psychology, Adorno left room for resistance to the social order. If the uneasy "fit" between the social totality and individual drives indicates the powerlessness of the individual, it also reveals the space in which resistance is possible. Despite the fact that social forces indirectly reinforce pathological behavior via the superego, the thesis of total integration overlooks the fact that for Adorno, the individual's "psychological dimension had not been totally obliterated."[41] Although individual consciousness had become increasingly dysfunctional and regressive—owing in part to the culture industry which, in principle at least, could control and coordinate "the beliefs and attitudes of countless people from some central location" (LC, 243)—Adorno continued to maintain that some, albeit limited, potential for resistance existed both on the instinctual level and on the more conscious level.

However, apart from a few pregnant and largely implicit references to instinctual resistance against the totally administered world, Adorno did not discuss such resistance in any detail. In this he differed from Herbert Marcuse who, in his *Essay on Liberation*, posited and elaborated on "the instinctual basis for freedom which the long history of class society has blocked."[42] Marcuse thought that some instinctually-based resistance was healthy and radical. Although both he and Adorno maintained that the demands and behavior of sixties radicals offered some resistance to the one-dimensional or totally administered world, Adorno was far more circumspect about the nature of that resistance and its potential to make a real difference.[43] Perhaps Adorno's lack of support for protest movements during the sixties can be explained by his views about the prevalence of narcissism which makes possible only a psychologically pathological resistance to the social totality.[44]

Despite Adorno's contention, then, that the instincts or drives are fundamentally antagonistic to the social order, only a few tentative and well-qualified remarks can be made about an Adornian version of instinctual resistance to that order. Fortunately, Adorno did not confine resistance to an instinctual basis. He realized that there were other bases for resistance when he held out the hope that individuals might become consciously aware of the functions and effects of the culture industry. The preconditions for "consciousness-raising" already exist. According to Adorno, the ideology of the culture industry is extremely weak, the consciousness of its consumers is duplicitous, and consumers have achieved a degree of "enlightenment" which cannot be revoked arbitrarily.

Adorno strongly criticized the view that individuals in late capitalism were blind and unwitting objects in an insuperable system of domination:

> [W]e cannot content ourselves with merely stating that spontaneity has been replaced by blind acceptance of the enforced material. Even the belief that people today react like insects and are degenerating into mere centers of socially conditioned reflexes, still belongs to the façade. Too well does it serve the purpose of those who prate about the New Mythos and the irrational powers of community. (PM, 47–48)

The belief that individuals react in predictable and controllable ways to certain stimuli is held by Nazi leaders, demagogues, and the culture industry. Endorsement of this belief would mean that Adorno shared with the latter a view of individual psychology which effectively supported their assertions about the efficacy of manipulatory techniques. However "pessimistic" or "élitist" he may have been, Adorno would not countenance that "inherent contempt of the masses" which underlies the assumption shared by both nazism and the culture industry that individuals are entirely malleable (FT, 119).

The culture industry does not succeed completely in controlling and reinforcing the consciousness of its consumers. In a much-celebrated passage from "Freizeit," one of his last essays, Adorno explicitly denied that complete control and reinforcement were possible. Quoting a passage from this essay, Axel Honneth characterizes it as "unusually strange" because, in it, Adorno conceded "the possibility that the messages [of the culture industry] could simply reverberate against the walls of an everyday world skeptical toward the pseudo-reality of the media."[45] Adorno is renowned for his pessimism; he allegedly thought that only an "eschatological rupture" would bring about the change needed to free individuals from their imprisonment in the iron cage of the "totally administered world." It is this influential but flawed interpretation of Adorno which blinds Honneth and other commentators to texts in which Adorno clearly stated that narcissistic individuals are not helpless pawns in an indefeasible system. Adorno was much less pessimistic than his commentators generally believe.

The passage in "Freizeit" to which Honneth refers is not at all unusually strange. The views expressed in this essay can be found as early as 1941, in "On Popular Music," where Adorno spoke of the thin veil separating consciousness from its knowledge of the lies purveyed in the threadbare ideology of the culture industry. Domination has become an open secret. This is a point Adorno reiterated throughout his work. Nazi leaders and the culture industry "bank" on the irrationality of contemporary consciousness. In their propaganda and ideology, they attempt to convince, not "through the rational statement of rational aims," but through statements "obviously based on psychological calculations" (FT, 118). However, these calculations do not always succeed completely because, at the very least, individuals have an unconscious awareness of the flimsiness of that very propaganda and ideology. In his 1953 essay, published in German as "Fernsehen als Ideologie," Adorno expressed the hope that education would debunk the culture industry's ideology, cultivating among television viewers "a public aversion to being led by the nose" (FI, 531).

Adorno reiterated this earlier claim about the weakness of the culture industry's ideology in "Transparencies on Film." But in this essay, Adorno also supplemented his discussion of the fragility of the culture industry's hold on consciousness by referring to the disparity which may exist between the film-goer's ideas and forms of behavior and the culture industry's ideology. This disparity creates a "gap" or breach between a film's "intentions" and its actual effects. Adorno thought that empirical communications research should give priority to exploring this gap because it could lead to important results.[46] This point was made earlier, in a more vague and indirect fashion, in "Culture Industry Reconsidered": although the culture industry "touches the lives of innumerable people, the function of something is no guarantee of its particular quality."[47] Adorno frequently described the culture industry's reinforcement techniques and ideology—the frank lie no one believes—as fragile. Moreover, he insisted that consumers of cultural commodities were already aware of the truth. According to Adorno, the consciousness of the consumers of cultural commodities is duplicitous.

In "On Popular Music," Adorno wrote that the truth about the culture industry "is subjectively no longer so unconscious as it is expected to be'' (PM, 47). In connection with this idea, Adorno also spoke of "the tremendous effort which each individual has to make in order to accept what is enforced upon him—an effort which has developed for the very reason that the veneer veiling the controlling mechanisms has become so thin" (PM, 48). On the one hand, then, a great deal of psychic energy is required to repress knowledge of the truth. People "need their will, if only in order to down the all too conscious premonition that something is 'phony' with their pleasure.'' On the other hand, Adorno also recognized that making people consciously aware of what they know unconsciously is "almost insuperably difficult" (PM, 47). People deceive themselves "with rationalizations or abstract statements like the one that television really 'entertains' them" (PF, 512). Self-deception is not easily defeated. Only a psychoanalytically oriented analysis can uncover what really lies behind duplicitous consciousness.

Since, by definition, self-deception is practised by consumers themselves, and not by the culture industry, Adorno could not content himself with the view that blind acceptance of cultural commodities had been substituted for a once spontaneous reception. If viewers and listeners were entirely passive and manipulated, they would not be capable of *self*-deception. Even in *Dialectic of Enlightenment*—the book most often cited by commentators to support their interpretation of a total manipulation thesis—Adorno and Horkheimer did not maintain that consumers succumbed completely to the blandishments of the culture industry. Consumers "suspect that the less anything costs, the less it is being given them." Their attitude is characterized by a double mistrust: the mistrust "of traditional culture as ideology is combined with mistrust of industrialized culture as a swindle" (*DE*, 161). This idea is reiterated in another passage from *Dialectic of Enlightenment*: "The triumph of advertising in the culture industry is that consumers feel compelled to buy and use its products even though they see through them" (*DE*, 167).[48]

Earlier in their chapter on the culture industry, Adorno and Horkheimer described resistance to "the pleasure industry" as exceptional, but they also added that it had become "increasingly difficult" to keep people in the unreflective condition that prevented resistance: "The rate at which they are reduced to stupidity must not fall behind the rate at which their intelligence is increasing" (*DE*, 145). While it is admittedly the case that, in much of this chapter in *Dialectic of Enlightenment*, Adorno and Horkheimer offer few reasons for believing that the rate at which people's intelligence is increasing will actually outstrip attempts to keep them in a state of stupidity, one should not, for all that, overlook their claim that it might.

Similar claims are made in other work. In "Prolog zum Fernsehen," Adorno refers to various "contradictions" or discrepancies in cultural commodities. Although the public does not appear to be bothered by the fact that the unbroken world of images is actually fragmented, it will "know this unconsciously." Consequently: "The suspicion will grow that the reality one serves is not what it pretends to be" (PF, 510). In a very interesting little essay written in 1963, "Kann das Publikum Wollen?" Adorno wrote the following:

> The millions of people who consume mass culture, which has been tailor-made for them and has really turned them into masses for the first time, have no inherently standardized consciousness. Beneath the level of weak ideology, they feel, on a preconscious level, that they are being deceived by the front page of every newspaper, by every cellophane-wrapped hit. They probably only approve so spasmodically of what they are force-fed because they are obliged to evade their consciousness of it as long as they have nothing else.[49]

Here Adorno repeats a number of ideas expressed in earlier essays and books: the culture industry's ideology is weak; people unconsciously know they are being deceived but actively seek to conceal this knowledge from themselves.

When *New German Critique* published a translation of Adorno's radio talk—broadcast in 1963 for the International Radio University Program—under the title "The Culture Industry Reconsidered," Andreas Huyssen contrasted the modified version of the "concept of a manipulated culture industry" presented in the broadcast to the "totally negative version presented in *Dialectic of Enlightenment*."[50] Seven years later, when the same journal published a translation of "Filmtransparente," Miriam Hansen was moved to make a similar contrast: readers of the translation would be surprised because the "essay seems to suspend some of the major fixations of Adorno's theory on Culture Industry."[51] However, given Adorno's comments in "On Popular Music" and *Dialectic of Enlightenment*, along with the remarks he made in other essays, such "surprise" seems quite unwarranted. One need not read Adorno against the grain in order to avoid attributing to his work a simple-minded thesis about the total manipulation of consciousness by the culture industry.

In his essay on free time, Adorno made even more explicit his earlier characterization of the consciousness of media consumers as duplicitous. Based on empirical work, carried out by the Institute for Social Research, on the German public's reception of the wedding of Holland's Princess Beatrix to Claus von Amsberg, Adorno claimed that "symptoms of a doubled consciousness"[52] came to the fore:

> What the culture industry presents people with in their free time . . . is indeed consumed and accepted, but with a kind of reservation. . . . Perhaps one can go even further and say it is not quite believed in. It is obvious that the integration of consciousness and free time has not yet completely succeeded. The real interests of individuals are still strong enough to resist, within certain limits, total inclusion. . . . [A] society, whose inherent contradictions persist undiminished, cannot be totally integrated even in consciousness. (Time, 170)

This idea of "doubled consciousness" finds more contemporary confirmation in the work of Jean Baudrillard. According to the latter, belief in the culture industry is similar to belief in myth: *"One believes in them and one does not believe in them."* People respond to what the system offers with "ambivalence," "disaffection," or with "an always enigmatic belief."[53] Baudrillard admonishes critics for presupposing that the "masses" are so naive and stupid that they would swallow the "myth" whole. Unfortunately, neither he nor Adorno elaborated on their idea that the consciousness of consumers of cultural commodities is duplicitous. More work needs to be done on this duplicity and on the self-deception that prevents consciousness from bringing to the surface what it allegedly already knows. The motives of the self-deceived should be explored along with the psychological (and logical) mechanisms involved in self-deception.

The culture industry cannot completely reinforce and control the consciousness and the unconscious of its consumers. It is unable to do so not only because of the contradictions inherent in late capitalism, and the transparency of its ideology; nor does the duplicitous consciousness of the consumers of cultural commodities account entirely for the limits to reinforcement. As Adorno had observed in "Theory of Pseudo-Culture," these limits are also a consequence of the fact that, to a certain extent, people have already been "enlightened." The same point is made in "Freudian Theory and the Pattern of Fascist Propaganda." In this latter essay, however, Adorno's bleak depiction of Nazi followers as "post-psychological deindividualized social atoms" (FT, 136) lends credence to some of the accusations leveled against his work. Yet, despite this depiction, Adorno went on to describe how the psychological impoverishment of Nazi followers dialectically reversed itself. The dynamics of group psychology were no longer able to function in nazism since the autonomy and spontaneity presupposed by group psychology were largely absent. As a result, the ego-ideal was not thoroughly internalized; demagogues and mass idols began to appear phony, and identification was only acted out, performed. Adorno wrote: "It is through this performance that they strike a balance between their continuously mobilized instinctual urges and the historical stage of enlightenment they have reached, and which cannot be revoked arbitrarily" (FT, 137).

In Adorno's work, liberal ideology, based historically in the Enlightenment, contains a speculative moment against which individuals can judge their own historical condition. For example, the liberal concept of autonomy or self-sufficiency serves as an historical and speculative ideal contrasting with the current lack of autonomy; a gap or breach arises between the autonomy promised in the normative ideal and its empirical and historical realization. As early as *Minima Moralia*, Adorno had insisted on the importance of preserving the speculative content in the liberal ideology of the Enlightenment.[54] (This idea is reiterated in *Negative Dialectics* in particular but it also appears in many of Adorno's essays.) In addition, Adorno maintained that the liberal ideology of the Enlightenment had so affected consciousness that it could not be expunged. Individuals have "absorbed" this ideology. Either consciously or unconsciously, they compare their current condition with liberal ideology's promises and claims. Despite all the passages in his work which seem to deny that the individual can make the distinction between what is and what ought to be, there are other passages which illustrate that Adorno believed individuals in late capitalist societies were at least marginally aware of the disparity.

In some of his essays, then, Adorno offered another explanation for the limits to reinforcement which is not incompatible with his claims that the culture industry's ideology is weak and the consciousness of its consumers duplicitous. For Adorno, the liberal ideology of the Enlightenment does not function solely as an instrument of domination and oppression but actually explains why people cannot be dominated and oppressed completely. Since they have already been "enlightened" to a certain extent, individuals are at the very least unconsciously aware of the culture industry's fraudulence and frank lies. But Adorno did not describe the enlightenment individuals have attained as "genuine" or authentic. In the passages from "Theory of Pseudo-Culture" and "Freudian Theory and the Pattern of Fascist Propaganda" cited above, Adorno only advanced the historical claim that the liberal ideology of the Enlightenment had acted as a force on people's consciousness and served as counter-force to the ideology of the culture industry and the propaganda of Nazi leaders.[55] The ideology of Enlightenment was valued for its oppositional effects. Adorno's claims about liberal ideology will be examined in greater detail in Chapter 4.

Nonetheless, even if one concedes that the individual's unconscious knowledge of the truth can be attributed to the achievement in history of a certain degree of maturity (*Mündigkeit*), Adorno neither explained how this knowledge had been acquired nor how it had managed to resist successfully the culture industry's attempts at anti-enlightenment. These questions should have been answered. By contrast, Adorno did attempt to show that the culture industry has limits. The "administrative manipulation" carried out by the culture industry is neither total nor, given the psychological makeup of its consumers, could it ever become so. In fact, the belief that the culture industry can totally manipulate consciousness is advanced by the very demagogues and political leaders whose actions and ideas Adorno excoriated. As Adorno repeatedly emphasized, however deformed it may have become, the consciousness of individuals within late capitalist societies "is unconsciously aware of its own deformation" (PC, 34).

Concluding Remarks

Axel Honneth maintains that if one studied the everyday lifeworld of social groups to locate in them "subcultural interpretive styles and forms of perception—that is cooperative interpretive accomplishments," one would discover that "the cooperative production of group-specific horizons of orientation was itself not subject to manipulation." According to Honneth, there is "an autonomous sphere of cultural action in which members of a social group bring their everyday experiences and interests into agreement in one common world view."[56] However, Honneth's claim is clearly too categorical. Manipulation is not only exercised from above; even on the "grassroots" level, individuals attempt to control and manipulate one another. Social theorists like Michel Foucault have demonstrated convincingly that there are few, if any, interpersonal relationships or social groups that are completely free of "micro-political" struggles.

It is just as false to posit a realm of human action or interaction entirely free of manipulation as it is to claim that manipulation is total. Furthermore, one could question Honneth's assertion that the effects of socio-economic domination and control are minimal or completely absent in the lifeworld. Adorno's theory provides an important corrective to such a view. In order to refute Adorno's theory, Honneth would have to show that the narcissism many psychologists describe as prevalent in contemporary Western societies is entirely independent of changes in the nature of capitalism. He would also have to refute Adorno's views about the effects of reification on consciousness. In addition, Honneth would have to address specifically Adorno's analysis of the techniques used by the culture industry to reinforce the status quo instead of creating a straw-man Adorno in order to rebut a simplistic thesis about complete control and manipulation.

Adorno's recognition of the self-deception practised by consumers of cultural industrial products did not take him "along the path of an inquiry into the subcultural orientation-horizons that are the result of an interpretive praxis based on the on-going common experiences of social groups."[57] For Adorno, the family no longer served as the basis for resistance against the social order, and other groups often exhibited psychological traits associated with nazism. Nonetheless, it would not be fruitless to explore what Honneth describes as the "orientation-horizons" of different social groups and Adorno's work might even prove useful here. Adorno did acknowledge that, in late capitalist societies, liberal ideology provided, if not a "subcultural" horizon, then at least a prevalent mode of self-understanding which occasionally had the effect of countering the culture industry's messages and techniques. Although individuals in late capitalist societies are not free, autonomous, and equal, they believe they are. (Perhaps this "orientation-horizon" also underlies Honneth's own criticism of Adorno.)

Most commentators on Adorno's analysis of the culture industry single out the late essays as indicative of his new appreciation of the limits to its powers. They tend to read all other work by Adorno in light of "The Culture Industry: Enlightenment as Mass Deception" in *Dialectic of Enlightenment*. These interpretations of Adorno, which are often only glosses on the widespread view that he was overwhelmingly pessimistic about manipulation, can and should be challenged. It should be clear that Adorno both posited and briefly examined the duplicity of consciousness very early in his work. Along with his belief in the continuing efficacy of liberal ideology, Adorno's assertions about consumer duplicity deserve to be taken seriously. Owing to their self-deception, consumers are facilitating practices of domination. Making them aware of their complicity in these practices could have far-reaching consequences.

Despite their questionable claim that Adorno subscribed to a thesis "of the total commercialization and manipulation" of consciousness in most of his work, theorists like Andreas Huyssen recognize that a more balanced theory of the culture industry "provides parameters for future investigations."[58] Although Adorno's insights were dated, Huyssen thought that they could be applied to media reception in the seventies on the condition that "we stay this side of the thesis of universal manipulation and delusion (*Verblendungszusammenhang*), while going beyond the thesis of absolute negativity of all art."[59] Even now in the nineties, Adorno's explanations for the limits to domination in the reception of cultural commodities should be corroborated and elaborated both in theory and in empirical work. Unfortunately, given the passage of time, it has become virtually impossible to confirm (or to disconfirm) many of Adorno's views concerning the psychology of domination and resistance. However, the fact that other writers—like Christopher Lasch—have made use of Adorno's work on the psychotechnics of the culture industry shows that this work still merits reflection. Adorno was too dialectical a thinker to fall prey to one-dimensional thinking. A number of important ideas in Adorno's social psychology remain untapped and deserve further exploration.

Chapter 4

Affirmative Culture and Enlightened Critique

In *Negative Dialectics*, Adorno laid the framework for a dialectical epistemology which served as the theoretical foundation for his views about both the culture industry's ideology and the nature and function of ideology critique. The epistemological primacy he accorded to the object in *Negative Dialectics* is reaffirmed in a short essay entitled "Subject and Object." An object can exist without a subject, but it is not possible to posit a subject without taking a detour through the objective world. The subject itself is an object known through consciousness, albeit an object "in a qualitatively different sense, in a sense more radical than the object." If the subject "is not something—and 'something' indicates an irreducible objective moment—the subject is nothing at all; even as *actus purus*, it still needs to refer to something active."[1] The subject owes its very capacity to grasp objects to the fact that it is also something objective.

Although they have often been intimated in such notions as the Kantian *Ding-an-sich*, the theoretical ramifications of the primacy of the object, of the fact that "by its very nature"[2] the subject is also an object, have barely been developed. With his assertion about the preponderance of the object, Adorno stressed again, as he did so often in his work, the primacy of the somatic, material moment in thought itself. The allegedly transcendental subject presupposes a living, bodily, and empirical one. By extension, the preponderance of the object also signifies the priority of the objective world—the social totality—over and against the individual subjects within it.[3] Individuals are not weightless spirits unfettered by historical reality. If Kant had spoken of a Copernican revolution in metaphysics, Adorno was resolutely anti-Copernican in the Kantian sense. Individual consciousness is capable of acting as a condition for objectivity only because it itself has an objectivity "borrowed" from sedimented history.

Another important theoretical consequence of the preponderance of the object in Adorno's epistemology can be found in his injunction to respect the object's particularity. By "particularity," Adorno meant the object's uniqueness, its concrete and determinate "haecceity." Owing to the abstract and universal character of cognition, the particular is often subsumed under the universal and identified with it. While conceding that knowledge is impossible without this moment of abstract universality and identity, Adorno also believed it possible for cognition to respect particulars. This is the task of negative dialectics, defined as the attempt to maintain the distinction between concept and object—as opposed to simply identifying the object with subjective categories and concepts. Such identification, the "totalitarian" subsumption of objects under subjective categories and concepts, is one of the foremost characteristics of what Adorno described as positivism.

In his splenetic reaction to the publication of *The Positivist Dispute in German Sociology*, Karl Popper took umbrage at being labeled a "positivist." Popper identified positivism with what he termed the "sensualistic empiricism" of the Vienna Circle[4] which he himself had criticized. Although he never succeeded in grasping its meaning for Adorno and his co-workers, Popper correctly, if somewhat simplistically, observed that critical theorists were employing the word "positivism" in quite a different way than he himself did. As David Held has remarked with reference to Critical theory's use of the word "enlightenment," this latter term "does not refer to a definite period or to a particular set of intellectual currents, but . . . to more encompassing principles."[5] The same holds true for Adorno's use of the term "positivism." Adorno maintained that positivism is a naive form of identity-thinking which attempts to mirror the objective world in allegedly neutral, descriptive-explanatory concepts and images.

The culture industry is one among many phenomena characterized by positivism in Adorno's sense. Its products embrace that form of identity-thinking which fails to respect the distinctions between particulars and universals. In their ostensibly "realistic" portrayal of the concrete world of particulars, cultural commodities ultimately become idealist in the sense Hegel described when he criticized Reason in *Phenomenology of Spirit*: they identify themselves with the world. Reproducing particulars in a standardized, stereotypical, and schematized way, cultural goods also promote the reified status quo. Only a thought that has become emphatically dialectical is capable of perceiving the differences between concept and object. In one of his more enigmatic descriptions of the task of negative dialectics, Adorno claimed: "It is up to philosophy to think the things which differ from the thought and yet make it a thought, exclusively, while their demon seeks to persuade the thought that it ought not to be" (*ND*, 192). Negative dialectics sublates identity-thinking, conceiving of the object as "non-identity through identity" (*ND*, 189).

In what follows, Adorno's account of positivism will be examined and a comparison will be made between positivist and liberal ideologies. This comparative analysis will also bring to light Adorno's views about the goals and functions of ideology critique. Since the culture industry is one of the principal vehicles for the form of identity-thinking characteristic of positivist pseudo-culture, the second part of the chapter is devoted to Adorno's discussion and critique of the industry's ideology. The third part of the chapter begins with a presentation of Jürgen Habermas's influential analysis of Adorno's views on ideology and ideology critique. Habermas has argued that Adorno's critique of the culture industry (and of instrumental reason as a whole) lacks a rational foundation; it "does not have anything in reserve to which it might appeal."[6] A critical evaluation of Habermas's objections to Adorno's ideology critique will end this section. The final section will show briefly how Adorno's ideology critique served as one of the prototypes for radical social practice.

Ideology and Identity

Karl Marx criticized philosophy because it merely interpreted the world without changing it. In response to this criticism, Adorno objected that Marx's "summary judgment" of philosophy represented the "defeatism of reason after the attempt to change the world miscarried." For Adorno, it was imperative that reason not succumb to such defeatism. In the continuing absence of the practice which Marx hoped would render philosophy obsolete, "philosophy is obliged ruthlessly to criticize itself" (*ND*, 3). This self-criticism makes use of dialectics which "says no more, to begin with, than that objects do not go into their concepts without leaving a remainder, that they come to contradict the traditional norm of adequacy" (*ND*, 5). If philosophy still has a purpose, it is in part to show how philosophical concepts fail to make sense of what is non-conceptual, particular, and individual. This means that one of the

tasks of contemporary philosophy consists in thematizing its own limitations.[7]

Despite the inadequacy of philosophical concepts, Adorno advocated
philosophical self-reflection, or reflection on the nature of thought itself. Since they are universals, concepts say both more and less than the
particulars they subsume. They say more because no particular object
or individual ever completely embodies the universal. Universal concepts are always larger than the life of the particulars to which they are
applied. On the other hand, concepts say less because every particular
thing has attributes which the concept—as singular—does not compre-
hend. Particulars are the concrete amalgamation of many singular concepts. The use of philosophical (and scientific) concepts is therefore
extremely problematic. It cannot, however, be eclipsed. The task of a
self-reflective and dialectical philosophy is to maintain the tension between universal concepts and particulars, to "strive, by way of the concept, to transcend the concept" (ND, 15). On one interpretation of
Adorno's work, Adorno was attempting to explore the "established relations of subject and object, attending to the universals that emerge
therein." He then probed "these relations for moments of domination,
for instances, like those found in Kant, where one moment is denied,
the objective-empirical, in favor of the other, the subjective-transcen-
dental."[8]

Adorno claimed that some Enlightenment thinkers exemplified the
ratio of negative dialectics in at least one respect: "Encyclopedic thinking—rationally organized and yet discontinuous, unsystematic, loose—
expressed the self-critical spirit of reason." The philosophes implicitly
reflected on the nature of thought itself by attempting to represent
"mundane experience," the particular, and then releasing it from the
tyranny of the concept (ND, 29). Experience was not simply subsumed
under universal concepts and identified with them. However, dialectical
thinking also requires a second moment because free thought counters
identity-thinking not only by thematizing it but also by surpassing it.
The concept has a speculative dimension; it reveals something "more"
to which the object does not yet correspond. If one aspect of negative
dialectics consists in immersion in particularity, probing for moments
of domination, the other aspect involves probing for moments of emancipation. This is possible owing to the freedom that thought has "to
step out of the object, a freedom which the identity claim cuts short"
(ND, 28).

Following Hegel, Adorno described the use of concepts and, by extension, thinking itself as acts of negation. And, like Hegel, Adorno

believed that these acts also had a positive dimension: universal concepts permit thought to transcend the given, the particular. Owing to their universality, concepts may resist submitting to the given facts: "The effort implied in the concept of thought itself, as the counterpart of passive contemplation, is negative already—a revolt against being importuned to bow to every immediate thing" (*ND*, 19). Thought has the capacity to envisage possibilities which have not yet been realized in the object; this capacity makes manifest its freedom with respect to the world of objects. Such freedom, which Adorno feared was increasingly compromised, implies that philosophical thought need not yield to the prevailing social order and partially grounds the critique of that order. Resistance to the social totality is possible because the "totally administered world" can be transcended in thought.

Negative dialectics, itself a type of ideology critique,[9] involves thinking against prevailing identitarian (or descriptive-explanatory) modes of thought. It discloses that what exists does not have to be what it is, or might yet become other than what it is now. It is grounded in the freedom enjoyed by thought to surpass identity, transcend the given. This speculative moment can also be found in the "false consciousness" of the bourgeois liberal ideology based historically in the Enlightenment. Following Marx, Adorno believed that false consciousness also had a purchase on truth. This is why, in *Minima Moralia*, Adorno insisted that the baby not be thrown out with the bathwater. The one-sided condemnation of culture as false consciousness "has a suspicious tendency to become itself ideology." To reduce all ideology to what is untrue, to something material which is "ruthlessly and openly formed according to the interests of the participants"[10] is to reject "with the false, all that was true also, all that, however impotently, strives to escape the confines of universal practice, every chimerical anticipation of a nobler condition, and so to bring about directly the barbarism that culture is reproached with furthering indirectly" (*MM*, 44).

Adorno made the same claim in "Cultural Criticism and Society": "Today, however, the definition of consciousness in terms of being has become a means of dispensing with all consciousness which does not conform to existence."[11] In other words, to reduce all thought to particular economic interests is to imply that thought is capable only of reproducing the economic base; it amounts to a denial of the speculative moment of thought. This reduction of thought to the simple reproduction of what exists underlies positivist ideology. Unlike liberal ideology, the positivist variant prides itself on presenting the facts and nothing but the facts, using "disenchanted" scientific concepts cleansed of their speculative residues. Positivist ideology lacks a speculative moment; it merely attempts to reproduce or duplicate what exists. By failing to reflect the incommensurability between concrete particulars and its own more general images or concepts, positivism also promotes reification.

The premise of negative dialectics is that thought does indeed have the capacity to surpass what exists, even though this capacity is increasingly threatened, often thwarted, and demands great effort. As a form of immanent ideology critique, one of the tasks of negative dialectics is to hold up the speculative moment of concepts against the reality these concepts subsume. To quote Gillian Rose: "This is the *utopian* aspect of identifying." When a concept identifies an object in this way, it refers to the object's "ideal existence" in which the object "would have . . . all the properties of its ideal state."[12] For example, the "self-evident" truth that all men are created equal contains an idea of equality which has not yet been realized and which can be used as the basis for a critique of existing inequalities. The idea of freedom, derived from the Enlightenment, is another concept whose ideational content transcends particular economic interests.[13] (In *Negative Dialectics* and other works, Adorno also found a speculative moment in the concepts of the individual, autonomy and spontaneity.) Adorno devoted an entire section of *Negative Dialectics* to exploring the rational potential in the bourgeois and Kantian concept of freedom. He wrote: "Emphatically conceived, the judgment that a man is free refers to the concept of freedom; but this concept in turn is more than is predicated of the man." Although it is also the case that "by other definitions the man is more than the concept of his freedom" (*ND*, 150), Adorno valued the Kantian concept for its transcendence of the historical condition of freedom and unfreedom in Kant's time.

It is this "more" expressed by the concept to which Adorno believed that thought should stubbornly cling:

> Living in the rebuke that the thing is not identical with the concept is the concept's longing to become identical with the thing. This is how the sense of nonidentity contains identity. The supposition of identity is indeed the ideological element of pure thought, all the way down to formal logic; but hidden in it is also the truth moment of ideology, the pledge that there should be no contradiction, no antagonism. (*ND*, 149)

The speculative moment in the concept of freedom, its rational potential, consists in this pledge: that society should allow each and every individual "to be as free as it promises" (*ND*, 219). Insofar as it is speculative, philosophical thought itself makes good on this pledge. It is one of the few activities which Adorno described as emancipated. The thought that "will not have its law prescribed for it by given facts," transcends these facts and is free (*ND*, 17).

Too much secondary literature on Adorno has overemphasized aesthetic emancipation—the cracks in modern art which let in the light of critique—at the expense of the speculative emancipation provided by immanent ideology critique. Indeed, critics and commentators have gone so far as to conflate the two forms of emancipation by locating the prospects for emancipation solely within Adorno's notion of mimesis. This interpretation gives to mimesis a role which it does not actually have in Adorno's work itself and stretches it to the breaking point. Inasmuch as negative dialectics insists on the priority of the nonconceptual, the particular, and the individual, it has an aesthetic dimension. But, according to Adorno, "A philosophy that tried to imitate art, that would turn itself into a work of art, would be expunging itself" (*ND*, 15). Thought's task is to think against the totalitarian animus of concepts by using concepts. It must endeavor to preserve the speculative and ideational content of its concepts without sacrificing the given.

In his work on Adorno, Albrecht Wellmer himself conflates the philosophical task of thinking against concepts by using concepts with the artistic and mimetic project. Wellmer argues that only because "there is a mimetic force at work in the life of meaning" could Adorno "demand of philosophy that it 'strive by means of the concept, to transcend the concept.' "[14] Adorno should have learned from Ludwig Wittgenstein that words can be used in many and various ways. Despite evidence to the contrary in works like *Dialectic of Enlightenment*,[15] Wellmer accuses Adorno of failing to recognize this simple fact; his general concepts are "rigid." Had he taken into account the multiplicity of meanings which a word may have, Adorno would have had to acknowledge the mimetic force of language which he actually presupposes.

There are a number of problems with Wellmer's criticism of Adorno. Wellmer does not seem to understand that no matter how many meanings each word may have, no matter how diverse and nuanced these meanings may be, the fact remains that all these meanings, qua meanings or concepts, still function as universals, subsuming particulars. Wellmer makes short shrift of the referential function of language, arguing that Adorno's philosophical project really amounts to reflecting what is non-identical in reality in "something non-identical in linguistic meanings."[16] But in Wellmer's argument, it is the diversity of a word's meanings which constitutes its non-identity. By contrast, for Adorno, no one of the many meanings a word may have in a given context is identical to the particular; as universal, each of them says both more and less than the particular. Wellmer uses the term "non-identity" to refer to linguistic meaning. Adorno uses the term to refer to the referential relationship between universal concepts and the particular objects they subsume. A non-identical meaning in Wellmer's sense continues to function in the "totalitarian" and "identitarian" way that Adorno criticized.

Adorno's critique of identity-thinking was most fully expressed in its theoretical form in *Negative Dialectics*. But Adorno also practised this critique throughout his work. One of the principal vehicles for the contemporary form of positivist ideology is the culture industry which puts a positivist spin on Nietzsche's injunction to become what one is: "If one were to compress within one sentence what the ideology of mass culture actually adds up to, one would have to represent this as a parody of the injunction 'Become what thou art': as the exaggerated duplication and justification of already existing conditions, and the deprivation of all transcendence and all critique."[17] Becoming what one is now entails remaining what one has become within a social totality which one is supposed to accept as an irrevocable state of affairs. This means that "The world as it is becomes the only ideology, and mankind, its component" (*ND*, 274). In what follows, I shall examine more closely this instantiation of identity-thinking within cultural commodities.

Affirmative Culture

In late capitalist societies, individuals have already been integrated (to a certain uneasy extent) into the social totality. One of the primary functions of the culture industry is to reinforce (*unterdrücken*), by means of the unstinting reproduction of what is, the behavior and norms society considers acceptable. The industry's reinforcement of socially acceptable behavior simply makes people "once more what they are already anyway under the obligation to conform to the system; it controls the gaps . . . provides them with models for imitation."[18] By reanimating the superego introjects and infantile defense mechanisms characteristic of the narcissism prevalent within late capitalist societies, the culture industry strengthens the psychological regression symptomatic of that pathology. But it also serves to promote the socio-economic conditions which led to narcissism in the first place. It does so through its positivist ideology.

Adorno provided a striking description of the new ideology in a passage in *Minima Moralia* which Martin Jay also quotes[19]:

> Irony's medium, the difference between ideology and reality, has disappeared. The former resigns itself to confirmation of reality by its mere duplication. Irony used to say: such it claims to be, but such it is; today, however, the world, even in its most radical lie, falls back on the argument that things are like this, a simple finding which coincides, for it, with the good. There is not a crevice in the cliff of the established order into which the ironist might hook a fingernail. Crashing down, he is pursued by the mocking laughter of the insidious object that disempowered him. The gesture of the unthinking That's-how-it-is is the exact means by which the world dispatches each of its victims, and the transcendental agreement inherent in irony becomes ridiculous in face of the real unanimity of those it ought to attack. Pitted against the deadly seriousness of total society, which has absorbed the opposing voice, the impotent objection earlier quashed by irony, there is now only the deadly seriousness of comprehended truth. (*MM*, 211–12)

The culture industry differs from liberal bourgeois culture in that its products lack a speculative moment. In the thoroughly commodified culture produced in late capitalist societies: "There are no more ideologies in the authentic sense of false consciousness, only advertisements for the world through its duplication and the provocative lie which does not seek belief but commands silence" (CCS, 34). As he did in the passage from *Minima Moralia* quoted above, Adorno frequently encapsulated the prevailing ideology of late capitalist societies in the phrase "That's just the way it is." Increasingly, the ideology of institutions or agencies like the culture industry is devoted to the endless repetition and reproduction of what exists. As positivistic, the new ideology never registers the contradictions between its duplication of the existing world in concepts or images and that world itself. In fact, Adorno described such duplication or reproduction as "pseudo-realistic." The culture industry falsely conflates its standardized, pseudo-individuated, stereotypical, and schematized reproductions with empirical reality.

In "Fernsehen als Ideologie," Adorno reiterated the claim he and Horkheimer had made earlier in *Dialectic of Enlightenment* when they wrote that the culture industry brazenly turns the truth that it is just business into ideology. It does this "in order to justify the rubbish" it produces.[20] This is another example of the positivism purveyed in cultural commodities. They do not pretend to have aesthetic value—or any other value, apart from that of exchange. The fact that what it produces is solely "a commodity and entertainment, does not frighten the culture industry. It has made this a part of its ideology for a long time."[21] The economic interests which lie behind the production of cultural commodities are now openly expressed: "No notion dares to be conceived any more which does not cheerfully include, in all camps, explicit instructions as to who its beneficiaries are—exactly what the polemics once sought to expose" (CCS, 29).

According to Adorno, the Marxist theory of base and superstructure has been superseded by historical reality "in which not only the machineries of production, distribution, and domination, but economic and social relations and ideologies are inextricably interwoven, and in which living people have become bits of ideology" (ND, 267–68).[22] At one time a part of the superstructure, culture itself is now interwoven with the economic base. (Adorno acknowledged that even the high modern art he championed had become commodified; it owes whatever autonomy it may have to its always precarious transcendence of the economic base.) As one of the weaker but expanding sectors of industry, the culture industry must bow to the wishes and whims of the more powerful conglomerates.[23] Culture monopolies "cannot afford to neglect their appeasement of the real holders of power if their sphere of activity in mass society (a sphere producing a specific type of commodity . . .) is not to undergo a series of purges" (DE, 122–23).

Adorno and Horkheimer described one of the ways in which products of the culture industry appease the captains of industry. As photographs of "stubborn life," endlessly reproducing this life in a pseudo-realistic way, cultural commodities suggest that what exists should exist. This is the "naked lie" which the culture industry disseminates (DE, 147). Elevating "unsatisfactory existence into the world of facts by representing it meticulously," the culture industry "makes existence itself a substitute for meaning and right" (DE, 148: translation modified). In order to sell its products, then, the culture industry does not glorify, but simply reproduces the "overwhelming existence-in-itself" (CCS, 31) of itself and of society. It leaves no room for the imagination: things are what they are. By implying that what exists ought to exist, the culture industry turns facts into values. Cultural commodities promulgate the idea that what exists *should* exist simply by virtue of the fact *that* it exists.

The culture industry need not conceal its appeasement of economic and political interests because its positivist ideology serves as an unapologetic and immanent legitimation of the economic order. In this sense too, Marx's distinction between the economic base and cultural superstructure is inadequate: "Where ideology is no longer added to things as a vindication or complement—where it turns into the seeming inevitability and thus legitimacy of whatever is—a critique that operates with the unequivocal causal relation of superstructure and infrastructure is wide of the mark" (*ND*, 268). Late capitalism "needs this tireless intellectual reduplication of everything that is, because without this praise of the monotonously alike and the waning efforts to justify that which exists on the grounds of its mere existence, men would ultimately do away with this state of affairs in impatience." Promoting the domination of the exchange principle with its implicit message that things cannot be changed, the culture industry now solidifies "existing forms of consciousness and the intellectual status quo."[24]

In their duplication or reproduction of the existing social-economic order, cultural commodities exhibit the effects of reification. The tension between the particular and the general (or universal) is not maintained. As standardized, schematized, and stereotypical, products of the culture industry have subordinated themselves to the economic imperatives driving the machinery of production; formulaic production replaces that attention to the particular and the unique found in some works of high modern art. Adorno wrote: "Owing to its openly commercial function in America, what the culture industry offers already promotes itself only as a commodity, as art for consumers . . . ."[25] While both cultural artifacts and individuals have become reified, the former not only fail to resist their subsumption under the abstract identity of the exchange principle, they frequently celebrate it. It is this positivist celebration of reification which Adorno subjected to ideology critique.

Adorno practised this critique in virtually all his work. Indeed, the continuity of Adorno's work is especially obvious when one takes into account his sustained ideology critique of the culture industry. It is not the case, as Martin Jay claims, that Adorno abandoned this critique altogether in the forties and fifties. However, it is true, as Jay himself notes, that "the comparison of ideologies with their alleged realization which he [Adorno] had used so frequently in his earlier work, was itself losing the capacity to provide a truly critical leverage on the world."[26] There is no longer any disparity between ideology and its realization. Since the nature of ideology has changed—it is no longer speculative but positivist—immanent critique must take a new tack. It must sound out this new ideology, exposing it for what it is: an implicit legitimation of what exists by its incessant duplication.

In late capitalist societies, ideology takes "the primal form of identity." With his ideology critique, Adorno attempted to break out of
the "objective context of delusion" produced by this form of identity-
thinking. Adorno described identity-thinking as the "authority for a
doctrine of adjustment" (ND, 148). Instead of claiming, as it once did
during the liberal era, that A = B (where B had a normative and legitimizing function), ideology now takes the analytic form of A = A: the
way things are is the way things are. Implied in this analytic and tautological form of identity is the idea that things cannot change and that
the only option open to individuals is to accept and conform to the
prevailing state of affairs. As the critique of such identity-thinking, ideology critique seeks to grasp "the coercive character of logic, hoping
that it may yield—for that coercion itself is the mythical delusion, the
compulsory identity" (ND, 406).

Despite their cogency, Adorno's views about the positivist ideology
of reified cultural goods demand closer scrutiny. Not only did Adorno
occasionally contradict his own assertion that the ideology of mass culture takes the form of analytic identity without speculative content, his
views have also been challenged indirectly by Jean Baudrillard, and
Ernesto Laclau and Chantal Mouffe. According to Baudrillard, the mass
media "treat us like subjects with desires, a will, free choice, in order
to negate us as subjects."[27] They do this by canvassing us in opinion
polls, the electoral process, and by engaging in other practices which
imply that we are free to choose. Although they generally invoke this
freedom only to negate it, the media do appeal to the liberal values
associated with enlightenment. For their part, Laclau and Mouffe contend that the prevailing ideology of late capitalist societies is embodied
in what they call the "democratic imaginary" of liberty and equality.
They attribute to this "imaginary" a speculative moment against which
people can measure their own condition: "Interpellated as equals in
their capacity as consumers, ever more numerous groups are impelled
to reject the real inequalities which continue to exist."[28]

In Dialectic of Enlightenment, Horkheimer and Adorno themselves
claimed that the culture industry was the vehicle for some liberal values.
At the same time, however, they also maintained that these values
lacked the force of attraction and motivation for consciousness which
they once had: "Even the abstract ideals of the harmony and benefi-
cence of society are too concrete in this age of universal publicity."
These "value judgments" are viewed cynically as sales propaganda;
they are perceived as "advertising or as empty talk" (DE, 147). Adorno
made a similar point in "How to Look at Television." While again

acknowledging that the culture industry does purvey liberal ideology, Adorno expressed the belief that consumers are "out of phase" with this ideology. Thus the messages contained in it misfire; traditional values end up being transformed "into norms of an increasingly hierarchical and authoritarian social structure."[29]

In some of his work, it would appear as if Adorno believed that liberal ideology—particularly the ideology of freedom—has lost its hold on consciousness. Freedom "comes to be a borderline value. Not even as a complementary ideology does one really dare to set it forth" (*ND*, 274). Despite his recognition of the fact that values and norms like freedom do appear in cultural commodities, Adorno sometimes held that they have little or no effect on human behavior. By contrast, in other work, Adorno claimed that liberal ideology does continue to have some force in contemporary consciousness. Individuals "are not what they should be and do not do what they should do according to their self-image."[30] Adorno thought that this self-image reflected a self-understanding derived from enlightened thought: "For once they are enlightened, the effective idea that they are free and autonomous and need not be deceived—no matter how unconscious it may be in all individuals in capitalist societies—demands that they at least behave as if it were true" (PC, 23–24). Although Adorno wrote in *Dialectic of Enlightenment* that enlightened ideas and values revert to mythology, in other work he held that these ideas continue to play a beneficial role in contemporary consciousness precisely because of their speculative content.

Even if they are only marginally effective because consumers are now cynical and out of sync with them and their legitimizing function has substantially weakened, Adorno should not have simply denied, as he did in some passages of his work, the important motivational role that ideas like freedom and equality continue to play in contemporary consciousness. The ideals and values of bourgeois liberal ideology may appear to be advertising and empty talk—indeed, they are often used in advertising[31]—but, as Adorno himself acknowledged in "Theory of Pseudo-Culture" and elsewhere, these ideas have not lost their power of attraction for consciousness. It would also be difficult to refute the claim that some products of the culture industry have become vehicles for liberal values and ideals. Baudrillard, Laclau, and Mouffe correctly point out that the media do appeal to consumers by making use of liberal ideology. While this appeal may simply take the form of calling on consumers to exercise their right to choose between different commodities, thereby affirming the values of freedom and equality only obliquely, remnants of these values can be found in cultural commodities. In Chapter 5, Laclau and Mouffe's ideas will be given closer consideration.

In much of his work, Adorno ignored the speculative dimension of the culture industry's ideology. In fact, he often denied it, focusing instead on the industry's positivist tendencies. These tendencies make the culture industry's ideology extremely weak. According to Adorno, the industry's ideology has become threadbare and this partially explains why the truth about the social totality lies very close to the surface of consumers' consciousness. As early as 1941, in his essay "On Popular Music," Adorno had written: "in the political praxis of authoritarian regimes the frank lie in which no one actually believes is more and more replacing the 'ideologies' of yesterday which had the power to convince those who believed in them."[32] What was true of the ideology of the authoritarian Third Reich is still true of the ideology of late capitalist societies: the latter has become positivist, open, and cynical.

One of the reasons why consumers of cultural industrial products have a latent awareness of the falseness of this ideology is because it "hardly says anything more than that things are the way they are" and "its own falsity also shrinks away to the thin axiom that it could not be otherwise than it is" (AS, 202). Ideology critique therefore has an important role to play in late capitalist societies. As Adorno wrote in "Fernsehen als Ideologie": "if ideology, which certainly uses a very modest number of constantly repeated ideas and tricks, were debunked, a public aversion to being led by the nose could be cultivated—however much the socially produced dispositions of countless viewers may accommodate ideology" (FI, 531). Adorno also cautioned individuals against succumbing "to defeatism" and allowing themselves "to be terrorized by the well-versed demand for affirmation which at most only tries to thwart the transformation of prevailing conditions" (FI, 530–31). This idea that individuals need not submit to the "compulsory identity" of affirmative culture is reiterated in a number of Adorno's essays, including "Kann das Publikum Wollen?" "Transparencies on Film," and "Free Time."

Education is the key. If individuals are capable of seeing through the thin veil of positivist ideology, it is in part because that ideology has become so flagrantly transparent. This capacity can also be explained by the degree of enlightenment individuals have reached. However tenuous the belief in freedom and autonomy may have become, it helps to counter the culture industry's frank or naked "lies." As an antidote to positivism, Adorno prescribed "a kind of inoculation of the public."

Based on a sociological and psychological investigation of those "plots and stereotypes" which "result in the stultification, psychological crippling and ideological mystification of the public," public awareness could be raised and people could be shown just how naked, how open and cynical, the lies really are. Moreover, Adorno's dialectical ideology critique is itself able to serve the function of making "phenomena like the ideological character of television conscious, and by no means only for those on the side of production, but also for the public" (FI, 531).

Andreas Huyssen believes that, in a later essay, "Culture Industry Reconsidered," Adorno retreated from his original condemnation of the Enlightenment in *Dialectic of Enlightenment*. Adorno "seems to imply that genuine enlightenment and gratification of needs may be possible after all" but he ultimately ends up with "a traditional 'enlightened' solution that relies on humanistic education."[33] Huyssen interprets *Dialectic of Enlightenment* as entirely pessimistic with respect to the prospects for enlightenment. However, as David Hoy points out, even in this early work, Horkheimer and Adorno found the antidote to enlightenment in enlightenment itself.[34] The authors of *Dialectic of Enlightenment* do not present "a completely different alternative to enlightenment" but instead offer criticisms which "are intended not to undercut and replace enlightenment but to lead to a more truly enlightened position."[35] Furthermore, in his remarks on education, it is not at all evident that Adorno specifically endorsed humanistic education as the solution to the problem of the false consciousness promoted by contemporary positivist ideology, as Huyssen suggests.[36]

False consciousness needs to become enlightened about its own role in maintaining the prevailing practices and ideology of domination. Hoy states quite succinctly that, for Adorno and Horkheimer, "the danger is not enlightenment as such, but its 'entanglement in blind domination.' "[37] The education that would counteract this entanglement includes the ideology critique Adorno himself practised in many of his essays and books. Especially in countries like Germany, where "economic interests do not directly control broadcasting," Adorno claimed that "something is to be hoped from attempts at enlightenment" (FI, 531). An enlightened critique would expose the conflation of fact and value inherent in contemporary ideology, while revealing the complicity of consciousness in domination, or "the fact that the mind has always been under a spell" (CCS, 32). Although Adorno provided very few indications of what the education he recommended would comprise, it is clear that he valued dialectical ideology critique precisely for its pedagogical function.

Yet even Hoy rejects Adorno's antidote to enlightenment by further enlightenment because he contends that one finds in it the "utopian illusion that genuine, enlightened knowledge will lead to increased freedom and progress."[38] In addition, Hoy argues that Adorno's later view of history as contingent and discontinuous calls into question the implicitly progressive view of history found in *Dialectic of Enlightenment*.[39] A number of commentators on Adorno's work who follow Habermas have also pointed out that Adorno has, so to speak, cut any possible ground for ideology critique out from underneath himself. Habermas was the first to raise the problem of the foundations for ideology critique in his 1982 essay—subsequently revised and reprinted as a lecture in *The Philosophical Discourse of Modernity*—"The Entwinement of Myth and Enlightenment: Re-reading *Dialectic of Enlightenment*."[40] In what follows, Habermas's objections to Adorno will be examined and criticized.

Enlightened Critique

The Philosophical Discourse of Modernity is a polemical work which often launches what can only be described as superficial broadsides against the menacing "irrationalism" of the "black writers" of "postmodern" theories. This is certainly true of Habermas's criticisms of Adorno. Habermas mistakenly sees in *Dialectic of Enlightenment* the complete and fully developed statement of Adorno's ideology critique; he claims that *Negative Dialectics* remains "faithful" to the "philosophical impulse" of *Dialectic of Enlightenment*.[41] Habermas fails to accept *Negative Dialectics* as the more mature theoretical basis for Adorno's on-going ideology critique. Although *Dialectic of Enlightenment* was an early example of such a critique, its theoretical foundations had not been fleshed out fully. Since Adorno believed that the nature and function of ideology had changed, ideology critique also had to change. Adorno discussed the ramifications of these changes in later essays and books.

The problems connected with Habermas's reading of Adorno would be serious enough to allow one to reject outright his criticism of Adorno if it were not for the influence his views have had on the work of other philosophers and commentators. For example, in her *Critique, Norm and Utopia*,[42] Seyla Benhabib takes up wholesale Habermas's criticisms of Adorno—criticisms expressed in their nascent form in "Modernity versus Post-Modernity"[43] in particular. This uncritical adoption of Habermas should be challenged because it has become all too prevalent in some circles. It is for this reason that Habermas's criticisms will be considered here. Before I counter them with Adorno's own views, I shall outline Habermas's objections to Adorno as well as Benhabib's further development of them.

In their *Dialectic of Enlightenment*, Horkheimer and Adorno supposedly rendered "critique independent even in relation to its own foundations." Ideology critique "*itself* comes under suspicion of not producing (any more) truths."[44] According to Habermas, Horkheimer and Adorno undermined ideology critique because they could not discover any rational potential in the liberal ideals of the Enlightenment. Their criticism of these ideals was undialectical; it one-sidedly rejected them without recognizing their emancipatory potential. While admitting that norms like freedom and equality do serve the particular interests of the dominant class, Habermas also contends that they highlight the disparity between the way things are and the way things ought to be, providing "the starting point for an immanent critique of structures that elevate to the status of the general interest what actually only serves the dominant part of society."[45]

In connection with this objection, Habermas contends that in *Dialectic of Enlightenment* "there is no longer any dynamism upon which critique could base its hope." Adorno and Horkheimer could not accept Marx's claim that the dynamics of class struggle would necessarily result in the overthrow of capitalism, inaugurating a qualitatively distinct socio-economic order. Furthermore, they allegedly abandoned the progressive (enlightenment) view of history which lay behind this claim. This meant that the foundations of ideology critique were shattered because the proletariat, which was supposed to bring to fruition the rational potential in bourgeois ideals, had itself become entangled in the web of domination.[46] Once they had rejected the proletariat's role as subject and object of history, Adorno and Horkheimer supposedly turned "against reason as the foundation of its own validity," their "critique becomes total." At this point in his discussion, Habermas proceeds to consider what he calls the "performative contradiction" in Adorno's "totalized critique."[47]

On Habermas's interpretation, Adorno and Horkheimer were harsh critics of the Enlightenment. They did not do justice "to the rational content of cultural modernity that was captured in bourgeois ideals."[48] Since they rejected the rational basis for ideology critique, which Habermas locates in enlightenment thought, the authors of *Dialectic of Enlightenment* actually undermined their own critique. If "myth is already enlightenment; and enlightenment reverts to mythology'' (*DE*, xvi), Horkheimer and Adorno's critique lacks a foundation. Habermas states that if the authors ''still want to *continue with critique*, they will have to leave at least one rational criterion intact for their explanation of the corruption of *all* rational criteria.''[49] That is, Horkheimer and Adorno should have salvaged at least some rational potential from enlightenment in order to ground their own critique. Ideology critique cannot be totalizing without contradicting itself.

Based on Habermas's objections to Adorno and Horkheimer's allegedly totalizing critique, Benhabib proceeds to describe two possible interpretations of their critique of instrumental reason.

First, one could claim that critique once again becomes mere criticism in the sense ridiculed by Marx in his early works, and that the critical theory of society must justify its explicit normative commitments. Second, one could argue that critical theory does not become mere criticism, for it still appeals to norms and values immanent to the self-understanding of late-capitalist societies, but that the *content* of the norms appealed to have [*sic*] been transformed.[50]

Benhabib asserts that even if one opts for the second, more charitable, interpretation, ''The charge that the critique of instrumental reason articulates the privileged discourse of a 'holy family' is still left unanswered.''[51] According to Benhabib, the norms to which Adorno appeals are juxtaposed to the present from a standpoint (a utopian future or edenic past) which transcends it. Presupposed in this standpoint is the self-righteous belief that one has privileged access to a truth (or truths) unavailable to the majority of one's fellows.

Like Habermas, Benhabib also objects to what she describes as the aesthetic basis for Adorno's critique. Adorno sought ''emancipation in those traces and moments of otherness, in those cracks in the crust of the totality of the administered world.'' Even in *Negative Dialectics*, ''this search for otherness, for a non-identitary logic, leads to the aesthetic realm.''[52] The crux of the problem for both Habermas and Benhabib lies in Adorno's romanticism, itself derived from Nietzsche's ''rebellion against everything normative.'' Unfortunately, Adorno follows Nietzsche who ''trusts only in art.''[53] The only response to such subjective romantic aestheticism lies in unpacking the rational potential in the bourgeois ideal of reaching agreement in situations of social interaction. In ''The Entwinement of Myth and Enlightenment,'' Habermas traces this ideal back to the historical Enlightenment. Rational consensus serves as the principle against which one can judge prevailing discursive practices.

Ironically, the ideal of rational consensus on which Habermas based his earlier version of critique shares an historical ground similar to the one found in the ideology critique Adorno developed in *Negative Dialectics* and elsewhere. Although one could still accuse him of holding to the subject-centered "philosophy of consciousness" Habermas rejects,[54] Adorno grounded his ideology critique on those ideas and concepts which have a speculative content and which therefore bear a remarkable resemblance to Habermas's own "speculative principle" of the ideal speech situation. The ideal speech situation, which Habermas salvages either from the Enlightenment notion of rationality or from the "enlightened" and universal norms embedded in communicative action (or both), eclipses current dialogical practice in which speech is often psychologically distorted and economically or politically coerced. As a normative ideal, rational consensus compares favorably to the speculative notions of autonomy, spontaneity, and freedom which ground Adorno's own ideology critique.

The question of the normative foundations for critique is one which has plagued Habermas. In *The Structural Transformation of the Public Sphere*, Habermas grounded critique historically in the ideals and values of eighteenth-century English Enlightenment. In fact, Habermas maintained that ideology itself first came into existence during the Enlightenment when citizens attempted to form a free and rational public sphere in which they claimed the maturity necessary to understand and criticize the political realm. In principle, all human beings belong to this sphere; in practice, of course, only some male property owners did. Nonetheless, the claims made for this sphere have had far-reaching consequences. The major claim made was that the "critical public debate of private people" was a "noncoercive inquiry into what was at the same time correct and right." This meant that "a legislation that had recourse to public opinion . . . could not be explicitly considered as domination."[55] Rational critical debate in an open public sphere became the model or standard which was opposed to the secret machinations of the monarch and the nobility.

This historical foundation for ideology critique in Habermas's work came under attack by critics who charged that it was incapable of supporting a critical theory because it idealized the bourgeois public sphere, illegitimately transforming a particular moment in history into a standard for the whole of history. While conceding this point, Habermas also criticized the progressive view of history on which these ideals were based—a view which had been betrayed by historical events in the twentieth century. In order to meet the objections to his historical grounding of critique, Habermas decided to reconceptualize its normative foundations and to ground them at a deeper level. This reconceptualized critique now finds its foundation in communication itself: there is a "rational potential intrinsic in everyday communication."[56] Communication allegedly has universal characteristics which serve as the basis for Habermas's project of rationalizing the democratic structures and procedures of the existing social order.

In the preface to the unrevised printing of the eighteenth German edition of *The Structural Transformation of the Public Sphere*, Habermas claimed that he had idealized the bourgeois public sphere "in a manner going way beyond any methodologically legitimate idealization of the sort involved in ideal-typical conceptualization."[57] By contrast, Adorno never recommended that the historical ideals of Enlightenment be viewed as ideal standards in the sense described by both Habermas and his critics. He valued bourgeois notions such as freedom and autonomy for their salutary effect on consciousness; as the rational basis for critique they permit consciousness to surmount, at least in thought, the contemporary social and historical context and act as a foil to positivism. Critique is possible when ideas like freedom and equality are used critically to make sense of the empirical world.

Adorno believed that the liberal ideals and values which stem from enlightened thought had become a part of the self-understanding of individuals in late capitalism, if only in a debased form. Adorno's own ideology critique is grounded on the way in which we, the progeny of enlightened thought, think about and experience ourselves. This grounding is necessary because it provides ideology critique with a rational basis. In Adorno's own words: "as the confrontation of ideology with its own truth, ideology critique is possible only insofar as ideology contains a rational element on which critique can work. This holds true for ideas like those of liberalism, individualism, the identity of the mind and reality" (BI, 465). Serving as the a posteriori foundation for Adorno's dialectical ideology critique, bourgeois liberal ideology evokes the breach between the way things are and the way they ought to be, implicitly referring to a reality which lies beyond our contemporary experience of freedom and unfreedom, autonomy and servitude, spontaneity and conformity. According to Gillian Rose, Adorno called this more speculative and utopian form of identification "*rational identity* (*rationale Identität*)."[58]

Whereas Hegel criticized the ideals of the Enlightenment, claiming that "principles" like equality and freedom remain "formal" because they "originated with abstract thought,"[59] Adorno insisted that the speculative ideology of the Enlightenment does have a concrete reality. Comparable in some respects to an Aristotelian *eidos* (*ND*, 150), an ideal like freedom does not hover "abstractly, impotently above things in being." In fact, "we can talk of it only insofar as it keeps arising in reality, in the guilty context of things as they are." Freedom and determinism are not primarily theoretical positions. Rather, they have an empirical, experiential basis, revealing the "contradiction in the subjects' way to experience themselves, as now free, now unfree." As free, individuals are "aware of and identical with themselves." At the same time, however, individuals are "unidentical with themselves because the subject is not a subject yet" (*ND*, 299). There is no universal and necessary basis for critique in Adorno's work. Following Marx, Adorno believed that the conditions of the possibility for change were immanent within history, not outside of it.

Although Adorno occasionally denied that liberal values have maintained a positive hold on consciousness, the continued efficacy of these values has been demonstrated repeatedly by recent historical events. Many examples could be cited, especially among the new social movements. For their part, Samuel Bowles and Herbert Gintis have described the historical impact of liberal ideology on working-class and civil rights movements:

> [M]ass radical political forces in the liberal democratic capitalist societies have not introduced a new language of politics; they have exploited the ambiguities and contradictions of liberal democratic discourse. One may bemoan the impressive hegemony of liberal discourse or one may celebrate it; but one need not dwell on it. It has simply been a part of the discursive landscape that political actors inhabit. We use it as we will and fashion it to our own ends if we can, but we seek to escape it only at the cost of becoming historically irrelevant.[60]

The "speculative moment" in these liberal values and ideals has served to motivate resistance to exploitation and repression under late capitalism by countering the identity-thinking which legitimates the status quo.

The formal condition for Adorno's ideology critique lies in the nonidentity between the particular and the universal, object and concept. Since thought is not entirely bound up with the particular and may contain a speculative moment which transcends what exists, ideology critique is possible. According to Adorno: "Thought as such, before all particular contents, is an act of negation, of resistance to that which is forced upon it'' (*ND*, 19). Negative dialectics is the thought which takes cognizance of itself as an act of negation and resistance and which foils identity-thinking by virtue of its speculative moment. (Adorno's unrelenting critique of positivism consists in a moral attack on a mode of thinking which refuses to bring the speculative moment of thought into play.) The substantive condition for ideology critique is found in that form of dialectical thinking which underscores the non-identity of concept and object—in order to reveal the identity-thinking which masks human suffering in ideology—and provides a basis for overcoming it.

Seyla Benhabib asks why ''the ideal of a non-repressive and non-regressive autonomy [is] not a moral and political, but an aesthetic one.''[61] However, in *Negative Dialectics*, Adorno insisted on the moral dimension in his speculative philosophy of freedom and autonomy. He announced that the employment of negative dialectics had become the new categorical imperative.[62] Its task is ''to lend a voice to suffering'' (*ND*, 17). The suffering to which Adorno wanted philosophy to lend its voice is caused by the current state of unfreedom and conformity, or by the ''unmet needs and unfulfilled desires''[63] of individuals within late capitalist societies. Thematizing its own limited ability to grasp by means of concepts ''the objectivity which weighs upon the subject'' in such societies (*ND*, 18), philosophy must attempt simultaneously to raise the specter of a qualitatively different reality which partially transcends the empirical one while being inadequately embedded in it. This speculative vision of reality serves as the conceptual prototype for social and political practices that may ultimately vindicate human suffering.

Both Habermas's and Benhabib's objections to Adorno rest on highly questionable readings of *Negative Dialectics* as well as of other work in which Adorno quite clearly defined the rational basis for ideology critique, the rational potential in the bourgeois ideology of the Enlightenment, and the moral—not aesthetic—imperative behind negative dialectics. Their objections are all the more perplexing given that Habermas himself first based ideology critique on the liberal ideals and values elaborated in the Enlightenment. Although he claims to have found a ''quasi-transcendental'' basis for his later idea of rational consensus, this claim is problematic and Habermas has shown not that such a basis is necessary for effective critique. Adorno recognized that ideology critique required a rational foundation but he discovered this foundation in historical ideas and values which could not be hypostatized and turned into a universal and necessary axiology.

Concluding Remarks

Adorno appropriated the speculative and normative insights of ideology critique from opposing tendencies within the repressive social structures his critique sought to impugn. He defined the speculative dimension of ideology critique in Hegelian terms: it is "the critical self-reflection of the intellect, of self-reflection's boundedness and self-correction" (*PD*, 5). Reflection or thought itself provides the critical categories and concepts with which it, and the reality of which it is a part, can be judged and criticized. Discussing the foundation for speculative reflection in *The Positivist Dispute in German Sociology*, Adorno wrote:

> The normative problems arise from historical constellations, and they themselves demand, as it were, mutely and "objectively," that they be changed. What subsequently congeals as values for historical memory are, in fact, question-forms [*Fragegestalten*] of reality. . . . For instance, as long as the forces of production are not sufficient to satisfy the primitive needs of all, one cannot declare, in abstract terms, as a value that all human beings must have something to eat. But if there is still starvation in a society in which hunger could be avoided here and now in view of the available and potential wealth of goods, then this demands the abolition of hunger through a change in the relations of production. This demand arises from the situation. . . . (*PD*, 62)

The "essence" against which "appearance" is judged is immanent within society itself.

Adorno defended the value of speculation over (and sometimes against) empirical research throughout his work. Although he readily admitted that speculative theory ran the risk of "venturing out too far" and could be accused of being wide of the mark in terms of its understanding of socio-historical reality, Adorno also valued it for its transcendence of the existing social order. Speculative thought does not transcend that order from a transcendent standpoint but rather from an immanent perspective which reflects the way in which people in late capitalist societies understand and make sense of their experience. It is not the case, as Seyla Benhabib claims, that Adorno had to abandon the emancipatory content of values found in the bourgeois public sphere and liberalism and to reground critique in the "utopian promise of culture, art and philosophy."[64] In essays like "Theory of Pseudo-Culture" and "Freudian Theory and the Pattern of Fascist Propaganda,"[65] Adorno explicitly stated that the debilitating effects of the culture industry and nazism could be countered because people had reached a certain degree of *Mündigkeit*, or historical enlightenment.

However, Adorno did not believe that the "enlightened" state people had achieved was sufficient to challenge the positivist ideology of the culture industry (or of nazism). An individual who "has grown up under the influence of the culture industry so entirely that it has become his second nature" will often fend off "insights which apply to the culture industry's functions and role in the social structure" (*PD*, 43). As a force in the service of anti-enlightenment, the culture industry constantly disputes the historically achieved state of enlightenment. This is why ideology critique is required: to expose the legitimation of the social totality effected by the pseudo-realism of the culture industry as it turns facts into values, compromising the ability of consciousness to oppose the status quo. Ultimately, however, even ideology critique with its pedagogical value is insufficient. In the final analysis, what is required are changes in the structure of the whole—"that whole which today, in terms of its own law, deforms rather than develops awareness" (*PD*, 43). Yet, as his critics have so often correctly charged, Adorno never developed this idea of structural change in any detail.

In Adorno's theory, the necessary—though not sufficient—condition for radical social, political, and economic change lies in thought itself. With the failure of the revolution in the East and its absence in the West, there was little historical evidence to support the idea that revolutionary changes were objectively determined and would take place by themselves. There was even less evidence to suggest that radical changes in political and economic conditions were sufficient to bring about a true revolution. Furthermore, the events which took place in Nazi Germany indicated that consciousness had regressed to a barbaric state. Indeed, even before Hitler rose to power, art and thought itself "had long been leading a severed and apocryphal existence." In the Weimar Republic, liberal culture was already deteriorating; its "line of least resistance" to intellectual wares "was continued undeflected in the line of least resistance to a political regime among whose ideological methods, as the Führer himself declared, comprehensibility to the most stupid ranked the highest" (*MM*, 57).

Like Lukács, Adorno believed that, unless consciousness were "raised" in some fashion, it would not be possible to challenge social, economic, and political conditions effectively. Individuals are implicated in the very practices of domination which hold them captive. Until they realize this, and resist, those practices will remain in place. Adorno feared that positivism, which attempts to expunge even that slim thread of hope represented by the ability to transcend prevailing conditions in thought, was gaining ground. One of the only alternatives to this situation was to find those avenues still open to thought to think beyond the status quo. If Adorno's *Aesthetic Theory* can be interpreted as an attempt to question "the possibility of emancipatory theory and practice in the need to maintain the tension between subject and object,"[66] *Negative Dialectics* evinces a similar concern. Adorno's work on non-identity thinking represents the exploration of one type of practice which not only maintains the tension between concept and object (as Sullivan and Lysaker's interpretation suggests), but also honors the pledge that there should be no such tension or antagonism between them.

Although he did not advocate any concrete and positive political action, or specify the structural transformations necessary for radical social change, Adorno did explore what he believed were the preconditions for this change. These preconditions appear in practices, both artistic and cognitive, which preserve a speculative moment, challenging the inroads positivism has made on our very ability to think. Adorno complained that speculation had become "a fact to be included in one of the departments of classification as proof that nothing changes." Not only did he think that speculation had been displaced and assimilated by science, it had also been "handed over as an object to science, whose subjectivity is extinguished with it" (*MM*, 69). This makes it all the more interesting that, even as Adorno lamented the loss of the capacity for speculative thought, he also discovered the vestiges of that thought in a moribund ideology whose value lies not so much in itself but in its experiential significance for us. The prospects for emancipation lie in those modes of thinking, making, and behaving which both respect and transcend the distinction between particular and universal, object and concept, fact and value.

Chapter 5

Reassessing the Culture Industry

A close reading of Adorno's work occasionally suggests a more balanced account of the culture industry and its products which Adorno himself never developed. It also reveals a number of inconsistencies and contradictions, superficialities and omissions. In his discussion of the commodification of culture, for example, Adorno is remarkably silent about what he himself recognized as one of the salient features of the culture industry, namely, its rationalization of distribution techniques. Other lacunae in Adorno's theory—especially his failure to take advertising and marketing into account—need to be addressed before any broader claims can be made about the effects of commodification on cultural goods. Furthermore, in spite of the empirical support for Adorno's claim that cultural goods have become standardized, schematized, and stereotypical, the fact that early stages in the cultural labor process resemble handicraft modes of production actually implies that certain less standardized and fetishized products might find their way to the market—even though formatting, with its rank imitation of successful products, serves to counteract this possibility.

When he discussed the reinforcement techniques used by the culture industry, Adorno quite explicitly stated that these techniques are only partially successful. Even as he described the regressive and narcissistic tendencies in the reception of cultural goods, Adorno insisted that consumers of these goods are not taken in entirely by the industry's reanimation of superego introjects, its mobilization of infantile defense mechanisms, wish-fulfillment, and use of stereotypes and schemata. The consciousness of consumers is duplicitous. They do not swallow the culture industry's products whole; their attitude is that of mistrust, suspicion, and disbelief. It is also the case that the often illusory and distortive satisfactions offered by cultural commodities result in consumer discontent and may promote resistance. Moreover, despite Adorno's doubts about the culture industry's gratification of needs, he implied on at least one occasion that some cultural commodities may gratify some needs which are not created by profit interests, thereby enhancing the lives of individuals.

In his essay on free time, Adorno stated that the individual's real interests were strong enough to resist, at least partially, total identification with the interests of the administered world. This implies that rational self-interest has not been undermined completely by the narcissistic tendencies which the culture industry reinforces. Among those concerns which Adorno considered rational are the interests in freedom, autonomy, and spontaneity inherited from the Enlightenment. In some cases, the culture industry itself is probably the vehicle for these interests; its ideology may contain implicitly critical elements. Yet, even and especially in its more negative, positivistic dimension, Adorno thought that the culture industry's ideology had become extremely weak. Its affirmation of the status quo, the "thin axiom" that things cannot be otherwise than they are, is almost embarrassingly transparent. Consumers can be taught to see through affirmative culture. The culture industry is particularly vulnerable to resistance on this ideological level.

Notwithstanding the more measured account of the culture industry implicit in Adorno's theory, Adorno often contrasted the industry's products to works of high modern art in an extremely polarized way. He believed that some instances of high modern art enjoy a greater degree of independence from the nearly ubiquitous reign of the exchange principle; they have not become completely reified. In addition, Adorno contended that the high modern art he championed does satisfy unfulfilled needs and desires rather than pandering to narcissistic tendencies. Finally, on the ideological level, Adorno attempted to show that some artworks also contain the speculative moment he wanted to see preserved. The first section of this chapter is devoted to examining the stark dichotomy in Adorno's work between high modern art and products of the culture industry. Citing Adorno's essays on the culture industry, I shall explore the various points of contrast between a thoroughly commodified culture and its less commodified "other half."

In the second section, I shall consider in greater depth than I have thus far the limits that Adorno himself either implicitly or explicitly ascribed to the commodification of culture, to the culture industry's reinforcement of narcissistic tendencies, and to its positivist ideology.

Given these limits, some cultural commodities may exhibit those features Adorno prized in autonomous works of high modern art—though, of course, not all cultural goods will do so, owing in particular to the degree to which they have become reified. Following this discussion, I shall examine "Transparencies on Film" where Adorno argues that some films do have an emancipatory potential. Consideration will also be given here to Adorno's early views on entertainment. These concluding remarks will point to the need for further research on the culture industry and its products. A thorough reassessment of the industry, based on Adorno's own tacitly more dialectical account, demands additional empirical and theoretical work.

Culture's Torn Halves

In his first critical response to Walter Benjamin's "The Work of Art in the Age of its Mechanical Reproduction," Adorno made the well-known comparison between great works of art and film: "Both bear the stigmata of capitalism, both contain elements of change. . . . Both are torn halves of an integral freedom, to which however they do not add up."[1] Earlier, in "On the Social Situation of Music," Adorno had used the same metaphor in his discussion of the relationship between serious and light music.[2] He reiterated these claims about the two spheres of music in "On the Fetish Character of Music and the Regression of Listening." Light and serious music

> do not hang together in such a way that the lower could serve as a sort of popular introduction to the higher, or the higher could renew its lost collective strength by borrowing from the lower. The whole can not [*sic*] be put together by adding the separated halves, but in both there appear, however distantly, the changes of the whole, which only moves in contradiction.[3]

Entangled inextricably within the political economy of late capitalism, serious art and its ostensibly more commodified, lighter half cannot combine to express the reconciliation of the particular and the universal.

Given Adorno's application of this holistic trope to the distinction between light and serious music, Fredric Jameson argues that Adorno's informal remark to Benjamin about the torn halves of an integral freedom refers, not to a distinction between high art and the culture industry, but to one between high art and light art.[4] However, it is quite clear from the context that Adorno was contrasting works of art "proper" to film or cinema as a more utilitarian art dependent on industrial production and reproduction. Although he had not yet developed his concept of the culture industry, Adorno's discussion of film in this letter foreshadows his subsequent distinction between the culture industry as heteronomous and works of art as autonomous. Jameson should also have taken into account Adorno's later assertion that the culture industry "forces together" light and serious art.[5] Forcing these spheres together, each cultural commodity presents itself as a compromise between autonomy and heteronomy. Each stands in opposition to the autonomy of a successful work of art as a falsely synthetic whole to an uncompromisingly antithetical half.

Despite the incommensurability of high modern art and the culture industry, these cultural spheres cannot be separated in Adorno's work. In fact, Andreas Huyssen has maintained that modernism and mass culture are engaged in a "compulsive *pas de deux*" in Adorno's theory of culture. Where modernism functions as a "reaction formation" to mass culture, the latter serves as modernism's Derridean "*supplément.*" Huyssen proceeds to criticize Jameson who maintains that Adorno opposed modernist high art and mass culture in a completely undialectical way.[6] Accusing Adorno of giving to great works of modern high culture the role of fixed points and eternal standards, Jameson recommends an approach to high and mass culture which sees them "as objectively related and dialectically interdependent phenomena, as twin and inseparable forms of the fission of aesthetic production under late capitalism."[7] Yet, as Huyssen observes, Jameson's approach actually mimics Adorno's own.

The opposition Adorno posits between modern high art and the culture industry is at least partially dialectical. Mass culture is modern art's commodified "other." It has sold out completely to the status quo and is dominated entirely by the exchange principle which it also promotes through its positivist ideology. Products of the culture industry are "planned and administrated," subordinate to the demands of the market economy.[8] By contrast, modern art is mass culture's guilty alter ego. Since it perpetuates the division between manual and mental labor, art generally lacks a vital relation to practice and is integrated more easily into society. Its alleged purity and independence from the market end up serving as an apology for the existing socio-economic order. As intellectualized, art's powerlessness is confirmed. Consequently, "the real life of people is given over to blind existence, blind changing relations."[9]

Although they are dialectically entwined, art and commodified culture do have separate histories within capitalism. The culture industry is not the historical outgrowth of developments in the realm of art. Rather, as the term "culture industry" itself suggests, it arises from the later, more industrialized, phase of capitalism and is from the beginning absorbed into its production processes. By contrast, high modern art originates in the classical liberal era and obeys the independent standards for artistic production characteristic of that period. Threatened—now perhaps even to the point of extinction—by the need to go to the market when artists lost their "feudal protectors during the latter part of the 18th Century,"[10] more autonomous forms of artistic production did manage to survive into the twentieth century and art continued to express its alienation from and disaffection with capitalism.

In *Dialectic of Enlightenment*, Adorno and Horkheimer described one of the reasons why such relatively autonomous art managed to survive more or less unscathed. They observed that even with their "feudal protectors," artists were dependent "on the buyer and his objectives." The works they produced "were always wares all the same."[11] Once this patronage system had collapsed, countries like Germany granted their artists "a measure of freedom from the power relations promulgated on the market, just as princes and feudal lords had done up to the nineteenth century" (*DE*, 133: translation altered). Of course, most artists were also forced increasingly to rely on the market, but it was only after the culture industry had developed that art met with almost insurmountable pressure. What prevented European artists from being assimilated by the industry was the cultural lag between pre-fascist Europe and the more industrially advanced United States. This lag "left intellect and creativity some degree of independence and enabled its last representatives to exist—however dismally" (*DE*, 132). In the early part of the twentieth century, art continued to derive some financial support from the state and was therefore exempted in part from the laws of supply and demand.

The artists who benefited from this cultural lag include the modernists Arnold Schönberg, Samuel Beckett, and Franz Kafka. Their works provide examples of that cultural production in the Western world which had not yet subordinated itself entirely to market mechanisms and become commodified. As Jameson himself notes, "the only form of 'high culture' which can be said to constitute the dialectical opposite of mass culture is that high cultural production contemporaneous with the latter, which is to say that artistic production designated as *modernism*."[12] In dialectical contrast to high cultural production, production in the culture industry was never protected from the laws of supply and demand and has always been geared, more or less exclusively, to profit interests. Consequently, cultural goods lack critical and oppositional elements; as standardized and homogenized, they are supposedly completely affirmative. This contrast between art and the products of the culture industry is found in many of Adorno's books and essays. In what follows, it will be explored briefly, primarily with reference to Adorno's essays on the culture industry.

One important distinction between cultural commodities and some modernist artworks can be seen in the differences between the techniques each uses. Adorno made this point succinctly:

> The concept of technique in the culture industry is only in name identical with technique in works of art. In the latter, technique is concerned with the internal organization of the object itself, with its inner logic. In contrast, the technique of the culture industry is, from the beginning, one of distribution and mechanical reproduction, and therefore always remains external to its object. The culture industry finds ideological support precisely insofar as it carefully shields itself from the full potential of the techniques contained in its products. It lives parasitically from the extra-artistic technique of the material production of goods, without regard for the obligation to the internal artistic whole implied by its functionality (*Sachlichkeit*), but also without concern for the laws of form demanded by aesthetic autonomy. (CIR, 14)

The most advanced artistic techniques serve to develop the inner substance of modernist works, allowing them to acquire meaning or import. While it also uses the most up-to-date techniques in the production of its goods, the culture industry imports these techniques from the sphere of industrial production; they are "extra-aesthetic." In Lambert Zuidervaart's words, the culture industry "embodies standards of technique . . . not much different from ones pertaining to other products on the market."[13]

If artistic techniques are concerned with the internal organization of the work, its inner logic, then they also help to mediate between parts of the work and the work as a whole. This relationship between part and whole in artworks offers a second point of contrast with products of the culture industry. In modern musical compositions, for example, the unity of parts and the whole is antagonistic. Although music has a structure which preserves "the unity of appearance" and protects it "from falling apart into diffuse culinary moments," it simultaneously reveals the incommensurability between the whole (the general or universal) and the part (the particular). In this way, music is able to evoke "the image of a social condition in which . . . those particular moments of happiness would be more than mere appearance." In popular music, however, parts are extraneous to the whole; they "suspend the critique which the successful esthetic totality exerts against the flawed one of society" (FC, 273). Yet, at the same time, parts or details of cultural commodities are also standardized and "subserve the formula which replaces the work." A formulaic whole replaces the unity of the work and "there is no antithesis and no connection" between whole and part (*DE*, 126).

As opposed to those works of high modern art Adorno defended, cultural commodities are completely standardized and schematized; they conform to formulaic patterns which present consumers with pre-digested experience and ideas. Adorno repeatedly stressed that formulaic production effectively eradicates critical or oppositional elements in culture. Since culture "is only true when implicitly critical,"[14] and its criticism is directed "towards the status quo and all institutions thereof" (CA, 100), products of the culture industry—which legitimate the status quo by reproducing it incessantly—are not instances of culture proper but rather of that pseudo-culture which Adorno deplored. For its part, high modern art is in principle able to express "the idea of harmony [between parts and whole] negatively by embodying the contradictions, pure and uncompromised, in its innermost structure" (CCS, 32). Unlike its dialectical counterpart, high modern art may fulfill a function analogous to social theory in its presentation and criticism of social problems (SSM, 130).

Adorno contended that art deals "with the protest of the unconscious disfigured by civilization."[15] Some modernist art satisfies needs that late capitalism has distorted, deflected, or repressed, thereby indirectly serving a political function. Such art also honors Adorno's categorical imperative by lending a voice to human suffering under late capitalism. In fact, Adorno insisted very early in his work that the task of music as art was to express "in the antinomies of its own formal language—the exigency of the social situation and to call for change through the coded language of suffering" (SSM, 130). Although it also deals with the unconscious, the culture industry misuses it by fostering instinctually motivated and regressive forms of behavior. In contradistinction to high modern art, products of the culture industry obstruct the work of making conscious to the ego the unconscious processes of the id; they perpetuate suffering by reinforcing narcissistic tendencies.

Successful works of art also exhibit what Adorno called aesthetic complexity. It is only by means of this complexity that these works evoke the unfulfilled promise of happiness, a utopian moment. Compared to the aesthetic depth of high modern art, the complexity of the culture industry's products is primarily psychological. In television, for example, producers "presuppose several psychological layers in viewers" which they attempt to penetrate using "psychotechnical" messages which may be both subliminal and explicit. In so doing, they have one overriding goal in mind: "the strengthening of conformity in viewers and the reinforcement of the *status quo.*"[16] On a depth-psychological level, then, there is an extreme polarity between some modernist artworks and commodified culture.

Another difference between art and commodified culture concerns the way in which each portrays the antagonistic whole. Andreas Huyssen mistakenly characterizes this difference as one between realism and abstraction.[17] But Adorno himself stated frequently that commodified culture was pseudo-realistic. Although it attempts to downplay the distinctions between culture and practical life by duplicating reality in detail, the culture industry's "sensuous individuation . . . contradicts the abstractness and self-sameness to which the world has shrunk."[18] Furthermore, this very form of individuation to which the culture industry lays claim is contradicted by its schematized and stereotypical reproduction of the real. The latter "fills empirical life with false meaning whose deception the viewer can scarcely see through" (FI, 522). In comparison to the culture industry's pseudo-realism, works of high modern art can be said to be more "realistic." While eschewing the techniques of aesthetic realism, these artworks do succeed in representing the antagonistic nature of capitalism through their abstractions. Each modern artwork depicts "within its own structure the social antinomies which are also responsible for its own isolation" (SSM, 130).

Presupposed in all these distinctions between modernist art and commodified culture is the autonomy of the former and the heteronomy of the latter. Yet Adorno carefully qualified his claims about the aesthetic autonomy of modernist art. Art's autonomy is "untrue" because "its universality remains allied to ideology as long as real hunger is perpetuated in hunger for the material in the aesthetic domain" (SMC, 55). Art's autonomy is also relative because even "non-conformist" works have been "incorporated into the distribution-mechanisms of large-scale capital."[19] Bound up as it is with the commodity economy of late capitalism, modern art is itself commodified. But if art has a commodity character, Adorno insisted that some instances of high modern art subvert or transcend the effects of commodification. One of the economic conditions for such subversion can be found in the cultural lag that Adorno and Horkheimer described in *Dialectic of Enlightenment*. Other extrinsic conditions for autonomy seem to lie in the advancement of artistic techniques—of objective tendencies within art itself—and in the psychological dispositions of the artist who has an acute, if latent, sense of his or her alienation.[20]

Apart from some suggestive ideas in ''Transparencies on Film,'' Adorno's explicit statements provide few grounds for asserting that the culture industry could ever transcend the socio-economic conditions which give rise to it. As commodified, pseudo-culture is wholly ''a means instead of an end, a fetish'' (SCR, 211). Of course, these claims about commodified culture have frequently come under attack. Both the culture industry and modernist art originate in the same socio-economic conditions and have become commodified as a result. If modernist art succeeds in subverting the fetish character of its commodity form despite its entanglement in exchange mechanisms, it may not be possible to preclude a priori the idea that some instances of commodified culture also succeed, expressing negatively that promise of happiness found in some modernist works. In what follows, I want to consider this possibility in more detail. Adorno's own work may provide grounds for asserting that, although products of the culture industry are *also* commodities, not all of them are commodities *through and through*.

Toward a Reassessment of the Culture Industry

A number of commentators, who are generally sympathetic to the main premises of Adorno's cultural theory, have been highly critical of what they see as his undialectical opposition of modernist art and products of the culture industry. For example, Andreas Huyssen, who believes that Adorno's view of the relationship between modernism and mass culture is dialectical, does not think that it is dialectical enough. Huyssen contends that there may be limits to the reification of mass culture. He infers these limits from an analysis of ''the signifying strategies of specific cultural commodities and the mesh of gratification, displacement and production of desires which are invariably put in play in their production and consumption.''[21] However, it is not at all clear that Huyssen's inference is valid. Even if one were to grant that cultural commodities open up spaces for resistive reception because of their signifying strategies and the needs they call into play, Huyssen must explain why this possibility necessarily implies that there are limits to the reification of mass culture. Mass culture may at one and the same time open up spaces for resistive reception *and* be thoroughly reified.[22]

Nicholas Garnham pursues a far more promising course for understanding the limits to both commodification and reification when he describes the economically contradictory nature of the absorption of culture by industry. Citing "contradictions" intrinsic to the development of capitalism itself—such as conflicts between labor and capital—as well as extrinsic conflicts—between, for example, developing capital and non-capitalist areas of life—Garnham claims that these antagonisms have also impacted on the mass media. He locates these displaced "contradictions" first "in resistances both actual and ideological to the industrialization of the artisanal modes of cultural production." He also discovers them "in the conflicts between national and international capitals, . . . or the existence of quotas on the importation of foreign film and TV material." Finally, "the growing Third World demand for a New World Information Order" provides further evidence for the impact on the media of capitalism's economic antagonisms.[23]

Referring to Marx in Volume One of *Capital*,[24] Garnham also points out that difficulties arise when cultural production is carried out by capitalist industries. Marx argues that there are definite limits to capitalist modes of production when these are applied to what he calls "non-material" production (the writing of books, painting of pictures, etc.) "even where it [non-material production] is undertaken purely for the sake of exchange, producing goods, etc." Since it employs "transitional forms" of capitalist production, cultural production "can only lead to a *capitalist mode of production in the formal* sense."[25] Garnham does not provide an extended analysis of this passage but Bill Ryan has found empirical evidence to support the continued relevance of Marx's claims about non-material production for an understanding of the production processes used by the culture industry.[26] While this evidence shows that there may be limits to commodification in the culture industry, it also lends some indirect support to Huyssen's suspicions about possible limits to reification. His suspicions are echoed by Lambert Zuidervaart who recommends that the use of concept of reification be restricted exclusively to the economic sphere. Alternatively, Zuidervaart also suggests that reification might not be as pervasive as Adorno asserted or that it might have "reversed itself in important respects during recent years."[27]

The claim that cultural production has been subsumed entirely under advanced industrial production is called into question as soon as the earlier stages of cultural production are taken into account. In fact, when Adorno argued that even film—one of the more industrialized sectors of the culture industry—has retained individual forms of production, he implicitly contradicted some of his own statements about the complete subsumption of culture by industry. Although many corporate producers in the culture industry do attempt to transfer the profit motive naked onto cultural forms, the success of their attempts in all cases may be disputed. If cultural production retains pre-industrial features in its earlier stages, there may well be conflicts between these stages and more industrialized ones. These conflicts may surface in cultural commodities themselves. Furthermore, if cultural workers are granted a degree of creative leeway in production, some cultural goods may manifest a degree of resistance to both commodification and reification.

It is not possible to make statements in advance about all products of the culture industry. Adorno's sweeping generalizations about the commodified and fetishized character of all cultural goods are easy targets for criticism. However, it is probably also the case that the prevailing economic tendencies of late capitalism, which Adorno outlined, will prevent all but a few cultural goods from resisting commodification— far fewer, perhaps, than can be found within whatever remains of the quasi-autonomous artistic sphere. Resistance is less likely in television, for example, where programs are often explicitly produced to attract both advertisers and consumers. The use-value of the majority of television and radio programs, of most newspapers and magazines, has been counterfeited by exchange-value. As Ben Bagdikian observes, the media have grown increasingly dependent on other industrial and corporate sectors for their revenues. As a result, they have also become ''partners in achieving the social and economic goals of their patrons and owners.''[28]

Yet, even if one were to grant the existence of less commodified instances of mass culture, it would remain to be shown that cultural goods exhibit the autonomy Adorno thought necessary if they were to present truths about the prevailing socio-economic order. Resistance to commodification is not strictly identical with autonomy. Although the autonomy of art does depend in part on fulfilling certain economic requirements, meeting these requirements does not constitute a sufficient condition for autonomy. In addition to being relatively independent of the market, a cultural good will also have to exhibit certain internal characteristics or features in order to be considered truly autonomous. Art's autonomy is primarily a consequence of an inner state or process.

Paradoxically, those features or characteristics which signal a work's autonomy are identical with some of the more important effects of reification itself.

According to Zuidervaart, Adorno defines autonomous artworks as defetishizing fetishes. As fetishes, these works conceal the labor "that has gone into them and appear to have a life of their own." They "appear to be superior cultural entities somehow detached from the conditions of economic production"; and they "seem to serve no use beyond their own existence." Nevertheless, this fetish character in art may dialectically reverse itself. Zuidervaart explains:

> By appearing to have a life of their own, works of art call into question a society where nothing is allowed to be itself and everything is subject to the principle of exchange. By appearing to be detached from the conditions of economic production, works of art acquire the ability to suggest changed conditions. And by appearing to be useless, works of art recall the human purposes of production that instrumental rationality forgets.[29]

By concealing or disguising their reification, some modern artworks also subvert it; they undermine the reifying effects of standardization, pseudo-individualism, stereotypes, and schemata.

In order to exhibit the autonomy found in artworks, products of the culture industry would themselves have to undermine reification from within. Although the creators of cultural goods may enjoy a measure of extrinsic independence from more industrialized production processes, such independence will not, in and of itself, guarantee the autonomy of their work. To achieve a measure of autonomy, cultural goods must also play the role of defetishizing fetishes, concealing their entanglement in commodity production. And, as Adorno repeatedly emphasized, this is precisely what the commodities produced by the culture industry do not do: they fail to disguise their fetish character and do not pretend to have any value apart from that of exchange. Governed directly and undisguisedly by "the principle of their realization as value" (CIR, 13), the industry's products actually promote the abstract identity of the exchange principle. This constitutes an intrinsic impediment to their autonomy.

Approaching the problem from another direction, Zuidervaart attempts to demonstrate that autonomy is not a necessary condition for successful works of art. Showing first that Adorno's claims about art's autonomy are problematic, because this autonomy is compromised extrinsically by art's entanglement in commodity production and by its functions within non-aesthetic institutions, Zuidervaart proceeds to re-define the concept by distinguishing between art's purposes and its in-stitutional functions. Artworks perform social and economic functions by serving as "agents of employment, socializing, corporate image-building, and civic pride."[30] At the same time, however, these same artworks may also serve to gratify human needs and desires. Zuider-vaart argues that such gratification or fulfillment is one of the purposes of art and should be considered to be the primary condition for its autonomy: "At best the concept of autonomy will imply that at least some of what is called art has come to serve certain human purposes more directly than have other institutions in society."[31]

The problem with Zuidervaart's argument here is that he defines au-tonomy extrinsically in terms of art's purposes: its gratification of human needs and desires. While it is clear that Adorno did believe that autonomous art met needs and desires which capitalism did not satisfy, he did not define art's autonomy in terms of its ability to serve this extrinsic purpose. Having redefined autonomy in this way, however, Zuidervaart questions the distinction Adorno makes between autono-mous and heteronomous art, claiming that heteronomous art may also occasionally reveal truths about existing society, challenging the status quo and evoking the image of a better world. After an impressively painstaking analysis of Adorno's concept of artistic autonomy in terms of both its intrinsic and extrinsic features, Zuidervaart ultimately ig-nores the implications of that analysis. In order to call into question Adorno's distinction between autonomous and heteronomous works, Zuidervaart must also show why art's intrinsic autonomy—its character as a "defetishizing fetish"—cannot or need not function as a necessary condition for truth. Art's autonomy may not be reduced to its fullfil-ment of purposes extrinsic to it as Zuidervaart has done.

If it does not have the character of defetishizing fetish, a cultural artifact cannot lay claim to the autonomy required for social signifi-cance or truth content in Adorno's sense of these terms. To reiterate, those economic conditions which may set limits to commodification are merely extrinsic factors determining a work's autonomy; the fact that production within the culture industry is not industrialized in the early stages proves little about the autonomy of the commodities produced. Zuidervaart implicitly undermines his own definition of art's autonomy when he observes that Adorno gave precedence in his aesthetic theory to judgments about internal processes in individual artworks. Adorno insisted that the primary criteria for determining whether a work is au-tonomous or successful are found neither in production nor in reception; rather they must be located within the individual work itself.[32] This means that each individual work must be judged on its own terms.

Nevertheless, Adorno himself did not observe this stricture when he indicted the culture industry. Apart from his few brief attempts at content analysis in essays like "Fernsehen als Ideologie" (and in its earlier English prototype "How to Look at Television"), Adorno seldom judged products of the culture industry on an individual basis. His assertion that all cultural goods fail to satisfy aesthetic criteria is far too sweeping. It could never be substantiated and need not be accepted at face value. Moreover, given his own analysis of the production of cultural goods, Adorno would have to concede that not all such goods are necessarily commodified through and through. As standardized as some products of the culture industry certainly are, one cannot generalize in advance about every one of them. The lacunae in Adorno's analysis of the political economy of the culture industry also make any more extensive claims about the effects of commodification on culture appear presumptuous.

In Adorno's work, limits to the commodification of cultural goods find their subjective complement in limits to the industry's reinforcement techniques. Since the consciousness of consumers is duplicitous and characterized by mistrust, a disparity emerges between the reinforcement techniques used by the culture industry and their effects on consumers. Adorno believed that the truth about products of the culture industry lay close to the surface of consciousness. Furthermore, while the culture industry does gratify some needs—however distorted these needs may be or however indirectly they are satisfied—Adorno was also aware that there were antagonisms between the industry's offers of gratification and the individual's needs and drives. These antagonisms result in an underlying sense of unease or discontent under late capitalism.

Despite this more positive reading of Adorno's work on reception, several important caveats must be introduced before it can be assessed adequately. Cultural theorists who accuse Adorno of being too pessimistic about the gratification of needs and the success of reinforcement techniques often presuppose that there is some sort of ahistorical psychological core in consumers which is at least partially untouched by capitalism and resistant to it. Adorno's theory offers an important corrective to such an assumption. Capitalist production processes have had a profound impact on consciousness. Commenting on Adorno's work, Eugene Lunn remarks that the labor process "is usually so enervating, tedious and exhausting" that the capacity to concentrate, to focus attention in a sustained and undivided manner, has been inhibited. Owing to the "deconcentration" of perception, consumers want products that can be digested easily and enjoyed without effort. Quoting "On Popular Music," Lunn continues: "What results is that although 'people want to have fun,' they want relief from both boredom and effort simultaneously, 'making it impossible to break out of the cycle of frustration.' "[33]

Adorno's discussion of the narcissistic tendencies typical of individuals within capitalist societies adds a similar note of caution to any claims made by contemporary cultural theorists about resistive elements in reception. As Oskar Negt points out, Adorno believed that individuals were largely "confined to socio-psychological dispositions, to behavioral modes characterized by regression."[34] These regressive tendencies act as a fundamental obstacle to resistive reception; the prevalence of narcissism may undermine the resistive force of needs. Even if one were to grant that some products of the culture industry do meet needs which generally remain unsatisfied within capitalism, such gratification will not necessarily abrogate or even diminish the debilitating effects of narcissism. The possibility advanced by Andreas Huyssen that some products of the culture industry might "speak to and activate" more authentic "pre-ego impulses in a non-regressive way"[35] is also compromised by narcissism's regressive traits. Moreover, since all needs are socially mediated, any gratification cultural goods do provide may simply result in satisfaction with capitalism or in the reinforcement of narcissistic tendencies.

In *Negative Dialectics*, Adorno wrote that neuroses "absorb an immense quantity of available human strength," preventing "that right action which inevitably runs counter to hidebound self-preservation." For Adorno:

> Neuroses are pillars of society; they thwart the better potential of men, and thus the objectively better condition which men might bring about. There are instincts spurring men beyond the false condition; but the neuroses tend to dam up those instincts, to push them back toward narcissistic self-gratification in the false condition. Weakness that will mistake itself for strength, if possible, is a hinge in the machinery of evil.[36]

In Adorno's work, it often appears as if the conditions for critical reception are identical with the elimination of (or reduction in) narcissistic tendencies. Despite their duplicity, consumers only partially see through cultural commodities. Whatever needs they may satisfy, these commodities generally help to reinforce the narcissism which impedes emancipation. No contemporary account of the emancipatory or resistive elements in reception should overlook Adorno's analysis of the impact of capitalist forms of domination on contemporary consciousness. It casts a long shadow over any discussion of the possibility for resistance and emancipation.

To compound these problems, Adorno thought that individuals were increasingly losing their capacity to identify and formulate their needs. The culture industry attempts to satisfy consumers' wishes but consumers no longer know how to wish or what they should wish for (PF, 516). In his work on the satisfaction of needs within capitalist societies, William Leiss often reinforces Adorno's own claims about needs. Advertising, in particular, has fragmented and isolated needs, making it "increasingly difficult for the person to integrate the components into a coherent ensemble of needs and a coherent personality structure."[37] Although he denies that it is possible in principle to distinguish between true and false needs, Leiss believes that individuals have "become confused about the nature and objectives of their wants."[38] This means that even if some cultural commodities do satisfy unfulfilled needs, the consumer may be unaware that these needs are being met at all.

If consumers have difficulty in identifying and expressing their needs, and the resistive and instinctual elements in reception are held in check by narcissism, then the prospects for instinctually motivated resistance to the socio-economic order are severely diminished. These problems also undermine Adorno's claims about the political function of high modern art. Zuidervaart criticizes Adorno on this point. Adorno's belief that some works of high modern art manage to " 'get through' to people, changing their political attitudes, and thereby changing their political behavior" must be qualified. While Zuidervaart does not mention Adorno's work on the narcissistic reception of cultural commodities in this context, his qualification is especially necessary precisely because of the problematic character of this reception. Adorno never convincingly demonstrated that autonomous works of art actually do have the political impact on consciousness which he ascribed to them. And, as Zuidervaart points out, it is "doubtful that artistic import can have a genuinely political impact unless extra-artistic factors make for appropriate receptivity."[39]

When he claimed that the culture commodity's illusory and distortive fulfillment of needs under late capitalism might itself perform a political function—because the system's failure to satisfy needs results in consumer dissatisfaction and discontent—Adorno also implied that cultural commodities indirectly promote resistance to the status quo.[40] Although, in this case as well, Adorno never demonstrated convincingly that such dissatisfaction actually had the political function he ascribed to it, it is obvious that he refused to abandon completely the idea that individuals are capable of resistance on the level of their instincts or drives. Adorno even contended that the culture industry's reinforcement of needs was countered by a tendency within individuals themselves to resist reinforcement (SMC, 69). However maladroitly, individuals do tend to resist the culture industry's offers of gratification. But, at the same time, Adorno also recognized that consumers generally prefer to adapt to prevailing conditions, ultimately renouncing resistance. Their renunciation "is ratified by regression" (SMC, 80).

Adorno presupposes that the audience for modernist works is more robust on both the rational and instinctual levels—despite the damage done by reification and the weakening of the ego. A stroke of good luck, a failure or inability to adjust to prevailing conditions, allow this audience to be able to identify at least some of its needs, finding some measure of gratification for them in modern art. By contrast, the audience for the culture industry is presumed to be narcissistic. Its drives have been harnessed by the culture industry and other agencies of socialization; its ability to identify and promote its own needs and rational self-interest has been thwarted. Any tendencies this audience may have toward resistance to cultural commodities have been compromised by its regressive tendencies. Adaptation and conformity are the norm.

Yet Adorno also claimed that it was primarily the middle and lower-middle classes who demand narcissistic gratification. This suggests that other socio-economic classes may not have suffered the psychological damage Adorno diagnosed in the "masses." Unfortunately, Adorno himself never explored this possibility. He contrasted the less narcissistic—but equally damaged—"unhappy few" to the thoroughly narcissistic "unhappy many." These generalizations reveal the limits to Adorno's own speculative theory. Although they may help to give shape to prevailing social and psychological tendencies, they can certainly also be called into question when they are applied to all socio-economic groups. As Adorno himself wrote, to contend that narcissistic pseudo-culture is universal is "simplistic and exaggerated." This concept "does not purport to include all peoples and classes indiscriminately" (PC, 22). By failing to identify what peoples and classes are not covered by the concept, Adorno makes short work of his analysis of the resistive potential in reception.

The conditions for politicized reception seem to be met more fully in the duplicitous consciousness of consumers. It is here that enlightenment has left its mark. Adorno even managed to discover the imprint of enlightenment among the followers of nazism. However, Adorno did not demonstrate how enlightenment ideology was able to penetrate those who would seem to be most recalcitrant to it. Correspondingly, he never explained fully how these followers succeeded in resisting the effects of anti-enlightenment perpetrated by nazism. In fact, it was blatantly obvious that enlightenment ideology had not been sufficient to counteract nazism's effects; nor could its critical elements completely foil the blandishments of the culture industry. The duplicity which characterizes contemporary media reception itself results in part from this quasi-enlightened, but relatively impotent, state of consciousness. When narcissism is added to the mix, undermining rational self-interest, the prospects for conscious resistance to the culture industry appear virtually hopeless. Adorno's analysis casts doubt on locating in all but a few socio-economic groups the degree of receptivity required for any cultural good—including works of art—to have a political function.

Adorno said very little about the psychological constitution of those individuals who have the capacity for resistance to the culture industry. Moreover, Adorno's analysis of narcissistic tendencies within contemporary modes of reception sometimes appears to nullify even that potential for resistance which he himself discovered in the limits to reinforcement: the duplicity of consciousness and the antagonisms between consumers' needs and the culture industry's offers of gratification. In many passages of his work, Adorno retracted his more positive reading of the state of contemporary consciousness under late capitalism. He took away with one hand what he gave with the other. Adorno's apparent vacillations concerning the likelihood of resistance can perhaps be better understood if one also takes into account his belief that most consumers of cultural commodities lack sufficient education. Adorno thought that consumers could eventually learn to recognize their own role in maintaining both prevailing practices of domination and the positivist ideology which serves to legitimate these practices.

Education has a real chance precisely because people know, at least subconsciously, that they are underwriting a false bill of goods. Adorno believed this duplicity should be exposed; he also hoped that the knowledge which the culture industry withholds would finally be communicated to the consumers of cultural commodities. Ideally, this education would begin in childhood.[41] Identifying the "socio-psychological norms of production," sociologists and psychologists would provide the research that is needed to eliminate those schemata and stereotypes which "result in the stultification, psychological crippling and ideological mystification of the public" (FI, 531). Even though he realized that more enlightened socio-psychological norms for cultural production could not be laid down in advance, Adorno also observed that "the canon for what is negative is not so far from the canon for what is positive" (FI, 532).

Of course, in light of the fact that socio-economic groups do not all suffer equally from the effects of reification and narcissism, there is also a real chance that some of these groups already exhibit those capacities for reception which are a condition for actual resistance. In principle, these groups would be able to recognize many of the illusory and distortive elements in the culture industry's gratification of needs. At the same time, they would also be able to identify any products which satisfy unmet needs and desires. Adorno implied that in some cases the culture industry does actually gratify needs that are not wholly a function of the "machinery of production" (LC, 238). And, despite his belief that the needs satisfied by cultural commodities were primarily narcissistic in character, Adorno also insisted that more work—especially depth-psychological studies of consumption—had to be done before one could draw any firm conclusions about what commodities like television programs really offer people. In the absence of such studies, one cannot dismiss summarily the possibility that cultural commodities do meet needs which are not tied directly to profit interests.

This examination of the reception of cultural commodities must be supplemented with a critical analysis of Adorno's ideas about the ideology of the culture industry. Duplicity in reception is also due in part to the flimsiness and transparency of the industry's positivist ideology. Expressed in the tautological assertion that things are the way they are, this ideology often takes the form of a pseudo-realistic depiction of the existing state of affairs. As a result: "Reality becomes its own ideology through the spell cast by its faithful duplication" (SMC, 55). Where liberal ideology contains a speculative and ironic moment of truth, owing to the contradictions between its norms and empirical reality, the industry's positivism supports no such incongruities. Its legitimation of the status quo is one-dimensional; Adorno frequently alleged that the industry's products were entirely affirmative.

The modernist works which Adorno championed themselves conceal a speculative moment against which prevailing conditions can be judged. Zuidervaart elucidates this point: "In a world where consumers are deceptively soothed by culture industry products, the image-character of art exposes the alienation of subject and object."[42] The non-identity between subject and object prefigures a world in which there would be no antagonism and no contradiction: "The stored-up nonidentical breaks into an exchange society without becoming fungible. . . . [A]rtworks hint at what life would be like were it emancipated from imposed identity."[43] As autonomous, art is able partially to escape the domination of the exchange principle, evoking negatively the promise of a happiness denied by prevailing conditions and allowing "those things be heard which ideology conceals."[44] By contrast, Adorno asserted that every cultural commodity "renounces its own autonomy and proudly takes its place among consumption goods" (*DE*, 157). Its ideology consists in simply affirming that what counts as happiness here and now is all that happiness is and could ever be.

In many passages of his work, Adorno claimed that cultural commodities espouse an analytic form of identity without speculative content. But in other passages, Adorno contradicted these statements about the culture industry's positivist ideology: "The curse of modern mass culture seems to be its adherence to the almost unchanged ideology of early middle-class society." Speculative in terms of their content, the values promulgated in this ideology target "a frame of mind which is no longer bound by these values."[45] Since the "perennial middle class conflict between individuality and society has been reduced to a dim memory," in their reception of traditional values, consumers have already decided in favor of conformity to the status quo. For Adorno, the "constant plugging of conventional values seems to mean that these values have lost their substance" (HLT, 141). In *Dialectic of Enlightenment*, Horkheimer and Adorno made a similar observation, arguing that value judgments are now viewed cynically. Liberal ideology has lost its hold on consciousness.

This assessment of reception is contradicted in other essays, such as "Freudian Theory and the Pattern of Fascist Propaganda" and "Theory of Pseudo-Culture," where Adorno maintained that the values and ideals of liberal ideology are still effective in contemporary consciousness and influence behavior in a positive way. On the one hand, then, Adorno asserted that the culture industry promotes a more speculative middle-class ideology but that consumers are no longer receptive to its values. On the other, he held that the ideology of the culture industry is entirely positivistic while acknowledging that consumers are motivated beneficially by the liberal values which they have inherited from enlightenment. These conflicting claims about both the culture industry's ideology and the consciousness of its audience need to be assessed critically.

There would appear to be a speculative moment in some cultural commodities, especially in those which either implicitly or explicitly promulgate the values of freedom, equality, autonomy, and spontaneity. But, more often than not, even these liberal values are affirmed in the positivistic way Adorno condemned. For example, freedom, which is often overtly promoted in cultural commodities, is generally identified with freedom to consume the wealth of commodities which capitalism has to offer. As Herbert Marcuse once quipped, freedom in capitalism is the freedom to choose between a hundred different brands of toilet paper. When Ernesto Laclau and Chantal Mouffe state that the media call upon individuals as equals, they qualify this statement when they add ''in their capacity as consumers.''[46] Only occasionally do cultural commodities advance the normative and inherently critical content in the notions of freedom and equality. Although the industry's ideology may not be completely positivistic, the liberal values it may purvey are often purged of their critical content. They are reduced to descriptive and explanatory concepts that are congruent with and affirmative of a society dominated entirely by the exchange principle.

Laclau and Mouffe maintain that the action of the media inevitably results in ''the reigning appearance of equality and . . . cultural democratization.''[47] The media portray values like equality and liberty as if they were already realized empirically. The authors believe that this imaginary portrayal actually motivates groups to reject the empirical reality which negates the norms of liberty and equality. But if the promulgation of these values by the media is generally affirmative in character—and Laclau and Mouffe seem to recognize this—their ability to motivate resistive behavior may certainly be contested. Once liberal values are stripped of their critical content, it is difficult to see how they could serve this function. Although Laclau and Mouffe claim that cultural commodities have speculative content, they do not locate this content convincingly in the more affirmative elements of media ideology which they discuss in the above passage.

It is highly unlikely that more than a few cultural commodities will promote values with a critical content. When a writer like Fredric Jameson proclaims that all ideology is utopian, he implies that all ideology—even that found within cultural commodities—contains a normative and critical dimension:

> If the function of the mass cultural text is meanwhile seen rather as the production of false consciousness and the symbolic reaffirmation of this or that legitimating strategy, even this process cannot be grasped as one of sheer violence . . . nor as one inscribing the appropriate attitudes upon a

blank slate, but must necessarily involve a complex strategy of rhetorical persuasion in which substantial incentives are offered for ideological adherence. We will say that such incentives, as well as the impulses to be managed by the mass cultural text, are necessarily Utopian in nature.[48]

On Jameson's reading, Adorno and Horkheimer showed that anti-Semitism itself was utopian because it manifests "a form of cultural envy which is at the same time a repressed recognition of the Utopian impulse."[49] Nonetheless, contra Jameson, Horkheimer and Adorno never identified the utopian elements in ideology with incentives and impulses. While "mass cultural texts" may satisfy these latter in a variety of ways, such satisfaction says little about their ideology. Moreover, when Adorno described the culture industry's ideology as positivistic, he called into question Jameson's claims about the more speculative or utopian elements in cultural commodities.

Adorno defined ideology as "the supposition of identity." Liberal ideology once hid within this very supposition "the pledge that there should be no contradiction, no antagonism" between subject and object (*ND*, 149). Cultural commodities conceal no such pledge. Adorno often ruled out in advance the possibility that these commodities might communicate speculative and "utopian" elements. Like his other generalizations, this one need not be accepted as a universal and necessary truth about pseudo-culture. However, Adorno's more negative assessment of the culture industry's ideology does act as a caution against Jameson's all too buoyant optimism. The problem with Jameson's generalizations about ideology is that they are equally exaggerated. Many cultural goods will be predominately positivistic, advertisements for the world as it is, dominated by the exchange principle.

When one takes into account Adorno's belief that enlightenment ideology continues to play a motivating role in behavior—a belief that can be confirmed empirically, especially in the case of the new social movements—it is difficult to conceive where this ideology could have been acquired if not from some of the commodities produced by the culture industry. It is probably also the case, then, that some of the critical elements in enlightenment ideology are occasionally disseminated by the culture industry. Only an analysis of individual cultural goods will determine whether or not they purvey a more speculative and utopian ideology in Adorno's terms: non-identity within identity. A number of commentators, including Jameson and Douglas Kellner,[50] have attempted to sound out popular culture for its more critical and oppositional themes, images and ideas. Unfortunately, they have not made use of Adorno's work. In order to have the critical force Adorno attributed to the ideological dimension of some works of high modern art, cultural goods must transcend their positivistic identification with the commodity form.

Adorno maintained that cultural goods obey the dictates of the exchange principle which is based on the abstract identity of human labor and its products. Inasmuch as they have become reified, these goods are identical with all other commodities. Through their positivist ideology, cultural goods also help to promulgate the identity imposed by the exchange principle. Adorno's discussion of ideology as a function of identity claims is closely intertwined with his analysis of commodification and reification. Since Adorno believed that ideology contains a moment of truth when it posits a moment of non-identity, it follows that cultural goods themselves will acquire truth value only when they reject or conceal their identity with the commodity form. In order to serve a political function, these goods will have to play the role of defetishizing fetishes, subverting the commodity form from within by appearing to have a life of their own as concrete and insubordinate particulars. Ultimately, a truly critical work will break the spell cast by the prevailing form of domination within capitalism—a form characterized in large measure by its increasing reification of subjects and objects.

Reification represents the triumph of the general social order over the particular—whether this latter is an individual subject or an individual work. According to Adorno, the "more total society becomes, the greater the reification of the mind and the more paradoxical its effort to escape reification on its own." Adorno expresses the fear that reification "is now preparing to absorb the mind entirely" (CCS, 34). As the individual mind is absorbed under the exchange principle, all antagonisms between the individual and society will effectively be suppressed. Expunging individual differences when they posit an identity between the universal and the particular, standardized cultural goods have also become reified. In such goods, "the commodified, reified content of culture survives at the expense of its truth content and its vital relation to living subjects" (PC, 23). Only by revealing the conflicts that arise between what historically remains of individuals as non-reified subjects and the socio-economic order of late capitalism (where the homogenizing exchange principle reigns virtually supreme), will cultural commodities succeed in indicting what is false in false consciousness.

Concluding Remarks

In his 1966 essay on film, Adorno observed that some of the work done in New German Cinema did have critical potential even though a "gap" continued to exist between "the most progressive tendencies in the visual arts and those of film."[51] Since it is a more representational medium, film generally tends to place "a higher intrinsic significance on the object, as foreign to subjectivity, than aesthetically autonomous techniques" (TF, 202). Adorno contended that the use of montage would prevent film from lapsing into a purely documentary and pseudo-realistic mode while also introducing the element of subjective intention into film. Although montage "does not interfere with things but rather arranges them in a constellation akin to that of writing," its refusal to interpret is "itself a subjective act and as such *a priori* significant" (TF, 203). To further counteract the intrusion of objective social elements, Adorno also suggested that the film-montage be composed of interior, subjective images. And, despite his disparagement of the *Gesamtkunst-werk*,[52] Adorno claimed that film's "most promising potential lies in its interaction with other media, themselves merging into film, such as certain types of music." Adorno endorsed Mauricio Kagel's "Antithèse" as an example of such a work (TF, 203).

These claims about the potentially critical and emancipatory elements in film also make it impossible to rule out in advance the possibility that other cultural commodities may possess this potential. But some of Adorno's more intriguing and suggestive remarks about this potential appear much earlier in his work. For example, Nicholas Garnham quotes an interesting passage from *Dialectic of Enlightenment* where Adorno and Horkheimer wrote:

'Nevertheless the culture industry remains the entertainment business. Its influence over the consumer is established by entertainment; that will ultimately be broken not by an outright decree, but by the hostility inherent in the principle of entertainment to what is greater than itself.'[53]

In a similar vein, Martin Jay insists that it would be wrong to view "Transparencies on Film" as a "totally new departure" in Adorno's work since Adorno was never entirely dismissive of the culture industry. Jay cites *Dialectic of Enlightenment*: " 'the culture industry does retain a trace of something better in those features which bring it close to the circus.' "[54] Eugene Lunn finds another reference to the circus in Adorno's *Aesthetic Theory* where Adorno compares the "purposeful purposelessness of art, its potential as a source of resistance to draconian utility'' to ''forms of entertainment, such as the circus, which have survived from the early industrial era.''[55]

As these remarks show, there are many aspects in Adorno's theory of the culture industry which remain to be plumbed. Adorno and Horkheimer railed against the deadly seriousness of the entertainment industry while at the same time expressing the hope that producers of culture would finally offer the entertainment they promised. The authors described entertainment or amusement as the ''relaxed self-surrender to all kinds of associations and happy nonsense'' (*DE*, 142). Amusement has an ''original affinity'' with business because both business and amusement defend society—''To be pleased means to say yes'' (*DE*, 144). Owing to this affinity, amusement is the ''antithesis of art.'' At the same time, however, it is also art's ''extreme role'' because, in its absurd features, amusement acts as a ''corrective'' to art's seriousness. Appealing to whatever historically remains of non-reified subjectivity, amusement can still be gleaned occasionally from ''some revue films, and especially in the grotesque and the funnies'' (*DE*, 142). Unfortunately, the culture industry more often than not cuts short amusement by ''intellectualizing'' it and controlling ''genuine personal emotion'' (*DE*, 143–44). With its formulaic production, its positivism and reinforcement techniques, the industry tends to foster conformity rather than the spontaneity which amusement presupposes.

Nevertheless, just as Adorno refused to abandon the idea that resistance was possible on both the instinctual and the more conscious levels, so too, in ''The Schema of Mass Culture,'' Adorno and Horkheimer held open the possibility that individuals had not adjusted completely to the reified status quo. Although the unreified subjective residue they claimed to find was itself largely a socio-historical product of the bourgeois liberal stage of capitalism—and should not be confused with the ahistorical psychological core that contemporary cultural theorists often presuppose in their discussions of resistive reception—it allegedly counteracted the fragmentation and isolation caused by reification and commodification. As subjects, individuals ''still represent the ultimate limit of reification.'' This means that ''mass culture must try and take hold of them again and again: the bad infinity involved in this hopeless effort of repetition is the only trace of hope that this repetition might be in vain, that men cannot be wholly grasped at all'' (SMC, 80).

On the one hand, then, Adorno often expressed the fear that the conscious mind and the unconscious drives were being overwhelmed by the effects of reification. In *Minima Moralia*, for example, Adorno argued that "by dint of reflecting on the psyche," artists "have found out more and more how to control themselves." This more recent form of self-control is repressive; it has resulted in "a kind of reification, technification of the inward as such" (*MM*, 214). On the other hand, Adorno also insisted that individuals "are not exhausted by the objectified control of nature which they reprojected—projected back upon themselves, from outward nature" (*ND*, 297). Once again, Adorno refused to relinquish what he often described as the extremely remote likelihood that something in individuals remains historically resistant to reinforcement and reification.

Since it fosters reification and reinforces the individual's narcissistic identification with in-groups, the entertainment industry fails to appeal to whatever remains of this less reified subject. With its stereotypes and schemata, the industry encourages only pathological forms of collectivity. By contrast (as Adorno pointed out in his discussion of New German Cinema), a more emancipated work would "wrest its *a priori* collectivity from the mechanisms of unconscious and irrational influence and enlist this collectivity in the service of emancipatory intentions" (TF, 203–4). In fact, Martin Jay has observed that, for Adorno, the subject of autonomous art is itself a collective subject, "a composite of the composer's personal skills and the means at his disposal bequeathed by the past."[56] On Zuidervaart's reading: "When an individual artist works with historical materials, collective sociohistorical experience enters specific works of art."[57] Successful artworks manage to maintain the tension between subject and object which is the precondition for the emergence of an emancipated "we," the subject of radical political practice.[58]

Michael Sullivan and John Lysaker even go as far as to claim that "Adorno's turn to aesthetic theory does not so much abandon the possibility of 'objective communication,' as it does seek out its exemplification in the practice of artworks." Adorno's work on the relationship between subject and object, "on the possibility of subjects and objects belonging together in forms of existence that are free of domination is, in Adorno's own view, work on the possibility of communication."[59] If some products of the culture industry succeed in achieving a degree of autonomy, they will do so by taking as their model those activities—both artistic and philosophical—which break the stranglehold of reification and its psychological counterpart narcissism, holding out the promise of independent forms of communication between more rationally and instinctually robust individuals. Although Adorno disparaged many contemporary forms of communication for "falsifying truth and selling it out,'' he also believed that some individuals are still able to make ''the moral and, as it were, representative effort to say what most of those for whom they say it cannot see, or, to do justice to reality, will not allow themselves to see'' (*ND*, 41).

While respecting the basic premises of Adorno's theory of culture, the supposition cannot be dismissed out of hand that some products of the culture industry already follow the model for cultural practice with political import which Adorno discovered in some works of high modern art. This supposition could only be confirmed by analyzing cultural goods on an individual basis. Furthermore, as I have tried to show, more autonomous subjects, receptive to the political import of culture, may also exist. They would be able to make use of whatever cultural commodities have to offer in the way of critical and emancipatory potential. However, as long as it has not been demonstrated that resistance to reification is actually occurring, this more balanced account of the culture industry implicit in Adorno's work remains abstract. A comprehensive reassessment of the culture industry demands empirically thorough and theoretically sound accounts of the nature of resistive works and practices themselves. Unfortunately, most of the studies that have been done in this area are unconvincing.[60] Yet, without this reassessment, Adorno's allegedly more pessimistic views about the anti-enlightenment perpetrated by culture industry seem more susceptible to empirical verification than the slim prospects for emancipation which he often held in abeyance.

Epilogue

The fundamental substance of an epoch and its unheeded impulses illuminate each other reciprocally.

— *Siegfried Kracauer*

In spite of the deficiencies in Adorno's analysis of mass culture, some of the more contemporary writers cited in this book have found many ideas in Adorno's brief excursus on the political economy of the culture industry which continue to prove relevant. They have extended his work while pointing to those features of cultural production, including its contradictions and inconsistencies, which Adorno himself sometimes identified but never pursued. For instance, if Adorno acknowledged the centrality of the industry's "rationalized" distribution techniques— which have allowed the culture industry to reach into the homes of hundreds of millions of people—he never carried out the critical work on these techniques that remains to be done. If the culture industry promises entertainment while promoting business interests, then the cultural commodity may harbor "an inherent contradiction, a contradiction which, as with the other contradictions within the capitalist mode of production, may be profoundly subversive."[1]

Adorno's work also needs to be reinforced with a critical examination of the connections between advertising and cultural commodities. Among the newer advertising techniques worthy of consideration is cross-promotion; advertisements for movies like *Congo* or *Pocahontas* serve a dual function when they are also used to promote products made by Taco Bell or services sold by Best Western. More important are the economic effects of advertising on the culture industry. Ben Bagdikian has gone as far as to attribute the increasing concentration of newspaper

131

ownership to mass advertising.² He also maintains that it was advertising which first allowed television to triumph over magazines. For Bagdikian, "the dynamics of advertising" even account for the standardization of television.³ Later in his book, he reveals how the corporate agenda of advertising has been successfully foisted on both entertainment and news or documentary programs.⁴

Graham Murdock and Peter Golding criticize Marxian theorists in general for their undeveloped analyses of the economic bases of cultural production. They believe that "Marxism's distinctiveness and promise as a framework for the sociological investigation of culture and communication lies precisely in the fact that it focuses on the complex connections *between* economics and intellectual production."⁵ Although the authors continue to claim that the base-superstructure relation provides a suitable framework for the study of cultural production—a claim Adorno refuted—their insistence on the value of economic analyses is all the more compelling precisely because the economic base now subsumes cultural production. Especially important in this regard is an analysis of marketing. When Bill Ryan attempts to provide such an analysis, demonstrating the central role of marketing in the circulation of cultural commodities, he makes a necessary contribution to a political economy of cultural production. Now enveloping advertising, marketing "involves several related activities including research, product planning and design, packaging, publicity and promotion, and sales and distribution and is closely tied with merchandising and retailing."⁶ As consumers of cultural goods themselves become commodities marketed and sold to advertisers, the study of marketing techniques and strategies acquires new relevance.

Complementing a more thorough critique of the political economy of the culture industry, researchers might undertake the depth-psychological studies which Adorno recommended but never completed. These studies would serve to support both the general account of narcissism provided by Adorno as well as the empirical validation of that account initiated by writers like Christopher Lasch. If narcissism is to our time what hysteria was to Freud's, further investigation of this pathology is required. To shore up this inquiry, clinical work on consumption patterns and habits—in the form of a critical study of the "psychotechnics" of cultural commodities and their effects on consumers—should be developed and elaborated. Adorno's more specialized discussion of the culture industry's reanimation of superego introjects, mobilization of infantile defense mechanisms, wish-fulfillment, and use of stereotypes and schemata would certainly also benefit from further empirical research.

Adorno advanced the speculative hypothesis that narcissism had become widespread under late capitalism. At the same time, however, he conceded that his hypothesis could not be taken as a universal and necessary statement about all individuals. Social psychologists might explore the possibility that some socio-economic groups do not suffer from narcissism to the same degree as do members of the middle and lower-middle classes. Similarly, Adorno's work on needs and their satisfaction deserves greater scrutiny. Writers like William Leiss have already taken important steps in this direction.[7] Although Leiss's rejection of Herbert Marcuse's theory of needs may also extend to Adorno's assertion that it is possible in principle to distinguish between true and false needs, researchers could study those needs whose gratification may foster greater ego autonomy and spontaneity. More generally, they could also examine non-narcissistic forms of the gratification of needs.

In addition to their examination of needs, sociologists and social psychologists might take a closer look at Adorno's ideas about the effects of liberal ideology on consciousness. How much a part of our self-understanding have the implicitly critical ideals of freedom, autonomy, and spontaneity really become? To what extent and under what conditions do such ideals motivate resistance to the inequalities, dependence, and conformity prevalent in late capitalist societies? Such questions have seldom been posed in empirical research. Although Ernesto Laclau and Chantal Mouffe make interesting comments about the effects of liberal ideology on consciousness, their remarks are not entirely convincing. History certainly has shown that people are willing to resist, even to lay down their lives, for what they perceive as freedom and equality. Yet history has also demonstrated that these ideals are usually not sufficient to motivate resistance to oppressive political and economic regimes. If culture industries like television really do reinforce regressive modes of behavior, which have been drummed in since the end of the seventeenth century and "internalized as second nature,"[8] more "enlightened" values and ideals may end up losing whatever resistive force they originally had. As facts become values under the prevailing spell of positivism, they may condense and displace what Laclau and Mouffe have described as the liberal democratic imaginary of freedom and equality,[9] compromising the prospects for political and economic opposition even further.

Cultural theorists interested in Adorno's work could apply Adorno's insights about the speculative dimension of bourgeois liberal ideology to an analysis of specific cultural commodities. While some theorists allege that many of these commodities have a "utopian" content, and foster resistive practices, they have not adopted Adorno's ideas about what makes up the emancipatory potential of culture. In fact, recent work on the consumption of allegedly "utopian" elements of mass culture often shows inadvertently how they serve to keep individuals content with capitalism. Capitalism appears to offer something for everyone, including the disempowered and dispossessed. For his part, David Sholle offers an alternative critique of the latest versions of limited effects theory when he observes that the resistances contemporary theorists of mass culture locate in receptive practices are "unorganized and unchanneled" and "can just as easily be interpreted as forms of resentment."[10] If liberal ideology does contain critical elements, and these elements are a necessary condition for resistance, cultural theorists would do well to use Adorno's ideas as a guide for their work on resistive consumption.

Adorno placed a great deal of emphasis on education. He recommended that pedagogues, sociologists, and psychologists identify the more debilitating effects of the "socio-psychological norms of production" and propose ways in which these effects could be counteracted or eliminated.[11] Adorno also maintained that more creative workers in the industry—writers, directors, and actors—manifest a certain degree of resistance to the standardization of cultural production. Supported by a social science that refuses "to be stultified and fobbed off with administrative research polls," creative workers would be "in a better position than their bosses and supervisors" to oppose the industry's techniques and ideology (FI, 531–32). Owing to their relative independence from industrial modes of production, writers, directors, and actors could also inject into cultural commodities some of the critical and oppositional elements which Adorno discovered in liberal ideology.

In keeping with Adorno's work on the culture industry, these often unexplored avenues for empirical research must be supplemented by theories of a more speculative nature. Theorists could focus their efforts on criticizing prevailing tendencies which may not as yet have been verified scientifically, projecting from these trends to future developments. The growing monopolization of both industrial and cultural production by ever fewer corporations (with the attendant threat of a postmodern feudalism), the increasing commodification of services and products once immune from market pressures, the general absence of resistance to capitalism (along with the introduction of a market economy to countries like China), the frenzied launching of ever more "new and improved" cultural and industrial commodities for immediate and oblivious consumption—all these observable tendencies should encourage reflection and speculation. Oppressive police and paramilitary measures, assisted by sophisticated surveillance techniques, are being sanctioned as never before in the Western world. Marx's theory of relative impoverishment—which Adorno once rejected as factually inaccurate because of the observable augmentation in workers' standard of living[12]—is being confirmed belatedly today as the underclass continues to grow, while what Habermas has described as the "legitimation crisis" facing Western democracies is coming to a head. These economic and political developments provide a modified framework for understanding the role and functions of the culture industry in the nineties and beyond.

One should not forget the use to which communications technology was put—for better or for worse—in Eastern bloc countries during the eighties. Such technology seems to offer the prospect of either growing social and political interaction or escalating isolation and fragmentation. Neil Postman warns of the latter,[13] while John Downing finds some hope in the former. Now disseminating both disinformation and the positivist ideology of corporate capital, the media may yet contribute to the democratization of political institutions and processes. The referendum will almost certainly become a more widely used venue for political decision-making as computers replace the television set or extend its functions. Although access to the increasingly commodified Internet may be reserved exclusively for those who can afford it, this problem is now being redressed with the spread of municipally funded "free-nets." These latter will facilitate democratic electoral processes while allowing many more people to obtain and monitor information about political, economic, and social events. Citing the examples of the collectively run *Libération* and *Tagezeitung*, along with the politicization of journalists' and writers' unions and the growing demand for open-access broadcasting, Downing maintains that the democratization of the media themselves "is firmly on the political map and processes are underway which can be used to open up media communications at certain points to control from underneath."[14] Nevertheless, pace Downing, given the mainstream media's unparalleled position in the culture industry, one wonders whether the more democratic potential of the media will ever be realized.

Will the couch potato syndrome also afflict the new "surfers" of the so-called Information Highway? Rather than actively informing themselves about available political options and exercising their right to vote, many North Americans prefer to be bombarded—more or less passively—with packaged entertainment and information emanating from an isolated screen. But even when they do engage in the political process, people frequently fall prey to what the French sociologist, Pierre-André Taguieff, has called ''videopolitics.'' Reviewing the literature on this new evangelized mediation of politics, Taguieff cites Elihu Katz and Daniel Dayan. For these media analysts, ''subordinating politics to the media seems to engender a new type of 'minor' people, treated as naturally incompetent or irresponsible.'' And, as Taguieff points out: ''This constitutes a democratic evil for the partisans of an active or participatory democracy. . . .''[15] Adorno never explored such problems in any of his books or essays. They are probably far more devastating in their depoliticizing effects than pseudo-culture's narcissistic and reifying tendencies have ever been.

In the wake of Habermas's *The Structural Transformation of the Public Sphere* and *Theory of Communicative Action*, the importance of more recent work on the viability of a politically active public sphere (or spheres) cannot be overemphasized. It holds out the promise that the media's depoliticizing effects can be reversed. Nevertheless, I have tried to show that there are limitations to Habermas's influential theory. Peter Hohendahl pinpoints the major limitation when he writes that ''Habermas's assessment of the contemporary public sphere relies on the apparatus of liberal theory, which tends to separate the economy from civil society.''[16] In *Civil Society and Political Theory*, Jean Cohen and Andrew Arato follow Habermas when they contend that the life-world has differentiated itself from economic and political systems (with their steering media of money and power).[17] Yet this claim about the relative autonomy of the lifeworld is more an article of faith than an empirically confirmed reality; it is meant to mark a break with Adorno's Marxist idea of the primacy of the economy in all realms of human behavior. Equally tendentious is Habermas's belief that the effects of the ''authoritarian potential'' of the media are precarious ''because there is a counterweight of emancipatory potential built into communicative structures themselves.''[18]

By contrast, Oskar Negt and Alexander Kluge have put forward the idea of interconnected proletarian public spheres—thereby emphasizing the ''de-differentiated'' relationship between the lifeworld and the economic system. Since Adorno's views about the persistence of economic stratification and exploitation in late capitalist societies have again been confirmed by recent historical trends, Negt and Kluge's ostensibly anachronistic idea could still prove useful to theorists of culture. Even as they recognize that the media cartel represents ''an extreme threat to any self-organization of human experience in the forms of autonomous proletarian public spheres,''[19] the authors also believe that human senses and faculties may eventually serve as the material ground for resistance from below. Along with work on needs and their gratification in different socio-economic groups, consideration should be given to Negt and Kluge's largely undeveloped theory.

As the primary vehicle for marketable entertainment and information, supported financially by corporate and monopoly capital, the culture industry now irrefutably undermines the potential for more democratically organized and politically active public spheres, colonizing free time and exercising unparalleled influence over the formation of interests and needs, opinions and ideas, throughout both the industrialized and the developing world. Adorno feared that, through its ideology and reinforcement of regressive narcissistic tendencies, the industry would help to eliminate resistive practice just as nazism was doing when he was forced to emigrate from Germany. Conformity to the status quo, abject dependence on the institutions and agencies of the totally administered world, and unprecedented economic and political exploitation by an oligarchical élite would continue unabated in late capitalist societies. Although they project an extremely somber picture of an irrational and fettered socio-historical reality, many of these hypotheses have found empirical confirmation.

If Adorno's work on the culture industry continues to open new prospects for contemporary media theory, this is largely due to his speculative vision of the historical reality that frames the culture industry and determines its features. Pitting late capitalism's political and economic tendencies against the instinctually-based needs and rational interests of individuals, Adorno deployed norms like freedom, autonomy, and spontaneity as immanent critical standards against which antagonistic reality could be judged. Such speculative thinking was also meant to serve as the prototype for social and political practices which might ultimately overcome reification and narcissism. It was the suffering the latter had caused, reinforced by the culture industry, that compelled Adorno to combat one-dimensional positivistic forms of thought which treat historical facts as universal and necessary values and foster conformity to the status quo. The possibility that positivism might triumph over speculative thought horrified Adorno. In *Negative Dialectics*, he warned: "If thought is not measured by the extremity that eludes the concept, it is from the outset in the nature of the musical accompaniment with which the SS liked to drown out the screams of its victims."[20]

Notes to the Chapters

Prologue

1. Readers interested in an intellectual history of Adorno and his connections to the Institute for Social Research should consult Martin Jay's *The Dialectical Imagination: A History of the Frankfurt School and the Institute of Social Research, 1923–50* (Boston and Toronto: Little, Brown and Company, 1973). They can also refer to Rolf Wiggershaus's *The Frankfurt School: Its History, Theories and Political Significance*, translated by Michael Robertson, (Cambridge, Mass.: The MIT Press, 1994).

2. My vision is derived from Denis Diderot's review of Jean-Honoré Fragonard's painting "Le Grand-prêtre Corésus se sacrifie pour sauver Callirhoé." This review is cited in P. N. Furbank's *Diderot: A Critical Biography* (London: Minerva, 1992) pp. 1–8. The review itself can be found in *Diderot*, Vol. XIV: *Salon de 1765: Essais sur la Peinture*, eds. Else Marie Bukdahl, Annette Lorenceau, and Gita May, (Paris: Hermann, 1984) pp. 253–64.

Chapter One

1. Theodor W. Adorno, "Sociology and Psychology," translated by Irving N. Wohlfarth, *New Left Review* 46 (1967) p. 69. (This is the first half of the translation of "Zum Verhältnis von Soziologie und Psychologie." The last half is found in the subsequent issue of *New Left Review*—number 47—and is cited below.) Cited in the text as SP1.

2. Martin Jay, *Adorno* (London: Fontana, 1984) p. 87. Hereafter cited in the notes as *Adorno*.

3. Alan Bullock, *Hitler and Stalin: Parallel Lives* (Toronto: McClelland & Stewart, 1993) p. 221. Hereafter cited in the notes as *Hitler and Stalin*.

4. Theodor W. Adorno, "Die Revidierte Psychoanalyse," *Soziologische Schriften* I (Frankfurt am Main: Suhrkamp Verlag, 1972) p. 27. All translations are my own. Cited in the text as RP.

5. Idem, *Minima Moralia: Reflections from Damaged Life*, translated by E. F. N. Jephcott, (London: Verso, 1974) p. 150. Cited in the text as *MM*.

6. Idem, "Society," translated by Fredric Jameson, *Salmagundi* III, no. 10–11 (1969–70) p. 152. Cited in the text as S.

7. Jürgen Habermas, "Questions and Counterquestions," translated by James Bohman, *Habermas and Modernity*, ed. Richard Bernstein, (Cambridge, Mass.: The MIT Press, 1985) p. 212. Hereafter cited in the notes as "Questions and Counterquestions."

8. Although Russell Jacoby does not adequately distinguish between the work of Herbert Marcuse and Theodor W. Adorno, he is correct when he points out that for both it is Freud's materialist instinct theory which "peels back and away the social 'norms' and 'values' to find the inner social dynamic." See *Social Amnesia: A Critique of Conformist Psychology from Adler to Laing* (Boston: Beacon Press, 1975) p. 32.

9. Theodor W. Adorno, "Sociology and Psychology," translated by Irving N. Wohlfarth, *New Left Review* 47 (1968) p. 80. Cited in the text as SP2.

10. Russell Jacoby, *Social Amnesia: A Critique of Conformist Psychology from Adler to Laing* (Boston: Beacon Press, 1975) p. 38.

11. Although I disagree with his claim that critical theorists evinced nostalgia for the bourgeois patriarchal family, Andrew Arato writes the following in his introduction to Part I of *The Essential Frankfurt School Reader*: "It is well known that . . . the Frankfurt School had more than a modicum of theoretical nostalgia for aspects of the earlier, liberal phase of capitalist development. The new was symbolized for them by the politics of fascism and the kitsch world of the *Kulturindustrie*. But on one point they were emphatic: since the earlier phase of capitalism was potentially or even inevitably the source of the later, all programs of return to liberalism would be bankrupt." See *The Essential Frankfurt School Reader*, eds. Andrew Arato and Eike Gebhardt (New York: Continuum, 1982) pp. 8–9.

12. Max Horkheimer and Theodor W. Adorno, *Dialectic of Enlightenment*, translated by John Cumming, (New York: The Seabury Press, 1972) p. 198. Cited in the text as *DE*.

13. Theodor W. Adorno, "Reflexionen zur Klassentheorie," *Soziologische Schriften* I (Frankfurt am Main: Suhrkamp Verlag, 1972) pp. 373–91. All translations are my own. Cited in the text as RK.

14. For a discussion of the idea of late capitalism, see Theodor W. Adorno, "Late Capitalism or Industrial Society," translated by Fred van Gelder, *Modern German Sociology*, eds. V. Meja, D. Misgeld, and N. Stehr, (New York: Columbia University Press, 1987) pp. 232–47.

15. Douglas Kellner, *Critical Theory, Marxism and Modernity* (Baltimore: Johns Hopkins University Press, 1989) p. 181.

16. Ibid., p. 182.

17. *Adorno*, p. 85.

18. David Riesman, in collaboration with Reuel Denney and Nathan Glazer,

The Lonely Crowd: A Study of the Changing American Character (New Haven: Yale University Press, 1950). For a defense of Riesman's position on the family against that of Talcott Parsons see Christopher Lasch, *Haven in a Heartless World: The Family Besieged* (New York: Basic Books, 1977) pp. 126–28. In the second section of the chapter, I examine both Christopher Lasch's and Jessica Benjamin's psychological analysis of the decline of the family as an agent of socialization. That Lasch's interpretation of this decline is still relevant is confirmed in a standard sociology textbook, *Family in Transition: Rethinking Marriage, Sexuality, Child Rearing, and Family Organization*, 7th ed., eds. Arlene S. Skolnick and Jerome H. Skolnick, (New York: Harper Collins, 1992). In their introduction (pp. 5–6), the editors cite Lasch's view of the family, contrasting it with feminist and left-wing views. They describe these views as current within contemporary sociological debates about the family.

19. Christopher Lasch, *Haven in a Heartless World: The Family Besieged* (New York: Basic Books, 1977) p. xxiii. Hereafter cited in the notes as *Haven in a Heartless World*.

20. Jürgen Habermas, *The Theory of Communicative Action*, Vol. 2: *Lifeworld and System: A Critique of Functionalist Reason*, translated by Thomas McCarthy, (Boston: Beacon Press, 1987) p. 367. Hereafter cited in the notes as *Lifeworld and System*.

21. *Lifeworld and System*, p. 388: "For some time now, psychoanalytically trained physicians have observed a symptomatic change in the typical manifestations of illness. Classical hysterias have almost died out; the number of compulsion neuroses is drastically reduced; on the other hand, narcissistic disturbances are on the increase. Christopher Lasch has taken this symptomatic change as the occasion for a diagnosis of the times that goes beyond the clinical domain. It confirms the fact that the significant changes in the present escape sociopsychological explanations that start from the Oedipal problematic, from an internalization of societal repression which is simply masked by parental authority. The better explanations start from the premise that the communication structures that have been set free in the family provide conditions for socialization that are as demanding as they are vulnerable." Habermas misinterprets Lasch here. In fact, Lasch quite clearly ties narcissism to both "the Oedipal problematic" and internalization. My discussion of Lasch's work on narcissism can be found in the next section of this chapter.

22. Pietro Bellasi, "Le Bébé et L'Eau du Bain," translated by Michel I. Makarius, *Présences d'Adorno* (Paris: Union Générale d'Editions, 1975) p. 62. My translation.

23. *Lifeworld and System*, p. 388.

24. Friedrich Pollock, "State Capitalism: Its Possibilities and Limitations," *Studies in Philosophy and Social Research* IX, no. 2 (1941) p. 207.

25. Helmut Dubiel, *Theory and Politics: Studies in the Development of Critical Theory*, translated by Benjamin Gregg, (Cambridge, Mass.: The MIT Press, 1985) p. 81.

26. Franz Neumann, *Behemoth: The Structure and Practice of National Socialism 1933–1944* (Toronto, New York, and London: Oxford University Press, 1944) p. 227.

27. Theodor W. Adorno, "Late Capitalism or Industrial Society," translated by Fred van Gelder, *Modern German Sociology*, eds. V. Meja, D. Misgeld, and N. Stehr, (New York: Columbia University Press, 1987) p. 237. Cited in the text as LC.

28. *Adorno*, p. 86.

29. Salvador Giner, *Mass Society* (London: Martin Robertson & Company Ltd., 1976) p. 143.

30. Ibid., p. 250.

31. Theodor W. Adorno, "Theory of Pseudo-Culture," translated by Deborah Cook, *Telos* 95 (Spring 1993) p. 28. Cited in the text as PC.

32. Jürgen Habermas provides some support for this claim. See *The Structural Transformation of the Public Sphere: An Inquiry into a Category of Bourgeois Society*, translated by Thomas Burger with the assistance of Frederick Lawrence, (Cambridge, Mass.: The MIT Press) p. 173: "[R]egular reading of weekend magazines, illustrated periodicals, and boulevard sheets, regular reception of radio and television, and regular visits to the movies are still more prevalent among relatively higher status groups and among city dwellers than in lower status groups and the rural population. Almost without exception, this kind of culture consumption increases directly with status, as measured by criteria of occupation, income and formal schooling, as well as with the degree of urbanization, ranging from village through small town to medium and large cities."

33. Theodor W. Adorno, "Freudian Theory and the Pattern of Fascist Propaganda," *The Essential Frankfurt School Reader*, eds. Andrew Arato and Eike Gebhardt, (New York: Urizen Books, 1978) p. 120. Cited in the text as FT.

34. Sigmund Freud, "Group Psychology and the Analysis of the Ego," translated by James Strachey, *The Penguin Freud Library* 12 (London: Penguin Books, 1991) p. 96.

35. Idem, "On Narcissism," translated by James Strachey, *The Standard Edition of the Complete Psychological Works of Sigmund Freud* 14 (London: The Hogarth Press, 1957) p. 88.

36. Christopher Lasch, *The Minimal Self: Psychic Survival in Troubled Times* (London and New York: W. W. Norton & Company, 1984) p. 184. Hereafter cited in the notes as *The Minimal Self*.

37. Idem, *The Culture of Narcissism: American Life in an Age of Diminishing Expectations* (New York: W. W. Norton & Company, 1979) p. 306. Hereafter cited in the notes as *The Culture of Narcissism*.

38. *The Culture of Narcissism*, p. 305.

39. *The Culture of Narcissism*, p. 299.

40. C. Fred Alford, *Narcissism: Socrates, the Frankfurt School, and Psychoanalytic Theory* (New Haven and London: Yale University Press, 1988) p. 94. Hereafter cited in the notes as *Narcissism*.

41. *The Minimal Self*, p. 179.
42. *Narcissism*, p. 199.
43. Jessica Benjamin, ''The End of Internalization: Adorno's Social Psychology,'' *Telos* 32 (1977) p. 54. Benjamin's critique will receive more extensive treatment in Chapter 3.
44. See Theodor W. Adorno, *Minima Moralia*, op. cit., p. 150: ''Socially, the absolute status granted to the individual marks the transition from the universal mediation of social relation—a mediation which, as exchange, always also requires curtailment of the particular interests realized through it—to direct domination, where power is seized by the strongest.'' See also ''Prolog zum Fernsehen,'' *Gesammelte Schriften* 10.2 (Frankfurt am Main: Suhrkamp Verlag, 1977) p. 508, which I am translating as follows: ''Freud taught that the repression of instinctive drives neither succeeded completely nor could it last and, for this reason, the individual's unconscious psychic energy is constantly squandered on further retaining in the unconscious what is not allowed to reach consciousness. Today, this Sisyphean labour of the individual economy of drives appears to be 'socialized,' taken in direct control by the institutions of the culture industry to the benefit of these institutions and of the powerful interests that lie behind them.''
45. *Haven in a Heartless World*, p. 177.
46. Jessica Benjamin, ''Authority and the Family Revisited: or, A World without Fathers?'' *New German Critique* 5 (Winter 1978) p. 53. Hereafter cited in the notes as ''Authority and the Family.''
47. ''Authority and the Family,'' p. 54.
48. As Martin Jay notes, in their work on *The Authoritarian Personality* researchers discovered that low-scorers on the F-scale valued the qualities of nurture and independence which they attributed to their mothers, whereas high-scorers typically rejected qualities and emotions connected with care and nurture. See Jay's *The Dialectical Imagination: A History of the Frankfurt School and the Institute for Social Research, 1923–1950* (Boston: Little, Brown and Company, 1973) p. 247. Complementing Jay's discussion (on pp. 247–48) of Horkheimer's ''Authoritarianism and the Family Today,'' Jessica Benjamin (see her ''Authority and the Family Revisited,'' pp. 46–49) finds in Horkheimer's ''Studies on Authority and the Family'' some noteworthy remarks about the role of the female parent in the early stages of childhood development. ''Authoritarianism and the Family Today'' was published in *The Family: Its Function and Destiny*, ed. Ruth Nanda Anshen, (New York: Harper, 1949) pp. 359–74; ''Studies on Authority and the Family'' was translated by John Cumming and published in *Critical Theory: Selected Essays* (New York: The Seabury Press, 1972) pp. 47–128.
49. ''Authority and the Family,'' p. 36.
50. Theodor W. Adorno, Else Frenkel-Brunswik, Daniel J. Levinson, R. Nevitt Sanford, *The Authoritarian Personality* (New York: Harper & Brothers, 1950) p. 386. Cited in the text as *AP*.

51. *The Minimal Self*, p. 175.

52. *The Culture of Narcissism*, pp. 267–68.

53. See *Dialectic of Enlightenment*, op. cit., p. 198, where Adorno and Horkheimer speak of identification with "stereotyped value scales."

54. Herbert Hyman and Paul Sheatsley, "*The Authoritarian Personality*—A Methodological Critique" in *Studies in the Scope and Method of "The Authoritarian Personality,"* eds. Richard Christie and Marie Jahoda, (Glencoe, Ill.: The Free Press, 1954) p. 99.

55. As historical background for this change in views, one should consult *The Frankfurt School: Its History, Theories and Political Significance*, translated by Michael Robertson, (Cambridge, Mass.: The MIT Press, 1994) p. 247. The author, Rolf Wiggershaus, writes: "The point of view from which the Institute's collective research had started was the conviction that authority was in a process of decay, at least in the long term. In the second half of the 1930s, there could be no more doubt about the ability of Nazism to survive, and the undermining of the family and the increasing reduction in unemployment seemed to match perfectly well the requirement that the individual's character should conform to authoritarian social conditions. Under these conditions, the Institute's original point of view could not be maintained. At the same time, the Roosevelt period in the USA showed that, even in non-fascist states, authoritarian (or subservient) thinking and behaviour was not decaying, even in the long term, but rather increasing."

56. *Haven in a Heartless World*, p. 88.

57. *Haven in a Heartless World*, p. 91.

58. See *Minima Moralia*, op. cit., p. 22: "Our relationship to our parents is beginning to undergo a sad, shadowy transformation. Through their economic impotence they have lost their awesomeness. Once we rebelled against their insistence on the reality principle. . . . But today we are faced with a generation purporting to be young yet in all its reactions insufferably more grown-up than its parents ever were; which, having renounced before any conflict, draws from this its grimly authoritarian, unshakeable power."

59. In *Escape from Freedom* (New York, Chicago, San Francisco: Holt, Rinehart and Winston, 1941), Erich Fromm described the personality type of individuals in non-totalitarian societies as conformist. Conformist and authoritarian personalities share the same socio-psychological origins. It is the "insignificance and powerlessness of the individual" which explain both the authoritarian personality and the compulsion to conform characteristic of the democratic "automaton." Fromm maintained that conformists lack autonomy and spontaneity in a world where "everybody and everything has [sic] become instrumentalized." Individuals believe they are "self-willing" (p. 253) but this belief is illusory because what they will is largely a product of forces they do not control. Since individuals have lost their identity, they conform to external standards and attempt to live up to the expectations of others (p. 254). Furthermore, the culture industry has destroyed their ability to think critically.

However, Fromm's account is impressionistic at best. For all its flaws, *The Authoritarian Personality* at least had the advantage of being based on actual case studies. Furthermore, by giving the same psychological roots to authoritarianism and conformism, Fromm could not explain why authoritarianism did not develop in North America as it did in Germany. In fact, in Fromm's account, both authoritarian and conformist personality structures are characterized by submission to authority. According to Fromm, conformists are "the prey of a new kind of authority": the "anonymous authority of common sense and public opinion" (p. 253). Fromm's distinction between authoritarian and conformist personalities is very blurred.

60. Martin Jay, *The Dialectical Imagination: A History of the Frankfurt School and the Institute of Social Research, 1923–50* (Boston and Toronto: Little, Brown and Company, 1973) p. 227. To support his interpretation, Jay quotes Adorno's "Social Science and Sociological Tendencies in Psychoanalysis," an unpublished paper which Leo Löwenthal made available to him. However, he also remarks that there was a German version of this paper which he does not name (see *Dialectical Imagination*, p. 319, n. 84). In fact, the German version is Adorno's "Die Revidierte Psychoanalyse," cited above.

61. *Hitler and Stalin*, p. 221. Bullock misquotes the title of Freud's essay in his notes; I have corrected it here.

62. The English translation reads "tend to falsify generalizations." Unfortunately, the editor of *Telos* took liberties which the translator did not. The German reads "zu falschen Generalisationen neigen" and was originally translated "tend towards false generalizations." I have substituted the original translation for the edited version here.

63. Theodor W. Adorno, et al., *The Positivist Dispute in German Sociology*, translated by Glyn Adey and David Frisby, (London: Heinemann, 1976) p. 47.

64. In his *The Culture of Narcissism*, op. cit., pp. 407–8, Christopher Lasch names some of the psychologists who have confirmed that narcissism is currently a pathology that is prevalent in the Western world. These psychologists include Peter L. Giovacchini, Allen Wheelis, Heinz Lichtenstein, Herbert Hendin, Michael Beldoch, Burness E. Moore, Joel Kovel, and Ilza Veith. Readers interested in this topic should also consult *Pathologies of the Modern Self: Postmodern Studies on Narcissism, Schizophrenia, and Depression*, ed. David Michael Levin, (New York and London: New York University Press, 1987).

65. Joel Whitebook, "Reason and Happiness: Some Psychoanalytic Themes in Critical Theory," *Habermas and Modernity*, ed. Richard Bernstein, (Cambridge, Mass.: The MIT Press, 1985) p. 150. Hereafter cited in the notes as "Reason and Happiness."

66. "Reason and Happiness," p. 151.

67. "Questions and Counterquestions," p. 212.

68. "Questions and Counterquestions," p. 213.

69. Adorno repeats this point in *The Jargon of Authenticity*, translated by Knut Tarnowski and Frederic Will, (Evanston, Ill.: Northwestern University

Press, 1973) p. 34. According to Adorno, "the fear of unemployment" lurks "in all citizens of countries of high capitalism. . . . This is a fear which is administratively fought off, and therefore nailed to the platonic firmament of stars, a fear that remains even in the glorious times of full employment. Everyone knows that he could become expendable as technology develops, as long as production is only carried on for production's sake: so everyone senses that his job is disguised unemployment. It is a support that has arbitrarily and revocably pinched off something from the total societal product, for the purpose of maintaining the status quo. He who has not been given a life ticket could in principle be sent away tomorrow."

70. "Reason and Happiness," p. 144.

71. See Martin Jay, *The Dialectical Imagination*, op. cit., p. 107.

72. Theodor W. Adorno, "Thesen über Bedürfnis," *Soziologische Schriften* I (Frankfurt am Main: Suhrkamp Verlag, 1972) p. 394. My translation. Adorno repeats these ideas virtually verbatim (but without the italics) in a paragraph of his essay on Aldous Huxley published in *Prisms*. Cited in Douglas Kellner's *Critical Theory, Marxism, and Modernity* (Baltimore: The Johns Hopkins University Press, 1989) p. 151: "If production is redirected towards the unconditional and unlimited satisfaction of needs, including precisely those produced by the hitherto prevailing system, needs themselves will be decisively altered. The indistinguishability of true and false needs is an essential part of the present phase. . . . One day it will be readily apparent that men do not need the trash provided them by the culture industry or the miserable high-quality goods proferred [*sic*] by the more substantial industries. The thought, for instance, that in addition to food and lodging the cinema is necessary for the reproduction of labour power is 'true' only in a world which prepares men for the reproduction of their labour power and constrains their needs in harmony with the interests of supply and social control."

Chapter Two

1. Michael Kausch, *Kulturindustrie und Populärkultur: Kritische Theorie der Massmedien* (Frankfurt am Main: Fischer Verlag, 1988) p. 84. (My translation.) Kausch is paraphrasing Adorno and Horkheimer in their "Culture Industry Reconsidered," *New German Critique* 6 (1975) p. 13: "Cultural entities typical of the culture industry are no longer *also* commodities, they are commodities through and through."

2. Theodor W. Adorno, "Reconciliation Under Duress," translated by Rodney Livingstone, *Aesthetics and Politics: Ernst Bloch, Georg Lukács, Bertolt Brecht, Walter Benjamin, Theodor Adorno*, ed. Ronald Taylor, (London: Verso, 1977) p. 160.

3. See, for example, Graham Murdock and Peter Golding in "Capitalism, Communication and Class Relations," *Mass Communication and Society*, eds.

James Curran, Michael Gurevitch, and Janet Woolacott, (London: Edward Arnold, 1977) pp. 12-43. On pages 18 and 19, the authors write: "Adorno's insistence that the process of cultural domination has its roots in the economic dynamics of the 'culture industry' is an indispensable starting point for any Marxist analysis. But it is only a starting point. It is not sufficient simply to assert that the capitalistic base of the 'culture industry' necessarily results in the production of cultural forms which are consonant with the dominant ideology. It is also necessary to demonstrate how this process of reproduction actually works by showing in detail how economic relations structure both the overall strategies of the cultural entrepreneurs and the concrete activities of the people who actually make the products the 'culture industry' sells—the writers, journalists, actors and musicians."

4. Karl Marx, *Capital*, Vol. 1, translated by Ben Fowkes, (New York: Vintage Books, 1976) p. 125. Hereafter cited in the notes as *Capital*.

5. *Capital*, p. 163.

6. Karl Marx, *Contribution to the Critique of Political Economy*, translated by S. W. Ryazanskaya, (New York: International Publishers, 1970) p. 27n.

7. Max Horkheimer and Theodor W. Adorno, *Dialectic of Enlightenment*, translated by John Cumming, (New York: The Seabury Press, 1972) p. 161. Cited in the text as *DE*.

8. Theodor W. Adorno, "On the Fetish-Character in Music and the Regression of Listening," translated by Maurice Goldbloom, *The Essential Frankfurt School Reader*, eds. Andrew Arato and Eike Gebhardt, (New York: Urizen Books, 1978) p. 279. Cited in the text as FC.

9. Idem, "Culture Industry Reconsidered," translated by Anson G. Rabinbach, *New German Critique* 6 (1975) p. 13. Cited in the text as CIR.

10. Idem, "Theory of Pseudo-Culture," translated by Deborah Cook, *Telos* 95 (Spring, 1993) p. 28. Cited in the text as PC.

11. *Capital*, p. 179.

12. Wolfgang Fritz Haug, *Critique of Commodity Aesthetics: Appearance, Sexuality and Advertising in Capitalist Society*, translated by Robert Bock, (Minneapolis: University of Minnesota Press, 1986) p. 25. Hereafter cited in the notes as *Critique of Commodity Aesthetics*.

13. *Critique of Commodity Aesthetics*, p. 100.

14. Jean Baudrillard, *Pour une Critique de l'Economie politique du Signe* (Paris: Gallimard, 1972) p. 47. (My translation.) For further work on this idea of the use-value of cultural commodities as social prestige, see Pierre Bourdieu, *Distinction: A Social Critique of the Judgement of Taste* (Cambridge, Mass.: Harvard University Press, 1984).

15. *Capital*, p. 126.

16. Terry Lovell, *Pictures of Reality: Aesthetics, Politics and Pleasure* (London: British Film Institute, 1980) p. 58. For a very interesting discussion and critique of Marx's theory of the commodity form, see William Leiss, *The Limits to Satisfaction: An Essay on the Problem of Needs and Commodities* (Kingston and Montreal: McGill-Queen's Press, 1988) pp. 74–82.

17. *Critique of Commodity Aesthetics*, p. 54.

18. Bill Ryan, *Making Capital from Culture: The Corporate Form of Capitalist Cultural Production* (New York: De Gruyter, 1992) p. 50. Hereafter cited in the notes as *Making Capital from Culture*.

19. *Making Capital from Culture*, pp. 39–40.

20. Martin Jay, *Adorno* (London: Fontana Paperbacks, 1984) p. 122.

21. See also "Theory of Pseudo-Culture," op. cit., p. 30. Commenting on the popularization of culture, Adorno wrote: "Only a linear and continuous view of intellectual progress recklessly glosses over the qualitative content of a culture which has been socialized into pseudo-culture."

22. Theodor W. Adorno, "A Social Critique of Radio Music," *Kenyon Review* VI, no. 2 (1945) p. 216.

23. Idem, "Thesen über Bedürfnis," *Soziologische Schriften* I (Frankfurt am Main: Suhrkamp Verlag, 1972) p. 395. All translations are my own. Cited in the text as TB.

24. See especially Theodor W. Adorno, "Theory of Pseudo-Culture," op. cit., pp. 32–33.

25. See John Fiske, *Understanding Popular Culture* (Boston: Unwin Hyman, 1989). For a critique of Fiske see my "*Ruses de Guerre*: Baudrillard and Fiske on Media Reception," *Journal for the Theory of Social Behaviour* 22, no. 2 (June 1992) pp. 227–38.

26. Graham Murdock and Peter Golding, "For a Political Economy of Mass Communications," *The Socialist Register 1973*, eds. Ralph Miliband and John Saville, (London: Merlin Press, 1974) p. 206.

27. Nicholas Garnham, "Contribution to a Political Economy of Mass-Communication," *Media, Culture and Society* I (1979) pp. 123–46. Hereafter cited in the notes as "Contribution to Political Economy."

28. Ben Bagdikian, *The Media Monopoly*, 4th ed., (Boston: Beacon Press, 1992).

29. "Contribution to Political Economy," p. 130.

30. "Contribution to Political Economy," p. 131.

31. Graham Murdock and Peter Golding, "Capitalism, Communication and Class Relations," *Mass Communication and Society*, eds. James Curran, Michael Gurevitch, and Janet Woolacott, (London: Edward Arnold, 1977) p. 19.

32. *Making Capital from Culture*, p. 106.

33. Nicholas Garnham, "Concepts of Culture: Public Policy and the Cultural Industries," *Cultural Studies* I, no. 1 (1987) p. 31.

34. Ibid., p. 31.

35. *Making Capital from Culture*, p. 58.

36. Theodor W. Adorno, with the assistance of George Simpson, "On Popular Music," *Studies in Philosophy and Social Research* IX (1941) p. 23. Cited in the text as PM.

37. *Making Capital from Culture*, p. 99.

38. *Making Capital from Culture*, p. 146.

39. In his "Culture Industry Reconsidered," op. cit., p. 14, Adorno wrote: "It [the culture industry] is industrial more in a sociological sense, in the incorporation of industrial forms of organization even where nothing is manufactured—as in the rationalization of office work—rather than in the sense of anything really and actually produced by technological rationality." In this passage, Adorno appears to contradict his earlier remarks in *Dialectic of Enlightenment* where he claimed that the technological "rationale" "has made the technology of the culture industry no more than the achievement of standardization and mass production, sacrificing whatever involved a distinction between the logic of the work and that of the social system" (*DE*, 121).

40. *Making Capital from Culture*, p. 146.

41. See Rolf Wiggershaus, *The Frankfurt School: Its History, Theories, and Political Significance*, translated by Michael Robertson, (Cambridge, Mass.: The MIT Press, 1994) p. 682 n. 177. As Wiggershaus observes, Adorno criticized Walter Benjamin's positive assessment of the culture industry's use of reproductive techniques. Benjamin's remarks can be found in his "The Work of Art in the Age of Mechanical Reproduction," translated by Harry Zohn in *Illuminations* (New York: Schocken Books, 1968). Adorno's criticisms appear in a letter to Benjamin dated March 18, 1936, translated by Harry Zohn, and published in *Aesthetics and Politics: Ernst Bloch, Georg Lukács, Bertolt Brecht, Walter Benjamin, Theodor Adorno,* ed. Ronald Taylor, (London: Verso, 1977) pp. 120–26. Adorno's scattered remarks about reproductive processes within the culture industry can also be found in some of his published essays including "On the Social Situation of Music," translated by Wes Blomster, *Telos* 35 (1978) pp. 146–51; *Minima Moralia: Reflections from Damaged Life*, translated by E. F. N. Jephcott, (London: Verso, 1974) p. 118; and "Music and Technique," translated by Wes Blomster, *Telos* 32 (1977) p. 83. In "Culture Industry Reconsidered," op. cit., p. 14, Adorno wrote: "The concept of technique in the culture industry is only in name identical with technique in works of art. In the latter, technique is concerned with the internal organization of the object itself, with its inner logic. In contrast, the technique of the culture industry is, from the beginning, one of distribution and mechanical reproduction, and therefore always remains external to its object." Unfortunately, Adorno simply posits here the predominate importance of "mechanical reproduction" for the economic viability of the culture industry; he does not examine its economic role in any detail.

42. Bernard Gendron, "Theodor Adorno Meets the Cadillacs," *Studies in Entertainment: Critical Approaches to Mass Culture*, ed. Tania Modleski, (Bloomington and Indianapolis: Indiana University Press, 1986) p. 28. Hereafter cited in the notes as "Adorno Meets the Cadillacs."

43. *Making Capital from Culture*, p. 145.

44. *Making Capital from Culture*, pp. 145–46.

45. Ernst Bloch elaborates on this idea in *The Principle of Hope*, Vol. I, translated by Neville Plaice, Stephen Plaice and Paul Knight, (Cambridge,

Mass.: The MIT Press, 1986) p. 442: "Where work no longer gives any plea-sure at all, art is forced to be good fun, merry swindle, tacked-on happy end. This keeps hold of the listeners; at the end of the Fascist national community or of the American way of life everyone will get something, and indeed without the least thing having to be changed in existing reality. The cinema-goers and the readers of magazine stories catch sight of rosy red upward paths, as if they were the norm in present society, and only chance has blocked them for the chance viewer. Indeed, the happy end becomes all the more unavoidable in capitalist terms, the smaller the chances of moving upwards have become in the society that exists today, the less hope the latter can offer."

46. "Adorno Meets the Cadillacs," p. 29.

47. *Making Capital from Culture*, p. 41.

48. *Making Capital from Culture*, p. 180.

49. Theodor W. Adorno, "Fernsehen als Ideologie," *Gesammelte Schriften* 10.2 (Frankfurt am Main: Suhrkamp Verlag, 1977) p. 531. All translations are my own. Cited in the text as FI.

50. Idem, "A Social Critique of Radio Music," *Kenyon Review* VII, no. 2 (1945) p. 216.

51. Idem, "Perennial Fashion—Jazz," translated by Samuel and Shierry Weber, *Critical Theory and Society: A Reader*, eds. Stephen Eric Bronner and Douglas MacKay Kellner, (New York and London: Routledge, 1989) p. 204.

52. "Adorno Meets the Cadillacs," p. 32.

53. "Adorno Meets the Cadillacs," p. 30.

54. *Making Capital from Culture*, p. 53.

55. Max Horkheimer and Theodor W. Adorno, "The Schema of Mass Cul-ture," translated by Nicholas Walker, *The Culture Industry: Selected Essays on Mass Culture*, ed. J. M. Bernstein, (London: Routledge, 1991) p. 55. Cited in the text as SMC.

56. J. M. Bernstein, editor of the collection of essays in which "The Schema of Mass Culture" appears, writes the following in his introduction: "The 'schema' of the title does not refer to Adorno's outline of the culture industry but rather to the culture industry's own schematizing (a Kantian term), pattern-ing or pre-forming of experience. Hence, the essay opens with what I shall suggest later is the controlling movement of postmodernism: the collapse of the difference between culture and practical life, which here is the same as the false aestheticization of the empirical world, an aestheticization of empirical life that does not transform it in accordance with the ideals of sensuous happiness and freedom, but rather secures the illusion that empirical life realizes those ends to the degree to which such is possible." See *The Culture Industry: Selected Es-says on Mass Culture*, op. cit., pp. 9–10. While I agree with Bernstein about the function of schemata—especially since, in the first few pages of "The Schema of Mass Culture," Adorno and Horkheimer do discuss explicitly the collapse of the distinction between culture and practical life brought about by the culture industry—the actual references made to schemata (I count five such

references in the essay) are oblique and do little to explain the specific links between the culture industry, business, advertising, and sports. Adorno and Horkheimer never clearly show how these particular schemata function nor do they provide concrete examples of such schemata except in the case of sports.

57. Idem, "How to Look at Television," *The Culture Industry: Selected Essays on Mass Culture*, ed. J. M. Bernstein, (London: Verso, 1991) p. 147. Cited in the text as HLT.

Adorno made the same point about the origin of the schemata in "'Beitrag zur Ideologienlehre," *Soziologische Schriften* I (Frankfurt am Main: Suhrkamp Verlag, 1972) p. 475: "The schemata of today's culture industry can be traced back historically to around 1700, to the early days of popular English literature in particular." See also, "Culture Industry Reconsidered," op. cit., pp. 13–14: "More than anything in the world, the culture industry has its ontology, a scaffolding of rigidly conservative basic categories which can be gleaned, for example, from the commercial English novels of the late 17th and early 18th centuries."

Readers should note that "How to Look at Television" was originally a study which Adorno wrote with Bernice T. Eiduson for the Hacker Foundation—see Martin Jay, *The Dialectical Imagination: A History of the Frankfurt School and the Institute of Social Research, 1923–1950* (Boston and Toronto: Little, Brown and Company, 1973) p. 196. It is unfortunate that the editor of *The Culture Industry* neither gave credit to Eiduson for her work on this piece nor credited Max Horkheimer for his work on "The Schema of Mass Culture."

58. Miriam Hansen, "Mass Culture as Hieroglyphic Writing: Adorno, Derrida, Kracauer," *New German Critique* 56 (Spring-Summer 1992) p. 50.

59. Ibid., p. 54.

60. For example, in his essay, "On the Social Situation of Music," *Telos* 35 (Spring 1978) p. 163, Adorno wrote: "[I]n its stereotyped figures, light music attempts to master the fact of its alienation by absorbing the reporting, observing and detached individual . . . into a fictive collective. This individual, in turn, finds his significance enforced through his participation in the objectivity of the refrain; indeed he experiences the content of the refrain text as his own content in the couplet. He then recognizes this content in the refrain with astonishment and elevation as a collective content. The psychological mechanism of hit song production, consequently, is narcissistic; the demand for arbitrary singability or hit tunes corresponds to this: in his ability to resing the melody with which he is manipulated, every listener identifies with the original vehicles of the melody, with leading personalities or with a collective of warriors which intones the song. He thus forgets his own isolation and accepts the illusion either that he is embraced by the collective or that he himself is a leading personality."

61. Martin Jay, *Adorno* (London: Fontana, 1984) p. 68.

62. Theodor W. Adorno, "Culture and Administration," translated by Wes Blomster, *Telos* 37 (Fall 1978) p. 97. Although Adorno occasionally referred to

the distinction between society and the individual as one between universal and particular, in "Society," translated by Fredric Jameson, *Salmagundi* III, no. 10–11 (1969–70) p. 145, Adorno states that society does not stand in relation to "its elements as a universal to particulars." Later, on page 148, he claims that "the abstraction implicit in the market system represents the domination of the general over the particular, of society over its captive membership."

63. *Making Capital from Culture*, p. 70.

64. *Making Capital from Culture*, p. 78.

65. See Ben H. Bagdikian, *The Media Monopoly*, 4th ed., op. cit., p. 149: "By 1928 there were thirty-nine universities teaching marketing, business promotion, and advertising. Advertising had become a big business of its own, growing from $200 million in 1880 to $3.5 billion just before the stock market crash of 1929. Advertising agencies once limited to placing ads in newspapers and magazines began to do 'creative' work—inventing slogans, brand names, and artistic designs and, eventually, conducting social science and psychological research on how to penetrate the emotions and subconscious of consumers. Especially with the emergence of television, with vivid images that came and went in seconds, appeals to the emotions—with sex, ambition, fear of rejection, and illness—became crucial. Advertising became a vital gear in the machinery of corporate power. It not only helped create and preserve dominance of the giants over consumer industries, it also helped create a picture of a satisfactory world with the corporations as benign stewards."

66. In his "Contribution to a Political Economy of Mass Communication," op. cit., p. 142, Nicholas Garnham makes reference to Dallas Smythe's early work in this area. See Dallas Smythe, "Communication: Blindspot of Western Marxism," in *Canadian Journal of Political and Social Theory* I, no. 3 (1977), as well as his "Rejoinder to Graham Murdock," *Canadian Journal of Political and Social Theory* II, no. 2.

67. "Contribution to Political Economy," p. 141. (Garnham describes the role played by the "creation, packaging and sale . . . of audiences to advertisers" on page 142.)

68. Andreas Huyssen, *After the Great Divide: Modernism, Mass Culture, Postmodernism* (Bloomington and Indianapolis: Indiana University Press, 1986) p. 24.

Chapter Three

1. Axel Honneth will serve here to represent this tendency in recent social theory. However, many other theorists also fit this description. They include John Fiske, Janice Radway, and Henry Jenkins. For a critical discussion of this tendency, see David Sholle, "Resistance: Pinning Down a Wandering Concept in Cultural Studies Discourse," *Journal of Urban and Cultural Studies* 1, no. 1 (1990) pp. 87–105.

2. Although I agree with Robert Hullot-Kentor that a discussion of Adorno's work in terms of the categories of optimism and pessimism is often not helpful and may lead to distortions (see Hullot-Kentor's "Back to Adorno," *Telos* 81 (Fall 1989) pp. 10–11), Adorno himself frequently used these categories. So, in one of the two large passages missing from *The Philosophical Forum*'s translation of "Fortschritt" (see *The Philosophical Forum* XV, no. 1–2 (Fall-Winter 1983–84) p. 66), Adorno wrote: "To stop what Schopenhauer called the self-unfolding wheel, what is certainly required is that human potential which is not absorbed completely by the necessity of historical movement. The idea of transcendent progress is blocked today because subjective moments of spontaneity in the historical process are beginning to wither away. To desperately oppose social omnipotence by referring, as the French existentialists do, to an isolated, allegedly ontological concept of subjective spontaneity is too optimistic, even as an expression of hope; the changing spontaneity cannot be conceived apart from social entanglement. It is illusory and idealistic to hope that such spontaneity would suffice here and now. It is only possible to approximate it in an historical moment where no basis for hope can be seen. Existential decisionism is only a reflex reaction to the unbroken totality of world spirit. Nonetheless, even the latter is also an illusion. Petrified institutions, relations of production, are not Being *per se*; rather, even as omnipotent, they are something made by people, revocable by people. In their relation to the subjects from whom they issue and whom they entrap, they remain thoroughly antagonistic. To avoid being destroyed, the totality not only demands its transformation but, owing to its antagonistic nature, it is also unable to enforce that complete identity with people which will be savoured in a negative utopia. For this reason, innerworldly progress, as an opponent of the other form [of progress], is also at the same time open to its possibility, however little it is capable of subsuming it under its own law." The original German essay appears in Adorno's *Stichworte: Kritische Modelle 2* (Frankfurt am Main: Suhrkamp Verlag, 1969) pp. 43–44.

3. Theodor W. Adorno, "Sociology and Psychology," translated by Irving N. Wohlfarth, *New Left Review* 46 (1967) p. 77. Cited in the text as SP1.

4. See for example, Adorno's discussion of classes in "Reflexionen zur Klassentheorie," *Soziologische Schriften* I (Frankfurt am Main: Suhrkamp Verlag, 1972) pp. 373–91. As I have already shown in Chapter 1, Adorno also analyzed the followers of National Socialism, using Freud's work on group psychology as his theoretical framework. In addition, Adorno wrote about the family and the historical changes in its functions throughout his work.

5. Theodor W. Adorno, "Sociology and Psychology," translated by Irving N. Wohlfarth, *New Left Review* 47 (1968) p. 85. (This is the last half of the translation of "Zum Verhältnis von Soziologie und Psychologie." The first half was published in the preceding issue of *New Left Review*—number 46—and is listed above.) Cited in the text as SP2.

6. Idem, "Die Revidierte Psychoanalyse," *Soziologische Schriften* I

(Frankfurt am Main: Suhrkamp Verlag, 1972) p. 33. All translations are my own. Cited in the text as RP.

7. Idem, *Minima Moralia: Reflections from Damaged Life*, translated by E. F. N. Jephcott, (London: Verso, 1974) p. 58.

8. Axel Honneth, *The Critique of Power: Reflective Stages in a Critical Social Theory*, translated by Kenneth Barnes, (Cambridge, Mass., and London: The MIT Press, 1991) p. 78. Hereafter cited in the notes as *Critique of Power*.

9. *Critique of Power*, p. 79.

10. *Critique of Power*, p. 72.

11. *Critique of Power*, p. 77.

12. *Critique of Power*, p. 83.

13. *Critique of Power*, p. 85.

14. *Critique of Power*, p. 84.

15. *Critique of Power*, p. 74.

16. On page 125 of "Freudian Theory and the Pattern of Fascist Propaganda," reproduced in Andrew Arato's and Eike Gebhardt's *The Essential Frankfurt School Reader* (New York: Urizen Books, 1978), Adorno writes that there is a "very subtle theoretical differentiation . . . between identification and introjection" which, unfortunately, he does not discuss. However, Freud himself used the terms synonymously. "Freudian Theory and the Pattern of Fascist Propaganda" will be cited in the text as FT.

17. Sigmund Freud, *New Introductory Lectures on Psychoanalysis*, translated by W. J. H. Sprott, (New York: W. W. Norton & Company, Inc., 1933) p. 94.

18. Max Horkheimer and Theodor W. Adorno, *Dialectic of Enlightenment*, translated by John Cumming, (New York: The Seabury Press, 1972) p. 198. Cited in the text as *DE*.

19. Jessica Benjamin, "The End of Internalization," *Telos* 32 (1977) p. 54.

20. Ibid., p. 55.

21. Among those Adorno considered revisionist psychoanalysts are Karen Horney, Alfred Adler, and the later Erich Fromm. See "Die Revidierte Psychoanalyse," op. cit., pp. 20–41.

22. Theodor W. Adorno, "How to Look at Television," *The Culture Industry: Selected Essays on Mass Culture*, ed. J. M. Bernstein, (London: Routledge, 1991) p. 138. Cited in the text as HLT.

23. Christopher Lasch, *Haven in a Heartless World: The Family Besieged* (New York: Basic Books, 1977) p. 177.

24. Miriam Hansen, "Mass Culture as Hieroglyphic Writing: Adorno, Derrida, Kracauer," *New German Critique* 56 (Spring-Summer 1992) pp. 51–52. Hereafter cited in the notes as "Mass Culture as Hieroglyphic Writing."

25. T. W. Adorno, "Prolog zum Fernsehen," *Gesammelte Schriften* 10.2 (Frankfurt am Main: Suhrkamp Verlag, 1977) p. 514. All translations are my own. Cited in the text as PF.

26. Idem, "Zum Verhältnis von Soziologie und Psychologie," *Soziologische Schriften* I (Frankfurt am Main: Suhrkamp Verlag, 1972) p. 74.

27. Sigmund Freud, *The Standard Edition of the Complete Psychological Works of Sigmund Freud* XX, translated by James Strachey, (London: The Hogarth Press, 1959) p. 164.

28. Anna Freud, *The Ego and the Mechanisms of Defense*, revised edition, translated by Cecil Baines, (New York: International Universities Press, 1966) p. 53.

29. Theodor W. Adorno, with the assistance of George Simpson, "On Popular Music," *Studies in Philosophy and Social Research* IX (1941) p. 41. Cited in the text as PM.

Although Adorno emphasized the deceptive character of the culture industry's fulfilment of wishes, Ernst Bloch provides an interesting counterpoint to Adorno when he focuses on the more positive dimension of wishing. Speaking of the "happy ending" in *The Principle of Hope*, Vol. I, translated by Neville Plaice, Stephen Plaice, and Paul Knight, (Cambridge, Mass.: The MIT Press, 1986) p. 443, Bloch writes: "An unmistakable drive is working in the direction of the good end, it is not only confined to gullibility. The fact that deceivers make use of this drive disproves it au fond almost as little as the 'socialist' Hitler disproved socialism. The deceivability of the happy end drive merely says something against the state of its reason; this, however, is as teachable as it is improvable. The deception represents the good end as if it were attainable in an unchanged Today of society or even the Today itself. But just because knowledge destroys rotten optimism, it does not also destroy urgent hope for a good end. For this hope is too indestructibly grounded in the human drive for happiness, and it has always been too clearly a motor of history. It has been so as expectation and incitement of a positively visible goal, for which it is important to fight and which sends a Forwards into barrenly continuing time. More than once, the fiction of a happy end, when it seized the will, when the will had learnt both through mistakes and in fact through hope as well, and when reality did not stand in too harsh contradiction to it, reformed a bit of the world; that is, an initial fiction was made real."

30. Max Horkheimer and Theodor W. Adorno, "The Schema of Mass Culture," *The Culture Industry: Selected Essays on Mass Culture*, ed. J. M. Bernstein, (London: Routledge, 1991) p. 80.

31. "Mass Culture as Hieroglyphic Writing," p. 51.

32. Theodor W. Adorno, "Fernsehen als Ideologie," *Gesammelte Schriften* 10.2 (Frankfurt am Main: Suhrkamp Verlag, 1977) p. 523. All translations are my own. Cited in the text as FI.

33. Idem, "Thesen über Bedürfnis," *Gesammelte Schriften* 8 (Frankfurt am Main: Suhrkamp Verlag, 1972) p. 395. All translations are my own. Cited in the text as TB.

34. Idem, "Late Capitalism or Industrial Society?" translated by Fred van Gelder, *Modern German Sociology* (New York: Columbia University Press, 1987) p. 242. Cited in the text as LC.

35. In his essay on Aldous Huxley in *Prisms*, where he repeats nearly verba-

tim his remarks about need in "Thesen über Bedürfnis," Adorno wrote the following: "The indistinguishability of true and false needs is an essential part of the present phase. . . . One day it will be readily apparent that men do not need the trash provided them by the culture industry or the miserable high-quality goods proffered by the more substantial industries." Compare "Thesen über Bedürfnis," op. cit., p. 394 to "Aldous Huxley and Utopia," *Prisms*, translated by Samuel and Shierry Weber (Cambridge, Mass.: The MIT Press, 1967) pp. 109–10.

36. *Critique of Power*, p. 86.

37. However, in *Dialectic of Enlightenment*, Adorno and Horkheimer had already partially undermined such an analysis by claiming that the culture industry represses sexual desire even while soliciting it. See *Dialectic of Enlightenment*, op. cit., p. 140: "The culture industry does not sublimate; it represses. By repeatedly exposing the objects of desire, breasts in a clinging sweater or the naked torso of the athletic hero, it only stimulates the unsublimated fore-pleasure which habitual deprivation has long since reduced to a masochistic semblance. There is no erotic situation which, while insinuating and exciting, does not fail to indicate unmistakably that things can never go that far. The Hays Office merely confirms the ritual of Tantalus that the culture industry has established anyway."

38. Theodor W. Adorno, "Theory of Pseudo-Culture," translated by Deborah Cook, *Telos* 95 (Spring 1993) pp. 32–33. Cited in the text as PC.

39. Herbert I. Schiller, *Culture, Inc.: The Corporate Takeover of Public Expression* (Oxford: Oxford University Press, 1989) pp. 152–53 *passim*.

40. *Critique of Power*, p. 86.

41. Martin Jay, *Adorno* (London: Fontana, 1984) p. 87.

42. Herbert Marcuse, *An Essay on Liberation* (Harmondsworth, Middlesex: Penguin Books, 1969) p. 14.

43. Commenting on Adorno's response to the student protests of the sixties, Rolf Wiggershaus observes that "Late Capitalism or Industrial Society" displays a kind of "reverence for the student movement." However, Wiggershaus is quick to add that in this essay Adorno never developed the far more promising ideas contained in "Anmerkungen zum sozialen Konflikt heute" (*Gesammelte Schriften* 8 (Frankfurt am Main: Suhrkamp Verlag, 1972) pp. 177–195). In the latter study, Adorno advanced "the hypothesis that class conflict had become latent, and was being displaced towards the margins of society—an idea that might have produced promising new directions for the New Left's theoretical analyses." By contrast, in "Late Capitalism," instead of elaborating on this idea, Adorno's positive comments about resistance in the sixties appear to interrupt the general train of his thought. According to Wiggershaus, Adorno "was thus showing his basic sympathy for the protest movement, and at the same time indicating that he did not regard this sympathy as having any implications for his thinking." See Rolf Wiggershaus, *The Frankfurt School: Its History, Theories, and Political Significance*, translated by Michael Robertson, (Cambridge, Mass.: The MIT Press, 1994) pp. 627–28 *passim*.

44. See Adorno's remark in *Negative Dialectics*, translated by E. B. Ashton, (New York: Continuum, 1973) p. 312: "A candid look at the predominance of the universal does all but unbearable psychological harm to the narcissism of all individuals and to that of a democratically organized society. To see through selfhood as nonexistent, as an illusion, would easily turn all men's objective despair into a subjective one. It would rob them of the faith implanted in them by individualistic society: that they, the individuals, are the substance."

45. *Critique of Power*, p. 80.

46. Theodor W. Adorno, "Transparencies on Film," translated by Thomas Y. Levin, *New German Critique* 24–25 (1981–82) p. 203. This recognition of the disparity between the ideology purveyed by cultural commodities and its reception is currently being exploited by some contemporary theorists of culture. According to John Fiske, for example, consumers undermine capitalist ideology by excorporating the cultural commodities in which it is reproduced and making their own "subcultures" out of these commodities. See John Fiske, *Understanding Popular Culture* (Boston: Unwin Hyman, 1989) p. 15. For a critique of Fiske see my "Symbolic Exchange in Hyperreality," *Baudrillard: A Critical Reader*, ed. Douglas Kellner, (Oxford: Basil Blackwell, 1994) pp. 155–58.

47. Idem, "Culture Industry Reconsidered," translated by Anson G. Rabinbach, *New German Critique* 6 (1975) p. 15.

48. In her "Mass Culture as Hieroglyphic Writing," op. cit., p. 54, Miriam Hansen points out that the translation of this sentence in *Dialectic of Enlightenment* is flawed. In German, the sentence reads: "Das ist der Triumph der Reklame in der Kulturindustrie, die zwangshafte Mimesis der Konsumenten an die zugleich durchschauten Kulturwaren"; see *Dialektik der Aufklärung* (Frankfurt am Main: S. Fischer Verlag, 1969) p. 176. Hansen translates this sentence as follows: "The 'triumph of advertising in the culture industry' . . . is made possible by . . . 'the compulsive mimesis of the consumers onto the cultural commodities, even as they see through them.' " For my purposes, however, this correction, albeit necessary, is not crucial.

49. Theodor W. Adorno, "Kann das Publikum Wollen?" *Gesammelte Schriften* 20.1 (Frankfurt am Main: Suhrkamp Verlag, 1986) p. 347. My translation.

50. Andreas Huyssen, "Introduction to Adorno," *New German Critique* 6 (1975) p. 9. Hereafter cited in the notes as "Introduction to Adorno."

51. Miriam Hansen, "Introduction to Adorno, 'Transparencies on Film' (1966)," *New German Critique* 24–25 (1981–82) p. 186.

52. Theodor W. Adorno, "Free Time," translated by Gordon Finlayson and Nicholas Walker, *The Culture Industry: Selected Essays on Mass Culture*, ed. J. M. Bernstein, (London: Routledge, 1991) p. 169. Cited in the text as Time.

53. Jean Baudrillard, *Simulacres et Simulation* (Paris: Galilée, 1981) p. 124. My translation.

54. See Theodor W. Adorno, *Minima Moralia*, op. cit., pp. 43–45.

55. Jürgen Habermas inadvertently lends some support to Adorno's observa-

tions about enlightenment ideology's hold on consciousness when he discusses "moral systems" (like those following in the wake of liberalism) in *Legitimation Crisis*, translated by Thomas McCarthy, (Boston: Beacon Press, 1975) p. 12: "A collectively attained stage of moral consciousness can, as long as the continuity of the tradition endures, just as little be forgotten as can collectively gained knowledge (which does not exclude regression)."

56. *Critique of Power*, p. 80.
57. *Critique of Power*, p. 80.
58. "Introduction to Adorno," p. 9.
59. "Introduction to Adorno," p. 11.

Chapter Four

1. Theodor W. Adorno, "Subject and Object," translated by E. B. Ashton, *The Essential Frankfurt School Reader*, eds. Andrew Arato and Eike Gebhardt, (New York: Urizen Books, 1978) p. 502.

2. Idem, *Negative Dialectics*, translated by E. B. Ashton, (New York: Continuum, 1973) p. 183. Cited in the text as *ND*.

3. For an interesting interpretation of the preponderance of the object, see Rolf Wiggershaus, *The Frankfurt School: Its History, Theories, and Political Significance*, translated by Michael Robertson, (Cambridge, Mass.: The MIT Press, 1994). On pages 602–3, Wiggershaus writes: "At the back of this there lay a simple insight: the world might also be able to exist without human beings, but human beings cannot exist without the world. Negative dialectics meant: be mindful of the Other. It did not round off into a system, did not represent a progress from one category to another, as in Hegel. Instead, it admonished one again and again, in every case, to 'release the non-identical' from which 'identitarian' thought, the self-satisfied spirit, could never tear itself away and which it could only distort, with unforeseeable consequences. Hypostatizations would never succeed in the long term, and the only reasonable solution must therefore be to recognize and accept the object, the Other, the alien: this was the conclusion of *Negative Dialectics*. . . . However, until this should come to pass, a predominance of the object, in the negative sense, was to be expected. As ever with Adorno, the central concepts were bipolar. Predominance of the object in the positive sense meant openness on the part of a differentiated subject towards an object perceived in qualitative differentiation. Predominance of the object in the negative sense meant domination over powerless individuals by social forces that had become autonomous—society's condition when it lacked an overall subject."

4. Theodor W. Adorno, et al., *The Positivist Dispute in German Sociology*, translated by Glyn Adey and David Frisby, (London: Heinemann, 1976) p. 299. Cited in the text as *PD*.

5. David Held, *Introduction to Critical Theory: Horkheimer to Habermas* (Berkeley and Los Angeles: University of California Press, 1980) p. 148.

6. Jürgen Habermas, *The Philosophical Discourse of Modernity: Twelve Lectures*, translated by Frederick Lawrence, (Cambridge, Mass.: The MIT Press, 1987) p. 118. Hereafter cited in the notes as *Philosophical Discourse of Modernity*.

7. In "The Actuality of Philosophy," translated by Bruce Mayo, *Telos* 31 (1977) pp. 129–30, Adorno even warns of a possible liquidation of philosophy. On page 130, he writes that "one of the first and most actual tasks" of philosophy "would appear to be the radical criticism of the ruling philosophic thinking."

8. Michael Sullivan and John T. Lysaker, "Between Impotence and Illusion: Adorno's Art of Theory and Practice," *New German Critique* 57 (Fall 1992) p. 107. Hereafter cited in the notes as "Between Impotence and Illusion."

9. In *Critical Theory* (Oxford: Basil Blackwell, 1994), a book he co-authored with Thomas McCarthy, David Hoy also recognizes that negative dialectics is a form of ideology critique while defending Adorno against the criticism that *Negative Dialectics* is a metatheoretical project which ultimately lacks a foundation. Hoy recommends that *Negative Dialectics* be read as "an account of how critical history is possible, and how immanent criticism can be effective without having to aspire to the status of theory in an ahistorical sense" (p. 124). Although I read *Negative Dialectics* as a work of epistemology, I also claim that in it Adorno attempted both to ground immanent ideology critique and to illustrate it by putting it into practice in his critique of Heidegger, Hegel, and Kant in particular.

10. Theodor W. Adorno, *Minima Moralia: Reflections from Damaged Life*, translated by E. F. N. Jephcott, (London: Verso, 1974) p. 43. Cited in the text as *MM*.

11. Idem, "Cultural Criticism and Society," *Prisms*, translated by Samuel and Shierry Weber, (Cambridge, Mass.: The MIT Press, 1967) p. 29. Cited in the text as CCS.

12. Gillian Rose, *The Melancholy Science: An Introduction to the Thought of Theodor W. Adorno* (New York: Columbia University Press, 1978) p. 44. Hereafter cited in the notes as *The Melancholy Science*.

13. See Theodor W. Adorno, "Beitrag zur Ideologienlehre," *Soziologische Schriften* I (Frankfurt am Main: Suhrkamp Verlag, 1972) pp. 472–73: "to be sure, ideologies are false consciousness but they are certainly not only false. The veil which necessarily lies between society and its insight into its own nature also expresses this nature at the same time by virtue of such necessity. Real ideologies first become false owing to their relationship to existing reality. They can be true 'in themselves,' as are the ideas of freedom, humanity and justice, but they behave as if they were already realized." All translations of "Beitrag zur Ideologienlehre" are my own. This essay will be cited in the text as BI.

14. Albrecht Wellmer, *The Persistence of Modernity: Essays on Aesthetics,*

Ethics and Postmodernism, translated by David Midgley, (Cambridge, Mass.: The MIT Press, 1991) pp. 71–2 *passim*. Hereafter cited in the notes as *Persistence of Modernity*.

15. In *Dialectic of Enlightenment*, Adorno and Horkheimer comment on the ruse of reason involved in Odysseus' encounter with Polyphemus in the *Odyssey*. Odysseus employs cunning to trick the Cyclops, calling himself "*Udeis*," a word which also means nobody. The authors claim that this *double entendre* can be interpreted as a "formalistic" recognition that words may have a number of meanings. Such a discovery opens a breach between words or concepts and the objects to which they refer, creating an antagonism between subject and object which will only increase as history progresses. See *Dialectic of Enlightenment*, translated by John Cumming, (New York: The Seabury Press, 1972) p. 60.

16. *Persistence of Modernity*, p. 71.

17. Frankfurt Institute for Social Research, *Aspects of Sociology*, translated by John Viertel, (Boston: Beacon Press, 1972) p. 202. Cited in the text as *AS*. This sentence repeats verbatim the remarks Adorno made in 1954 in "Beitrag zur Ideologienlehre," *Soziologische Schriften* I (Frankfurt am Main: Suhrkamp Verlag, 1972) p. 476. Adorno made a similar remark, already quoted in the previous chapter, in "Prolog zum Fernsehen," *Gesammelte Schriften* 10.2 (Frankfurt am Main: Suhrkamp Verlag, 1977) p. 514.

18. Theodor W. Adorno, "Reflexionen zur Klassentheorie," *Soziologische Schriften* I, (Frankfurt am Main: Suhrkamp Verlag, 1972) pp. 390–91. My translation.

19. Martin Jay, *Adorno* (London: Fontana, 1984) p. 43. Hereafter cited in the notes as *Adorno*.

20. Max Horkheimer and Theodor W. Adorno, *Dialectic of Enlightenment*, translated by John Cumming, (New York: The Seabury Press, 1972) p. 121. Cited in the text as *DE*.

21. Theodor W. Adorno, "Fernsehen als Ideologie," *Gesammelte Schriften* 10.2 (Frankfurt am Main: Suhrkamp Verlag, 1977) p. 530. All translations are my own. Cited in the text as *FI*.

22. This passage adopts, nearly verbatim, many of the ideas expressed in "Cultural Criticism and Society," op. cit., pp. 29–31, concerning the relationship between base and superstructure.

23. In his *Media Monopoly*, 4th ed., (Boston: Beacon Press, 1992) pp. 152–73, Ben Bagdikian shows that the culture industry has been forced to include in its programming the corporate agenda of its sponsors. For his part, Reinhold Wagnleitner documents some of the postwar links between Hollywood's motion picture industry and the US military in his essay "American Cultural Diplomacy, Hollywood, and the Cold War in Central Europe," *Rethinking Marxism* 7, no. 1 (1994) pp. 31–47.

24. Theodor W. Adorno, "Society," translated by Fredric Jameson, *Salmagundi* III, no. 10–11 (1969–70) p. 152; translation altered.

25. Idem, "Prolog zum Fernsehen," *Gesammelte Schriften* 10.2 (Frankfurt am Main: Suhrkamp Verlag, 1977) p. 510. My translation.
26. *Adorno*, p. 43.
27. Jean Baudrillard, "The Masses," translated by Marie Maclean, *Jean Baudrillard: Selected Writings*, ed. Mark Poster, (Stanford: Stanford University Press, 1988) p. 219.
28. Ernesto Laclau and Chantal Mouffe, *Hegemony and Socialist Strategy: Towards a Radical Democratic Politics* (London: Verso, 1985) p. 164.
29. Theodor W. Adorno, "How to Look at Television," *The Culture Industry: Selected Essays on Mass Culture*, ed. J. M. Bernstein, (London: Routledge, 1991) p. 140.
30. Idem, "Theory of Pseudo-Culture," translated by Deborah Cook, *Telos* 95 (Spring 1993) p. 32. Cited in the text as PC.
31. One television commercial broadcast recently says that if we do not like the rules we should change them. Implied in this message is the idea that we have the freedom to do so. By contrast, in its advertisement for Lotto 649, the government of Ontario asks us to "imagine the freedom" a winning lottery ticket would offer. Here freedom is equated with buying power.
32. Theodor W. Adorno, with the assistance of George Simpson, "On Popular Music," *Studies in Philosophy and Social Research* IX (1941) p. 47. Cited in the text as PM.
33. Andreas Huyssen, "Introduction to Adorno," *New German Critique* 6 (1975) p. 5.
34. David Couzens Hoy and Thomas McCarthy, *Critical Theory* (Oxford: Basil Blackwell, 1994) p. 124. Hereafter cited in the notes as *Critical Theory*.
35. *Critical Theory*, p. 115.
36. In *The Melancholy Science*, op. cit., p. 138, Gillian Rose claims that, along with other German writers in the period between the two world wars, Adorno was attracted to "an anti-humanist stance." He rejected "the humanist legacy of historicism, philosophical anthropology, 'realism' in art, and epistemology, for these were seen as bankrupt, incapable of providing any analysis of a much-changed historical reality."
37. *Critical Theory*, p. 115.
38. *Critical Theory*, p. 115.
39. *Critical Theory*, pp. 116–17.
40. Jürgen Habermas, "The Entwinement of Myth and Enlightenment: Rereading *Dialectic of Enlightenment*," translated by Thomas Y. Levin, *New German Critique* 26 (1982) pp. 13-30.
41. *Philosophical Discourse of Modernity*, p. 120.
42. Seyla Benhabib, *Critique, Norm and Utopia: A Study of the Foundations of Critical Theory* (New York: Columbia University Press, 1986). Hereafter cited in the notes as *Critique, Norm and Utopia*.
43. Jürgen Habermas, "Modernity versus Postmodernity," translated by Seyla Benhabib, *New German Critique* 22 (Winter 1981).

44. *Philosophical Discourse of Modernity*, p. 116.
45. *Philosophical Discourse of Modernity*, p. 117.
46. *Philosophical Discourse of Modernity*, p. 118.
47. *Philosophical Discourse of Modernity*, p. 119.
48. *Philosophical Discourse of Modernity*, p. 113.
49. *Philosophical Discourse of Modernity*, pp. 126–27.
50. *Critique, Norm and Utopia*, p. 179.
51. *Critique, Norm and Utopia*, p. 182.
52. *Critique, Norm and Utopia*, p. 222.
53. *Philosophical Discourse of Modernity*, p. 123.
54. But, as Peter Dews points out in *Logics of Disintegration: Post-Structuralist Thought and the Claims of Critical Theory* (London: Verso, 1987) p. 230: ''Adorno refuses to take the self-understanding of the philosophy of consciousness at face value: in accordance with the logic of disintegration, the claim to absolute identity, to the extent that it is realized, can only take the form of unprecedented fragmentation, and this contradiction points towards the possibility of another form of subjectivity, however difficult to conceptualize. By contrast, post-structuralist thought takes the repressive self-enclosure of consciousness to be definitive of subjectivity as such, with the consequence that 'emancipation' can only take the form of a breaking open of the coercive unity of the subject in order to release the diffuseness and heterogeneity of the repressed.''
55. Jürgen Habermas, *The Structural Transformation of the Public Sphere: An Inquiry into a Category of Bourgeois Society*, translated by Thomas Burger with the assistance of Frederick Lawrence, (Cambridge, Mass.: The MIT Press, 1989) p. 82.
56. Idem, ''Further Reflections on the Public Sphere,'' translated by Thomas Burger, *Habermas and the Public Sphere*, ed. Craig Calhoun, (Cambridge, Mass.: The MIT Press, 1992) p. 442.
57. Ibid., p. 442.
58. *The Melancholy Science*, p. 44.
59. G. W. F. Hegel, *The Philosophy of History*, translated by J. Sibree, (New York: Dover, 1956) p. 444. Cited in Jean Hyppolite, *Genèse et Structure de la "Phénoménologie de l'Esprit" de Hegel* (Paris: Editions Montaigne, 1946) p. 414.

Ernst Bloch discusses Hegel's view of ideals in *The Principle of Hope*, Vol. 1, translated by Neville Plaice, Stephen Plaice, and Paul Knight, (Cambridge, Mass.: The MIT Press, 1986) p. 169: ''For Hegel, ideals in general can only occur in art and not in the rest of reality, least of all in political and social reality; here they are for Hegel, in so far as he is a Restoration philosopher, solely chimeras of an imaginary perfection.'' Although Bloch criticized the abstract and static character of ideals, he claimed that, along with aesthetic ideals, there were ethical ideals which, if ''corrected,'' could serve as models for a less abstract and more dynamic model of perfection: ''For example, the supreme variation of the highest good in the socio-political sphere is the class-less society; consequently, ideals like freedom and also equality act as a means to this end, and derive their value-content . . . from the highest good in socio-political terms'' (*The Principle of Hope*, Vol. 1, op. cit., p. 173). Like Adorno, Bloch also recognized that ideology was more than simply chimerical, false consciousness. Stephen Bronner writes that, for Bloch: "The ideology of a given period is . . . never entirely 'false,' . . . since a set of 'not-yet-realized' utopian possibilities remains 'latent' and waiting for self-conscious appropriation." See Bronner's *Of Critical Theory and its Theorists* (Oxford: Basil Blackwell, 1994) p. 68.

60. Samuel Bowles and Herbert Gintis, *Democracy and Capitalism: Property, Community, and the Contradictions of Modern Social Thought* (New York: Basic Books: 1986) p. 62.

61. *Critique, Norm and Utopia*, p. 212.

62. According to the editor of the *Pléiade* edition of Marx's work, Marx himself used this term in *The Jewish Question* to refer to the moral necessity of "overcoming all conditions in which human beings are humiliated, subjugated, abandoned and scorned." See the interview with Maximilien Rubel, "Un Penseur du XXe Siècle et non du XIXe," *Le Monde des Livres* (Friday, September 29, 1995) p. viii.

63. Lambert Zuidervaart, *Adorno's Aesthetic Theory: The Redemption of Illusion* (Cambridge, Mass.: The MIT Press, 1991) p. 304.

64. *Critique, Norm and Utopia*, pp. 180–81.

65. See Theodor W. Adorno, "Freudian Theory and the Pattern of Fascist Propaganda," *The Essential Frankfurt School Reader*, eds. Andrew Arato and Eike Gebhardt (New York: Continuum, 1992) pp. 136–37: "Just as little as people believe in the depth of their hearts that the Jews are the devil, do they completely believe in the leader. They do not really identify themselves with him but act this identification, perform their own enthusiasm, and thus participate in their leader's performance. It is through this performance that they strike a balance between their continuously mobilized instinctual urges and the historical stage of enlightenment they have reached, and which cannot be revoked arbitrarily."

66. "Between Impotence and Illusion," p. 108.

Chapter Five

1. Theodor W. Adorno, "Letters to Walter Benjamin," translated by Harry Zohn, *Aesthetics and Politics: Ernst Bloch, Georg Lukács, Bertolt Brecht, Walter Benjamin, Theodor Adorno*, ed. Ronald Taylor, (London: Verso, 1977) p. 123.

2. Idem, "On the Social Situation of Music," translated by Wes Blomster, *Telos* 35 (Spring 1978) pp. 131–32: "From a social perspective, present-day

musical activity, production and consumption can be divided drastically into that which unconditionally recognizes its commodity character ... and orients itself according to the demands of the market and that which in principle does not accept the demands of the market. . . . The traditional distinction between 'light' and 'serious' music . . . ostensibly corresponds to this division—but only ostensibly. For a great share of supposedly 'serious' music adjusts itself to the demands of the market. . . . On the other hand, it is precisely 'light' music . . . which develops certain elements portraying the satisfaction of the drive of present society, whose official claims, however, stand in conflict to such satisfaction. In a certain sense, such music thus transcends the society which it supposedly serves. . . . For this reason, the distinction between light and serious music is to be replaced by a different distinction which views both halves of the musical globe equally from the perspective of alienation: namely, as halves of a totality which to be sure could never be reconstructed through the addition of the two halves." "On the Social Situation of Music" will be cited in the text as SSM.

3. Idem, "On the Fetish Character in Music and the Regression of Listening," translated by Maurice Goldbloom, *The Essential Frankfurt School Reader*, eds. Andrew Arato and Eike Gebhardt, (New York: Urizen Books, 1978) p. 275. Cited in the text as FC.

4. Fredric Jameson, *Late Marxism: Adorno, or, The Persistence of the Dialectic* (London: Verso, 1990) p. 133.

5. Theodor W. Adorno, "Culture Industry Reconsidered," translated by Anson G. Rabinbach, *New German Critique* 6 (1975) p. 12. Cited in the text as CIR.

6. Andreas Huyssen, "Adorno in Reverse: From Hollywood to Richard Wagner," *After the Great Divide: Modernism, Mass Culture, Postmodernism* (Bloomington, Ill., and Indianapolis: Indiana University Press, 1986) pp. 24–25 *passim*. Hereafter cited in the notes as "Adorno in Reverse."

7. Fredric Jameson, "Reification and Utopia in Mass Culture," *Social Text* 1 (1979) pp. 133–34. Hereafter cited in the notes as "Reification and Utopia."

8. Theodor W. Adorno, "Culture and Administration," translated by Wes Blomster, *Telos* 37 (Fall 1978) pp. 94–96 *passim*. Cited in the text as CA.

9. Idem, "Theory of Pseudo-Culture," translated by Deborah Cook, *Telos* 95 (Spring 1993) p. 16.

10. Idem, "A Social Critique of Radio Music," *Kenyon Review* VI, no. 2 (1945) p. 211. Cited in the text as SCR.

11. Max Horkheimer and Theodor W. Adorno, *Dialectic of Enlightenment*, translated by John Cumming, (New York: The Seabury Press, 1972) p. 157. Cited in the text as *DE*.

12. "Reification and Utopia," p. 134.

13. Lambert Zuidervaart, *Adorno's Aesthetic Theory: The Redemption of Illusion* (Cambridge, Mass.: The MIT Press, 1991) p. 235. Hereafter cited in the notes as *Adorno's Aesthetic Theory*.

14. Theodor W. Adorno, "Cultural Criticism and Society," *Prisms*, translated by Samuel and Shierry Weber, (Cambridge, Mass.: The MIT Press, 1967) p. 22. Cited in the text as CCS.

15. Idem, "Prolog zum Fernsehen," *Gesammelte Schriften* 10.2 (Frankfurt am Main: Suhrkamp Verlag, 1977) p. 515. All translations are my own. Cited in the text as PF.

16. Idem, "Fernsehen als Ideologie," *Gesammelte Schriften* 10.2 (Frankfurt am Main: Suhrkamp Verlag, 1977) p. 520. All translations are my own. Cited in the text as FI.

17. "Adorno in Reverse," p. 25.

18. Max Horkheimer and Theodor W. Adorno, "The Schema of Mass Culture," translated by Nicholas Walker, *The Culture Industry: Selected Essays on Mass Culture*," ed. J. M. Bernstein, (London: Routledge, 1991) p. 57. Cited in the text as SMC.

19. Theodor W. Adorno, *Minima Moralia: Reflections from Damaged Life*, translated by E. F. N. Jephcott, (London: Verso, 1974) p. 207. Cited in the text as *MM*.

20. I say "seem to lie" because it is not entirely clear what Adorno believes the necessary conditions for autonomy are. In *Adorno's Aesthetic Theory* (op. cit.), Lambert Zuidervaart offers an explanation for art's autonomy which supplements his later claim (see p. 218) that the conditions for such autonomy lie in political and economic conditions. On page 91, Zuidervaart writes: "The artifactual character of the work is a necessary condition for its autonomy." He further elaborates on this idea on pages 183–84.

21. "Adorno in Reverse," p. 28.

22. The reader should note that the terms "commodification" and "reification" are not strictly synonymous. As Adorno's discussion of successful works of art shows, such works may be commodified without being reified. In this book, I have followed Martin Jay, using the word "reification" to refer to the subsumption of the particular under the universal; see Jay's *Adorno* (London: Fontana, 1984) p. 68. While all cultural goods have become commodified, some subvert the reifying effects of standardized pseudo-culture. How they do so will be examined in what follows.

23. Nicholas Garnham, "Contribution to a Political Economy of Mass-Communication, *Media, Culture and Society* I (1979) p. 140. Hereafter cited in the notes as "Contribution to Political Economy."

24. "Contribution to Political Economy," pp. 140–41.

25. Karl Marx, *Capital: A Critique of Political Economy*, Vol. I, translated by Ben Fowkes, (New York: Vintage Books, 1976) p. 1048.

26. Bill Ryan, *Making Capital from Culture: The Corporate Form of Capitalist Cultural Production* (New York: De Gruyter, 1992) p. 99.

27. *Adorno's Aesthetic Theory*, p. 267.

28. Ben Bagdikian, *Media Monopoly*, 4th ed., (Boston: Beacon Press, 1992) p. 151.

29. *Adorno's Aesthetic Theory*, p. 89.

30. *Adorno's Aesthetic Theory*, p. 228.

31. *Adorno's Aesthetic Theory*, p. 229.

32. *Adorno's Aesthetic Theory*, p. 90.

33. Eugene Lunn, "The Frankfurt School in the Development of the Mass Culture Debate," *The Aesthetics of the Critical Theorists: Studies on Benjamin, Adorno, Marcuse, and Habermas*, ed. Ronald Roblin, (Lewiston, N. Y.: The Edwin Mellen Press, 1990) p. 40. Hereafter cited in the notes as "Frankfurt School."

34. Oskar Negt, "Mass Media: Tools of Domination or Instruments of Liberation? Aspects of the Frankfurt School's Communications Analysis," translated by Leslie Adelson, *New German Critique* (Spring 1978) p. 74.

35. "Adorno in Reverse," p. 27.

36. Theodor W. Adorno, *Negative Dialectics*, translated by E. B. Ashton, (New York: Continuum 1973) p. 298. Cited in the text as *ND*.

37. William Leiss, *The Limits to Satisfaction: An Essay on the Problem of Needs and Commodities* (Kingston and Montreal: McGill-Queen's University Press, 1988) p. 18. Oskar Negt and Alexander Kluge make a similar remark about perception in their *Public Sphere and Experience: Toward an Analysis of the Bourgeois and Proletarian Public Sphere*, translated by Peter Labanyi, Jamie Owen Daniel, and Assenka Oksiloff, (Minneapolis and London: University of Minnesota Press, 1993) p. 152: "*The development of these media* [traditional and advanced] *corresponds to a reception situation in which people's entire perceptual system is itself, through a division of labor, fragmented. The senses are enlisted in a specialized manner: radio monopolizes hearing; books, newspapers and television develop reading and seeing, film is concerned with movement . . . ; and, lastly, education incorporates learning processes, noting, memorizing, and recalling.*" Adorno himself was cognizant of the problems associated with this fragmentation. In *The Jargon of Authenticity*, translated by Kurt Tarnowski and Frederic Will, (Evanston, Ill.: Northwestern University Press, 1973) p. 67, Adorno speaks of the "real division of the subject into separated functions" which "negates the person's total principle." The person becomes "simply the sum of his functions," and the functions themselves "turn against the self which they are supposed to serve."

38. Ibid., p. 20.

39. *Adorno's Aesthetic Theory*, p. 272.

40. Theodor W. Adorno, "Late Capitalism or Industrial Society?" translated by Fred van Gelder, *Modern German Sociology* (New York: Columbia University Press, 1987) p. 242. Cited in the text as LC.

41. Idem, "Kann das Publikum Wollen?" *Gesammelte Schriften* 20.1 (Frankfurt am Main: Suhrkamp Verlag, 1986) pp. 346–47 *passim*. My translation.

42. *Adorno's Aesthetic Theory*, p. 184.

43. *Adorno's Aesthetic Theory*, pp. 185–86.

44. Theodor W. Adorno, "Lyric Poetry and Society," translated by Bruce Mayo, *Telos* 20 (1974) p. 58.

45. *Idem*, "How to Look at Television," *The Culture Industry: Selected Essays on Mass Culture*, ed. J. M. Bernstein, (London: Verso, 1991) p. 140. Cited in the text as HLT.

46. Ernesto Laclau and Chantal Mouffe, *Hegemony and Socialist Strategy: Towards a Radical Democratic Politics* (London: Verso, 1985) p. 164.

47. Ibid., pp. 164–65.

48. Fredric Jameson, *The Political Unconscious: Narrative as Socially Symbolic Act* (Ithaca, N. Y.: Cornell University Press, 1981) p. 287.

49. Ibid., p. 288.

50. See Fredric Jameson's discussion of "Jaws" in "Reification and Utopia," op. cit., pp. 142–44. See also Douglas Kellner's reading of "Rambo" in "Critical Theory and Ideology Critique," *The Aesthetics of the Critical Theorists: Studies on Benjamin, Adorno, Marcuse, and Habermas*, ed. Ronald Roblin, (Lewiston, N. Y.: The Edwin Mellen Press, 1990) pp. 91–99.

For an extremely suggestive though indirect critique of Jameson's and Kellner's ideas about utopian elements in mass culture see Michael Sullivan and John T. Lysaker, "Between Impotence and Illusion: Adorno's Art of Theory and Practice," *New German Critique* 57 (Fall 1992). On page 121, the authors write: "Achieving emancipation is not a matter of producing new contents that depict unsundered life, a matter of producing new ends toward which present practices could be directed. Instead, and this is Adorno's contribution to the question of political activity, the road to emancipation begins with analyzing practices, like art, that do not dissolve the tension between subject and object."

In his most recent book, *Media Culture: Cultural Studies, Identity and Politics between the Modern and the Postmodern* (London and New York: Routledge, 1995) pp. 57–58, Kellner develops his own view of ideology and is especially critical of what he describes as the Frankfurt School's dominant ideology thesis. In lieu of a response to Kellner's criticism, I shall quote Terry Eagleton's *Ideology: An Introduction* (London: Verso, 1991) p. 36: "The truth, surely, is that the diffusion of dominant values and beliefs among oppressed peoples in society has *some* part to play in the reproduction of the system as a whole, but that this factor has been typically exaggerated by a long tradition of Western Marxism for which 'ideas' are allotted too high a status."

51. Theodor W. Adorno, "Transparencies on Film," translated by Thomas Y. Levin, *New German Critique* 24–25 (Fall-Winter 1981–82) p. 202. Cited in the text as TF.

52. See "Prolog zum Fernsehen," op. cit., pp. 507–8. See also *Dialectic of Enlightenment*, op. cit., p. 124, where Adorno and Horkheimer described the process of fusing "all the works into one work" as the "triumph of invested capital."

53. "Contribution to Political Economy," p. 136n.

54. Martin Jay, *Adorno* (London: Fontana, 1984) p. 127. Hereafter cited in the notes as *Adorno*.

55. "Frankfurt School," p. 39.
56. *Adorno*, p. 138.
57. *Adorno's Aesthetic Theory*, p. 118.
58. See *Negative Dialectics*, op. cit., p. 265: "There is no available model of freedom save one: that consciousness, as it intervenes in the total social constitution, will through that constitution intervene in the complexion of the individual. This notion is not utterly chimerical, because consciousness is a ramification of the energy of drives; it is part impulse itself, and also a moment of that which it intervenes in. If there were not that affinity which Kant so furiously denies, neither would there be the idea of freedom, for whose sake he denies the affinity."
59. Michael Sullivan and John T. Lysaker, "Between Impotence and Illusion: Adorno's Art of Theory and Practice," *New German Critique* 57 (Fall, 1992) p. 122.
60. For a critique of contemporary theories of resistive consumption (the latest versions of the limited effects theory), see David Sholle's "Resistance: Pinning Down a Wandering Concept in Cultural Studies Discourse," *Journal of Urban and Cultural Studies* I, no. 1 (1990) pp. 87–105. See also Herbert Schiller's critical discussion of the thesis of an active and resistive audience in *Culture, Inc.: The Corporate Takeover of Public Expression* (Oxford: Oxford University Press, 1989) pp. 143–56. Tania Modleski briefly criticizes this thesis in her introduction to *Studies in Entertainment: Critical Approaches to Mass Culture*, Bloomington, Ill., and Indianapolis: Indiana University Press, 1986) pp. x–xiii. Douglas Kellner also offers a brief critical discussion of contemporary limited effects theory in *Media Culture: Cultural Studies, Identity and Politics between the Modern and the Postmodern*, (London and New York: Routledge, 1995), pp. 36–40. I have also criticized the active audience thesis in "Symbolic Exchange in Hyperreality," *Baudrillard: A Critical Reader*, ed. Douglas Kellner, (Oxford: Basil Blackwell, 1994) pp. 150–67.

Epilogue

1. Nicholas Garnham, "Contribution to a Political Economy of Mass-Communication," *Media, Culture and Society* I (1979) p. 136.
2. Ben Bagdikian, *The Media Monopoly*, 4th ed., (Boston: Beacon Press, 1992) p. 131.
3. Ibid., p. 132.
4. Ibid., pp. 152–73.
5. Graham Murdock and Peter Golding, "Capitalism, Communication and Class Relations," *Mass Communication and Society*, eds. James Curran, Michael Gurevitch, and Janet Woolacott, (London: Edward Arnold, 1977) p. 19.
6. Bill Ryan, *Making Capital from Culture: The Corporate Form of Capitalist Cultural Production* (Berlin and New York: Walter de Gruyter, 1991) p. 186.

Notes to Chapters

169

7. William Leiss, *The Limits to Satisfaction: An Essay on the Problem of Needs and Commodities* (Kingston and Montréal: McGill-Queen's Press, 1988).
8. Theodor W. Adorno, "Prolog zum Fernsehen," *Gesammelte Schriften* 10.2 (Frankfurt am Main: Suhrkamp Verlag, 1977) p. 514. My translation.
9. The success of the culture industry's positivist ideology partially depends on people wanting to believe they are free and equal despite massive evidence to the contrary. As Michael Lind writes in "To Have and Have Not: Notes on the Progress of the American Class War" in *Harper's Magazine* (June 1995) p. 36: "The American oligarchy spares no pains in promoting the belief that it does not exist, but the success of its disappearing act depends on equally strenuous efforts on the part of an American public anxious to believe in egalitarian fictions and unwilling to see what is hidden in plain sight." On the other hand, it may now have become somewhat easier to refute the conflation of fact and value characteristic of positivism. As Gore Vidal notes in "Andy Kopkind, 1935–94," *The Nation* (June 12, 1995) p. 836: "the disparity between what the United States thinks it is and what it actually is is now too great to be reconciled. One can only chip away at the edges."
10. David Sholle, "Resistance: Pinning Down a Wandering Concept in Cultural Studies Discourse," *Journal of Urban and Cultural Studies* I, no. 1 (1990) p. 97.
11. Theodor W. Adorno, "Fernsehen als Ideologie," *Gesammelte Schriften* 10.2 (Frankfurt am Main: Suhrkamp Verlag, 1977) p. 531. All translations are my own. Cited in the text as FI.
12. Idem, "Reflexionen zur Klassentheorie," *Soziologische Schriften* I (Frankfurt am Main: Suhrkamp Verlag, 1972) pp. 383–86. My translation.
13. See Neil Postman, *Technopoly: The Surrender of Culture to Technology* (New York: Knopf, 1992).
14. John Downing, *Radical Media: The Political Experience of Alternative Communication* (Boston: South End Press, 1984) p. 28.
15. Pierre-André Taguieff, "Le 'Populisme' devant la Science politique: Du Mirage conceptuel aux vrais Problèmes," unpublished manuscript, p. 39. My translation.
16. Peter Uwe Hohendahl, "Recasting the Public Sphere," *October* 73 (Summer 1995) p. 32.
17. Jean Cohen and Andrew Arato, *Civil Society and Political Theory* (Cambridge, Mass.: The MIT Press, 1992). See especially Chapter 9: "Social Theory and Civil Society," pp. 421–91.
18. Jürgen Habermas, *The Theory of Communicative Action*, Vol. II: *Lifeworld and System*, translated by Thomas McCarthy, (Cambridge, Mass.: The MIT Press, 1987) p. 390.
19. Oskar Negt and Alexander Kluge, *Public Sphere and Experience: Toward an Analysis of the Bourgeois and Proletarian Public Sphere*, translated by Peter Labanyi, Jamie Owen Daniel and Assenka Oksiloff, (Minneapolis and London: University of Minnesota Press, 1993) p. 158.
20. Theodor W. Adorno, *Negative Dialectics*, translated by E. B. Ashton, (New York: Continuum, 1973) p. 365.

Bibliography

Works by Theodor W. Adorno

Section A

In this section of the bibliography, works by Adorno cited in abbreviated form in the text are listed alphabetically in order of their abbreviations.

AP   *The Authoritarian Personality*, by Theodor W. Adorno, Else Frenkel-Brunswik, Daniel J. Levinson, and R. Nevitt Sanford. New York: Harper & Brothers, 1950.

AS   *Aspects of Sociology*, by the Frankfurt Institute for Social Research. Translated by John Viertel. Boston: Beacon Press, 1972.

BI   "Beitrag zur Ideologienlehre." *Soziologische Schriften* I, pp. 457–77. Frankfurt am Main: Suhrkamp Verlag, 1972.

CA   "Culture and Administration." Translated by Wes Blomster. *Telos* 37 (1978) pp. 93–111.

CCS   "Cultural Criticism and Society." *Prisms*, pp. 19–34. Translated by Samuel and Shierry Weber. Cambridge, Mass: The MIT Press, 1967.

CIR   "Culture Industry Reconsidered." Translated by Anson G. Rabinbach. *New German Critique* 6 (1975) pp. 12–19.

DE   *Dialectic of Enlightenment*, by Max Horkheimer and Theodor W. Adorno. Translated by John Cumming. New York: The Seabury Press, 1972.

FC   "On the Fetish Character in Music and the Regression of Listening." Translated by Maurice Goldbloom. *The Essential Frankfurt School Reader*, pp. 270–99. Edited by Andrew Arato and Eike Gebhardt. New York: Urizen Books, 1978.

FI   "Fernsehen als Ideologie." *Gesammelte Schriften* 10.2, pp. 518–32. Frankfurt am Main: Suhrkamp Verlag, 1977.

171

FT   "Freudian Theory and the Pattern of Fascist Propaganda." *The Essential Frankfurt School Reader*, pp. 118–37. Edited by Andrew Arato and Eike Gebhardt. New York: Urizen Books, 1978.

HLT   "How to Look at Television." *The Culture Industry: Selected Essays on Mass Culture*, pp. 136–53. Edited by J. M. Bernstein. London: Routledge, 1991.

LC   "Late Capitalism or Industrial Society?" Translated by Fred van Gelder. *Modern German Sociology*, pp. 232–47. Edited by V. Meja, D. Misgeld, and N. Stehr. New York: Columbia University Press, 1987.

MM   *Minima Moralia: Reflections from Damaged Life*. Translated by E. F. N. Jephcott. London: Verso, 1974.

ND   *Negative Dialectics.* Translated by E. B. Ashton. New York: Continuum, 1973.

PC   "Theory of Pseudo-Culture." Translated by Deborah Cook. *Telos* 95 (Spring 1993) pp. 15–38.

PD   *The Positivist Dispute in German Sociology*, by Theodor W. Adorno, et al. Translated and edited by Glyn Adey and David Frisby. London: Heinemann, 1976.

PF   "Prolog zum Fernsehen." *Gesammelte Schriften* 10.2, pp. 507–17. Frankfurt am Main: Suhrkamp Verlag, 1977.

PM   "On Popular Music," with the assistance of George Simpson. *Studies in Philosophy and Social Research* IX, no. 1 (1941) pp. 17–48.

RK   "Reflexionen zur Klassentheorie." *Soziologische Schriften* I, pp. 373–91. Frankfurt am Main: Suhrkamp Verlag, 1972.

RP   "Die Revidierte Psychoanalyse." *Soziologische Schriften* I, pp. 20–41. Frankfurt am Main: Suhrkamp Verlag, 1972.

S   "Society." Translated by Fredric Jameson. *Salmagundi* III, no. 10–11 (1969–70) pp. 144–53.

SCR   "A Social Critique of Radio Music." *Kenyon Review* VII, no. 2 (1945) pp. 208–17.

SMC   "The Schema of Mass Culture," by Max Horkheimer and Theodor W. Adorno. Translated by Nicholas Walker. *The Culture Industry: Selected Essays on Mass Culture*, pp. 53–84. Edited by J. M. Bernstein. London: Routledge, 1991.

SP1   "Sociology and Psychology." Translated by Irving N. Wohlfarth. *New Left Review* 46 (1967) pp. 67–80.

SP2   "Sociology and Psychology." Translated by Irving N. Wohlfarth. *New Left Review* 47 (1968) pp. 79–97.

SSM   "On the Social Situation of Music." Translated by Wes Blomster. *Telos* 35 (1978) pp. 128–64.

TB   "Thesen über Bedürfnis." *Soziologische Schriften* I, pp. 392–96. Frankfurt am Main: Suhrkamp Verlag, 1972.

TF   "Transparencies on Film." Translated by Thomas Y. Levin. *New German Critique* 24–25 (1981–82) pp. 199–205.

Time   "Free Time." Translated by Gordon Finlayson and Nicholas Walker. *The Culture Industry: Selected Essays on Mass Culture*, pp. 162–70. Edited by J. M. Bernstein. London: Routledge, 1991.

Section B

In this part of the bibliography, works by Adorno to which less frequent reference is made are listed in order of their publication dates.

"Aldous Huxley and Utopia." *Prisms*, pp. 95–118. Translated by Samuel and Shierry Weber. Cambridge, Mass: The MIT Press, 1967.

"Fortschritt." *Stichworte: Kritische Modelle 2*, pp. 29–50. Frankfurt am Main: Suhrkamp Verlag, 1969.

"Anmerkungen zum sozialen Konflikt heute." *Gesammelte Schriften* 8, pp. 177–95. Frankfurt am Main: Suhrkamp Verlag, 1972.

The Jargon of Authenticity. Translated by Kurt Tarnowski and Frederic Will. Evanston, Ill.: Northwestern University Press, 1973.

"Lyric Poetry and Society." Translated by Bruce Mayo. *Telos* 20 (1974) pp. 56–71.

"The Psychological Technique of Martin Luther Thomas' Radio Addresses." *Gesammelte Schriften* 9.1. Frankfurt am Main: Suhrkamp Verlag, 1975.

"Letters to Walter Benjamin." Translated by Harry Zohn. *Aesthetics and Politics: Ernst Bloch, Georg Lukács, Bertolt Brecht, Walter Benjamin, Theodor Adorno*, pp. 110–33. Edited by Ronald Taylor. London: Verso, 1977.

"Reconciliation under Duress." Translated by Rodney Livingstone. *Aesthetics and Politics: Ernst Bloch, Georg Lukács, Bertolt Brecht, Walter Benjamin, Theodor Adorno*, pp. 151–76. Edited by Ronald Taylor. London: Verso, 1977.

"The Actuality of Philosophy." Translated by B. Snow. *Telos* 31 (1977) pp. 120–33.

"Music and Technique." Translated by Wes Blomster. *Telos* 32 (1977) pp. 79–94.

"Subject and Object." Translated by E. B. Ashton. *The Essential Frankfurt School Reader*, pp. 497–511. Edited by Andrew Arato and Eike Gebhardt. New York: Urizen Books, 1978.

Gesammelte Schriften. Vol. 1–20. Frankfurt am Main: Suhrkamp Verlag, 1986.

"Progress." Translated by Eric Krakauer. *The Philosophical Forum* XV, no. 1–2 (Fall-Winter 1983–84) pp. 55–70.

Aesthetic Theory. Translated by C. Lenhardt. London, Boston, Melbourne, and Henley: Routledge & Kegan Paul, 1984.

"Kann das Publikum Wollen?" *Gesammelte Schriften* 20.1. Frankfurt am Main: Suhrkamp Verlag, 1986.

"Perennial Fashion—Jazz." Translated by Samuel and Shierry Weber. *Critical Theory and Society: A Reader*, pp. 199–209. Edited by Stephen Eric Bronner and Douglas MacKay Kellner. New York and London: Routledge, 1989.

Secondary Works

This section of the bibliography includes works which are cited in the notes, or which are relevant to a discussion of Adorno's theory of the culture industry. Multiple works by an author are listed in order of their publication dates.

Abercrombie, Nicholas; Hill, Stephen; and Turner, Bryan S. *The Dominant Ideology Thesis.* London: George Allen & Unwin, 1980.

Agger, Ben. *The Discourse of Domination: From the Frankfurt School to Postmodernism.* Evanston, Ill.: Northwestern University Press, 1992.

Alford, C. Fred. *Narcissism: Socrates, the Frankfurt School and Psychoanalytic Theory.* New Haven, Conn., and London: Yale University Press, 1988.

Allen, Richard W. "The Aesthetic Experience of Modernity: Benjamin, Adorno, and Contemporary Film Theory." *New German Critique* 40 (Winter 1987) pp. 225–40.

Anderson, Karen, L. "Historical Perspectives on the Family." *Family Matters: Sociology and Contemporary Canadian Families.* Edited by Lorraine Fairley. Scarborough, Ontario: Nelson Canada, 1988.

Arato, Andrew, and Gebhardt, Eike, eds. *The Essential Frankfurt School Reader.* Translated by Various. New York: Urizen Books, 1978.

Aronowitz, Stanley. *The Crisis in Historical Materialism: Class, Politics and Culture in Marxist Theory.* South Hadley, Mass.: J. F. Bergin Publishers, 1981.

Bagdikian, Ben H. *The Media Monopoly*, 4th ed. Boston: Beacon Press, 1992.

Baudrillard, Jean. *Pour une Critique de l'Economie politique du Signe.* Paris: Gallimard, 1972.

———. *Simulacres et Simulation.* Paris: Galilée, 1981.

Benhabib, Seyla. *Critique, Norm and Utopia: A Study of the Foundations of Critical Theory.* New York: Columbia University Press, 1986.

Benjamin, Andrew, ed. *The Problems of Modernity: Adorno and Benjamin.* London and New York: Routledge, 1989.

Benjamin, Jessica. "The End of Internalization: Adorno's Social Psychology." *Telos* 32 (1977) pp. 42–64.

————. "Authority and the Family Revisited: or, A World without Fathers?" *New German Critique* 5 (Winter 1978) pp. 35–57.

Benjamin, Walter. "The Work of Art in the Age of Mechanical Reproduction." *Illuminations*, pp. 217–51. Translated by Harry Zohn. Edited by Hannah Arendt. New York: Schocken Books, 1969.

Berman, Russell A. *Modern Culture and Critical Theory: Art, Politics and the Legacy of the Frankfurt School.* Madison, Wis.: The University of Wisconsin Press, 1989.

Bernstein, Richard J., ed. *Habermas and Modernity.* Cambridge, Mass.: The MIT Press, 1985.

Bloch, Ernst. *The Principle of Hope.* Translated by Neville Plaice, Stephen Plaice, and Paul Knight. Cambridge, Mass.: The MIT Press, 1986.

Bottomore, Tom. *The Frankfurt School.* New York: Tavistock Publications, 1984.

Bourdieu, Pierre. *Distinction: A Social Critique of the Judgement of Taste.* Cambridge, Mass.: Harvard University Press, 1984.

Bowles, Samuel, and Gintis, Herbert. *Democracy and Capitalism: Property, Community, and the Contradictions of Modern Social Thought.* New York: Basic Books, 1987.

Brantlinger, Patrick. *Bread and Circuses: Theories of Mass Culture as Social Decay.* Ithaca, N. Y., and London: Cornell University Press, 1983.

Bronner, Stephen Eric. *Of Critical Theory and Its Theorists.* Oxford: Basil Blackwell, 1994.

Bronner, Stephen Eric, and Kellner, Douglas MacKay, eds. *Critical Theory and Society: A Reader.* New York and London: Routledge, 1989.

Buck-Morss, Susan. *The Origin of Negative Dialectics: Theodor W. Adorno, Walter Benjamin and the Frankfurt School.* New York: The Free Press, 1977.

Bullock, Alan. *Hitler and Stalin: Parallel Lives.* Toronto: McClelland and Stewart, 1993.

Casty, Alan, ed. *Mass Media and Mass Man.* New York: Holt, Rinehart and Winston, 1988.

Chomsky, Noam, and Herman, Edward, S. *Manufacturing Consent: The Political Economy of the Mass Media.* New York: Pantheon Books, 1988.

Cohen, Jean L., and Arato, Andrew. *Civil Society and Political Theory.* Cambridge, Mass., and London: The MIT Press, 1992.

Connerton, Paul. *The Tragedy of Enlightenment: An Essay on the Frankfurt School.* Cambridge: Cambridge University Press, 1980.

Dallmayr, Fred. *Between Freiburg and Frankfurt: Toward a Critical Ontology.* Amherst, Mass.: The University of Massachusetts Press, 1991.

Davison, Peter; Meyersohn, Rolf; and Shils, Edward, eds. *Literary Taste and Mass Communication.* Vol. I: *Culture and Mass Culture.* Cambridge: Chadwyck-Healey, 1978.

Debord, Guy. *La Société du Spectacle.* Paris: Editions Gérard Lebovici, 1989.

De Laurentis, Teresa, et al., eds. *The Technological Imagination.* Madison, Wis.: The University of Wisconsin Press, 1980.

Dews, Peter. *Logics of Disintegration: Post-Structuralist Thought and the Claims of Critical Theory.* London and New York: Verso, 1987.

Diderot, Denis. *Diderot.* Vol. XIV: *Salon de 1765: Essais sur la Peinture.* Edited by Else Marie Bukdahl, Annette Lorenceau, and Gita May. Paris: Hermann, 1984.

Downing, John. *Radical Media: The Political Experience of Alternative Communication.* Boston: South End Press, 1984.

Dubiel, Helmut, and Söllner, Alfons, eds. *Horkheimer/Pollock/Neumann/Gurland/Kirchheimer/Marcuse: Wirtschaft, Recht und Staat im Nationalsozialismus: Analysen des Instituts für Sozialforschung 1939–1942.* Frankfurt am Main: Europäische Verlagsanstalt, 1981.

Dubiel, Helmut. *Theory and Politics: Studies in the Development of Critical Theory.* Translated by Benjamin Gregg. Cambridge, Mass.: The MIT Press, 1985.

Eagleton, Terry. *Ideology: An Introduction.* London and New York: Verso, 1991.

Enzensberger, Hans Magnus. *The Consciousness Industry: On Literature, Politics and the Media.* Translated by Various. New York: The Seabury Press, 1974.

Ewen, Stuart, and Ewen, Elizabeth. *Channels of Desire: Mass Images and the Shaping of American Consciousness*, 2nd ed. Minneapolis and London: University of Minnesota Press, 1992.

Feenberg, Andrew. *Lukács, Marx and the Sources of Critical Theory.* Oxford: Oxford University Press, 1986.

———. *Critical Theory of Technology.* Oxford: Oxford University Press, 1991.

Fiske, John. *Reading the Popular.* Boston: Unwin Hyman, 1989.

———. *Understanding Popular Culture.* Boston: Unwin Hyman, 1989.

Freud, Sigmund. *New Introductory Lectures on Psychoanalysis.* Translated by W. J. H. Sprott. New York: W. W. Norton & Company, Inc., 1933.

———. *The Basic Writings of Sigmund Freud.* Translated and edited by A. A. Brill. New York: Modern Library, 1938.

———. ''On Narcissism: An Introduction.'' Translated by James Strachey. *The*

Standard Edition of the Complete Psychological Works of Sigmund Freud. Vol. XIV. London: The Hogarth Press, 1957.

―――. "Inhibitions, Symptoms and Anxiety." *The Standard Edition of the Complete Psychological Works of Sigmund Freud.* Vol. XX. Translated by James Strachey. London: The Hogarth Press, 1959.

―――. *The Ego and the Id.* Translated by Joan Riviere. New York: W. W. Norton & Company, Inc., 1960.

―――. *Beyond the Pleasure Principle.* Translated by James Strachey. New York: W. W. Norton & Company, Inc., 1961.

―――. *Civilization and its Discontents.* Translated by Joan Riviere. London: The Hogarth Press, 1975.

―――. "Group Psychology and the Analysis of the Ego." *The Penguin Freud Library* XII: *Civilization, Society and Religion*, pp. 95–178. Translated by James Strachey. Harmondsworth, Middlesex: Penguin Books, 1985.

―――. "Thoughts for the Times on War and Death." *The Penguin Freud Library* XII: *Civilization, Society and Religion*, pp. 61–89. Translated by James Strachey. Harmondsworth, Middlesex: Penguin Books, 1985.

Friedman, George. *The Political Philosophy of the Frankfurt School.* Ithaca, N. Y., and London: Cornell University Press, 1981.

Fromm, Erich. *Escape from Freedom.* New York: Holt, Rinehart and Winston, 1969.

Gans, Herbert. *Popular Culture and High Culture: An Analysis and Evaluation of Taste.* New York: Basic Books, 1974.

Garnham, Nicholas. "Contribution to a Political Economy of Mass Communication." *Media, Culture and Society* I (1979) pp. 123–46.

―――. "Concepts of Culture: Public Policy and the Culture Industries." *Cultural Studies* I, no. 1 (1987) pp. 23–37.

Geuss, Raymond. *The Idea of a Critical Theory: Habermas and the Frankfurt School.* Cambridge: Cambridge University Press, 1981.

Giner, Salvador. *Mass Society.* London: Martin Robertson & Company Ltd., 1976.

Gurevitch, Michael; Bennett, Tony; Curran, James; and Woollacott, Janet, eds. *Culture, Society and the Media.* London and New York: Methuen, 1982.

Habermas, Jürgen. *Legitimation Crisis.* Translated by Thomas McCarthy. Boston: Beacon Press, 1975.

―――. "Psychic Thermador and the Rebirth of Rebellious Subjectivity." *Berkeley Journal of Sociology* XXV (1980) pp. 1–12.

―――. "Modernity—An Incomplete Project." Translated by Seyla Ben Habib. *The Anti-Aesthetic: Essays on Postmodern Culture.* Edited by Hal Foster. Port Townsend, Washington: Bay Press, 1983.

————. "Theodor Adorno: The Primal History of Subjectivity—Self-Affirmation Gone Wild." *Philosophical-Political Profiles*. Translated by Frederick Lawrence. Cambridge, Mass.: The MIT Press, 1983.

————. *The Philosophical Discourse of Modernity: Twelve Lectures*. Translated by Frederick Lawrence. Cambridge, Mass.: The MIT Press, 1987.

————. *The Structural Transformation of the Public Sphere: An Inquiry into a Category of Bourgeois Society*. Translated by Thomas Burger. Cambridge, Mass.: The MIT Press, 1989.

————. *The Theory of Communicative Action*. Vol. I: *Reason and the Rationalization of Society*; and Vol. II: *Lifeworld and System*. Translated by Thomas McCarthy. Boston: Beacon Press, 1989.

Hansen, Miriam B. "Introduction to Adorno, 'Transparencies on Film' (1966)." *New German Critique* 24–25 (1981–82) pp. 186–98.

————. "Mass Culture as Hieroglyphic Writing: Adorno, Derrida, Kracauer." *New German Critique* 56 (Spring-Summer 1992) pp. 43–73.

Hareven, Tamara K. "American Families in Transition: Historical Perspectives on Change." *Family in Transition: Rethinking Marriage, Sexuality, Child Rearing, and Family Organization*, 7th ed. Edited by Arlene S. Skolnick and Jerome H. Skolnick. New York: Harper Collins Publishers, 1992.

Haug, Wolfgang. *Critique of Commodity Aesthetics: Appearance, Sexuality and Advertising in Capitalist Society*. Translated by Robert Bock. Minneapolis: University of Minnesota Press, 1986.

————. *Commodity Aesthetics, Ideology and Culture*. Translated by Wolfgang Haug, Karen Ruoff Kramer, and Susan P. Brown. New York: International General, 1987.

Hegel, G. W. F. *The Philosophy of History*. Translated by J. Sibree. New York: Dover, 1956.

————. *Phenomenology of Spirit*. Translated by A. V. Miller. Oxford: Oxford University Press, 1977.

Heinlein, Bruno. *"Massenkultur" in der Kritischen Theorie*. Erlangen: Verlag Palm & Enke, 1985.

Held, David. *Introduction to Critical Theory: Horkheimer to Habermas*. Berkeley and Los Angeles: University of California Press, 1980.

Hohendahl, Peter Uwe. "The Dialectic of Enlightenment Revisited: Habermas' Critique of the Frankfurt School." *New German Critique* 35 (Spring-Summer 1985) pp. 3–26.

————. *Reappraisals: Shifting Alignments in Postwar Critical Theory*. Ithaca, N. Y., and London: Cornell University Press, 1991.

————. "Recasting the Public Sphere." *October* 73 (Summer, 1995) pp. 27–54.

Honneth, Axel. *The Critique of Power: Reflective Stages in a Critical Social Theory.* Translated by Kenneth Baynes. Cambridge, Mass.: The MIT Press, 1991.

Horkheimer, Max. "Art and Mass Culture." *Studies in Philosophy and Social Research* IX (1941) pp. 290–304.

———. "Authoritarianism and the Family Today." *The Family: Its Function and Destiny*, pp. 359–74. Edited by Ruth Nanda Anshen. New York: Harper, 1949.

———. "Begriff der Bildung. Immatrikulationsrede Wintersemester 1952/53." *Bildungstheorien Probleme und Positionen.* Edited by Jürgen-Eckardt Pleines. Freiburg, Basel and Vienna: Herder, 1954.

———. *Kritische Theorie: Eine Dokumentation* Vols. I and II. Frankfurt am Main: S. Fischer Verlag, 1968.

———. "Studies on Authority and the Family." Translated by John Cumming. *Critical Theory: Selected Essays*, pp. 47–128. New York: Herder and Herder, 1972.

———. "Traditional and Critical Theory." Translated by Matthew J. O'Connell. *Critical Theory: Selected Essays*, pp. 188–243. New York: Herder and Herder, 1972.

———. *Eclipse of Reason.* New York: The Seabury Press, 1974.

———. "Egoism and the Freedom Movement: On the Anthropology of the Bourgeois Era." Translated by David J. Parent. *Telos* 54 (1982–83) pp. 10–60.

Hullot-Kentor, Robert, "Back to Adorno." *Telos* 81 (Fall 1989) pp. 5–29.

Huyssen, Andreas. "Introduction to Adorno." *New German Critique* 6 (1975) pp. 3–11.

———. "Critical Theory and Modernity: Introduction." *New German Critique* 26 (1982) pp. 3–11.

———. *After the Great Divide: Modernism, Mass Culture, Postmodernism.* Bloomington, Ill., and Indianapolis: Indiana University Press, 1986.

Hyman, Herbert, and Sheatsley, Paul. "*The Authoritarian Personality*—A Methodological Critique," *Studies in the Scope and Method of "The Authoritarian Personality."* Edited by Richard Christie and Marie Jahoda. Glencoe, Ill.: The Free Press, 1954.

Hyppolite, Jean. *Genèse et Structure de la "Phénoménologie de l'Esprit" de Hegel.* Paris: Editions Montaigne, 1946.

Jacobs, Norman, ed. *Culture for the Millions? Mass Media in Modern Society.* Princeton: O. van Nostrand Company, Inc., 1961.

Jacoby, Russell. *Social Amnesia: A Critique of Conformist Psychology from Adler to Laing.* Boston: Beacon Press, 1975.

Jameson, Fredric. *Marxism and Form: Twentieth Century Dialectical Theories of Literature*. Princeton: Princeton University Press, 1971.

———. "Reification and Utopia in Mass Culture." *Social Text* 1 (1979) pp. 130–48.

———. *The Political Unconscious: Narrative as Socially Symbolic Act*. Ithaca, N. Y.: Cornell University Press, 1981.

———. *Late Marxism: Adorno, or, the Persistence of the Dialectic*. London: Verso, 1990.

———. *Postmodernism, or, the Cultural Logic of Late Capitalism*. Durham, N. C.: Duke University Press, 1991.

Jay, Martin. *The Dialectical Imagination: A History of the Frankfurt School and the Institute for Social Research: 1923–1950*. Boston: Little, Brown and Company, 1973.

———. *Adorno*. London: Fontana, 1984.

———. *Marxism and Totality: The Adventures of a Concept from Lukács to Habermas*. Berkeley and Los Angeles: University of California Press, 1984.

———. *Permanent Exiles: Essays on the Intellectual Migration from Germany to America*. New York: Columbia University Press, 1985.

Jimenez, Marc. *Adorno: Art, Idéologie et Théorie de l'Art*. Paris: Union Générale d'Editions, 1973.

Kausch, Michael. *Kulturindustrie und Populärkultur: Kritische Theorie der Massmedien*. Frankfurt am Main: Fischer Verlag, 1988.

Kellner, Douglas. *Critical Theory, Marxism and Modernity*. Baltimore: Johns Hopkins University Press, 1989.

———. "Critical Theory and Ideology Critique." *The Aesthetics of the Critical Theorists: Studies on Benjamin, Adorno, Marcuse and Habermas*. Edited by Ronald Roblin. Lewiston, N. Y.: The Edwin Mellen Press, 1990.

———. *Television and the Crisis of Democracy*. San Francisco: Westview Press, 1990.

———. *Media Culture: Cultural Studies, Identity and Politics between the Modern and the Postmodern*. London and New York: Routledge, 1995.

Kellner, Douglas, and Roderick, Rick. "Recent Literature on Critical Theory." *New German Critique* 23 (1981) pp. 141–170.

Kracauer, Siegfried. *From Caligari to Hitler: A Psychological History of the German Film*. New York: Dennis Dobson, 1947.

———. *The Mass Ornament: Weimar Essays*. Translated and edited by Thomas Y. Levin. Cambridge, Mass., and London: Harvard University Press, 1995.

Laclau, Ernesto, and Mouffe, Chantal. *Hegemony & Socialist Strategy: Towards a Radical Democratic Politics*. London: Verso, 1985.

Lasch, Christopher. *Haven in a Heartless World: The Family Besieged.* New York: Basic Books, 1977.

——. *The Culture of Narcissism: American Life in an Age of Diminishing Expectations.* New York: Warner Books, 1979.

——. *The Minimal Self: Psychic Survival in Troubled Times.* New York and London: W. W. Norton & Company, 1984.

Leiss, William. *The Limits to Satisfaction: An Essay on the Problem of Needs and Commodities.* Kingston, Ontario and Montreal: McGill-Queen's Press, 1988.

Lovell, Terry. *Pictures of Reality: Aesthetics, Politics, Pleasure.* London: British Film Institute, 1980.

Löwenthal, Leo. *Communication in Society.* Vols. I–IV. New Brunswick, N. J.: Transaction Books, 1984.

Lukács, Georg. *History and Class Consciousness: Studies in Marxist Dialectics.* Translated by R. Livingstone. Cambridge, Mass.: The MIT Press, 1968.

——. *The Theory of the Novel: A Historico-philosophical Essay on the Forms of Great Epic Literature.* Translated by Anna Bostock. Cambridge, Mass.: The MIT Press, 1971.

Lunn, Eugene. *Marxism and Modernism: An Historical Study of Lukács, Brecht, Benjamin and Adorno.* Berkeley and Los Angeles: University of California Press, 1982.

——. ''The Frankfurt School in the Development of the Mass Culture Debate.'' *The Aesthetics of the Critical Theorists: Studies on Benjamin, Adorno, Marcuse and Habermas.* Edited by Ronald Roblin. Lewiston, N. Y.: The Edwin Mellen Press, 1990.

MacCabe, Colin, ed. *High Theory/Low Culture.* Manchester: Manchester University Press, 1986.

Marcus, Judith, and Tar, Zoltan, eds. *Foundations of the Frankfurt School of Social Research.* New Brunswick, N. J.: Transaction Books, 1984.

Marcuse, Herbert. *Eros and Civilization: A Philosophical Inquiry into Freud.* New York: Vintage Books, 1955.

——. *One-Dimensional Man: Studies in the Ideology of Advanced Industrial Society.* Boston: Beacon Press, 1964.

——. *Negations: Essays in Critical Theory.* Boston: Beacon Press, 1968.

——. *An Essay on Liberation.* Harmondsworth, Middlesex: Penguin Books, 1969.

——. *The Aesthetic Dimension.* Boston: Beacon Press, 1978.

Marx, Karl. *The Economic and Philosophic Manuscripts of 1844.* Translated by Martin Milligan. New York: International Publishers, 1964.

——. *The German Ideology*, Part One (With Selections from Parts Two and

Three, together with Marx's "Introduction to a Critique of Political Economy"). Translated by Various. New York: International Publishers, 1970.

———. *Contribution to the Critique of Political Economy*. Translated by S. W. Ryazanskaya, 1970. New York: International Publishers, 1970.

———. *Capital: A Critique of Political Economy*. Translated by Ben Fowkes. New York: Vintage Books, 1977.

Mayo, Bruce. "Introduction to Adorno's 'Lyric Poetry and Society'." *Telos* 20 (1974) pp. 52–55.

McCarthy, Thomas, and Hoy, David. *Critical Theory*. Oxford: Basil Blackwell, 1994.

McKinney, David W., Jr. *The Authoritarian Personality Studies: An Inquiry into the Failure of Social Science Research to Produce Demonstrable Knowledge*. The Hague and Paris: Mouton, 1973.

Modleski, Tania. *Studies in Entertainment: Critical Approaches to Mass Culture*. Bloomington, Ill., and Indianapolis: Indiana University Press, 1986.

Moscovici, Serge. *The Age of the Crowd: A Historical Treatise on Mass Psychology*. Translated by J. C. Whitehouse. Cambridge: Cambridge University Press, 1985.

Murdock, Graham, and Golding, Peter. "For a Political Economy of Mass Communications." *Socialist Register 1973*, pp. 205–34. London: Merlin Press, 1974.

———. "Capitalism, Communication and Class Relations." *Mass Communication and Society*, pp. 12–43. Edited by James Curran, Michael Gurevitch, and Janet Woolacott. London: Edward Arnold, 1977.

Naremore, James, and Brantlinger, Patrick, eds. *Modernity and Mass Culture*. Bloomington, Ill. and Indianapolis: Indiana University Press, 1991.

Negt, Oskar. "Mass Media: Tools of Domination or Instruments of Enlightenment? Aspects of the Frankfurt School's Communications Analysis." Translated by Leslie Adelson. *New German Critique* 5 (Spring 1978) pp. 61–80.

Negt, Oskar, and Kluge, Alexander. *Public Sphere and Experience: Toward an Analysis of the Bourgeois and Proletarian Public Sphere*. Translated by Peter Labanyi, Jamie Owen Daniel, and Assenka Oksiloff. Minneapolis: University of Minnesota Press, 1993.

Neumann, Franz. *Behemoth: The Structure and Practice of National Socialism 1933–1944*. Toronto, New York, and London: Oxford University Press, 1944.

New German Critique 56: Theodor W. Adorno, (Spring-Summer 1992).

O'Neill, John, ed. *On Critical Theory*. New York: The Seabury Press, 1976.

Pizer, John. "Jameson's Adorno, or, the Persistence of the Utopian." *New German Critique* 58 (Winter 1993) pp. 127–151.

Pollock, Friedrich. "State Capitalism: Its Possibilities and Limitations." *Studies in Philosophy and Social Research* IX, no. 2 (1941) pp. 200–225.

―――. "Is National Socialism a New Order?" *Studies in Philosophy and Social Research* IX, no. 3 (1941) pp. 440–55.

―――. *Stadien des Kapitalismus*. Munich: Verlag C. H. Beck, 1975.

Poster, Mark. *Critical Theory and Poststructuralism: In Search of a Context*. Ithaca, N. Y.: Cornell University Press, 1989.

―――. *The Mode of Information: Poststructuralism and Social Context*. Chicago: University of Chicago Press, 1990.

Prokop, Dieter, ed. *Kritische Kommunikationsforschung: Aufsätze aus der Zeitschrift für Sozialforschung*. Munich: Carl Hanser Verlag, 1973.

Pütz, Peter. "Nietzsche and Critical Theory." *Telos* 50 (1981–82) pp. 103–114.

Revault d'Allonnes, Olivier, ed. *Présences d'Adorno*. Paris: Union Générale d'Editions, 1975.

Ridless, Robin. *Ideology and Art: Theories of Mass Culture from Walter Benjamin to Umberto Eco*. New York: Peter Lang, 1984.

Riesman, David, in collaboration with Denney, Reuel, and Glazer, Nathan. *The Lonely Crowd: A Study of the Changing American Character*. New Haven, Conn.: Yale University Press, 1950.

Rose, Gillian. *The Melancholy Science: An Introduction to the Thought of Theodor W. Adorno*. New York: Columbia University Press, 1978.

Rosenberg, Bernard, and White, David Manning, eds. *Mass Culture: The Popular Arts in America*. Glencoe, Ill.: The Free Press, 1957.

Ryan, Bill. *Making Capital from Culture: The Corporate Form of Capitalist Cultural Production*. Berlin and New York: Walter de Gruyter, 1991.

Schiller, Herbert I. *The Mind Managers*. Boston: Beacon Press, 1973.

―――. *Culture Inc.: The Corporate Takeover of Public Expression*. Oxford: Oxford University Press, 1989.

Sherover-Marcuse, Erica. *Emancipation and Consciousness: Dogmatic and Dialectical Perspectives in the Early Marx*. Oxford: Basil Blackwell, 1986.

Shils, Edward. *The Intellectuals and the Powers and Other Essays*. Chicago: University of Chicago Press, 1972.

Sholle, David. "Resistance: Pinning Down a Wandering Concept in Cultural Studies Discourse." *Journal of Urban and Cultural Studies* I, no. 1 (1990) pp. 87–105.

Slater, Phil. *Origin and Significance of the Frankfurt School: A Marxist Perspective*. Boston: Routledge & Kegan Paul, 1977.

Snow, Benjamin. "Introduction to Adorno's 'The Actuality of Philosophy.' " *Telos* 31 (1977) pp. 113–19.

Sullivan, Michael, and Lysaker, John T. "Between Impotence and Illusion: Adorno's Art of Theory and Practice." *New German Critique* 57 (Fall 1992) pp. 87–122.

Swingewood, Alan. *The Myth of Mass Culture*. London: The Macmillan Press, Ltd., 1977.

Tar, Zoltan. *The Frankfurt School: The Critical Theories of Max Horkheimer and Theodor W. Adorno*. New York: John Wiley & Sons, Inc., 1977.

Taylor, Ronald, ed. *Aesthetics and Politics: Ernst Bloch, Georg Lukács, Bertolt Brecht, Walter Benjamin, Theodor Adorno*. Translated by Various. London: Verso, 1977.

Tesson, Geoffrey. "Socialization and Parenting." *Family Matters: Sociology and Contemporary Canadian Families*. Edited by Lorraine Fairley. Scarborough, Ontario: Nelson Canada, 1988.

Wagnleitner, Reinhold, "American Cultural Diplomacy, Hollywood, and the Cold War in Central Europe." *Rethinking Marxism* 7, no. 1 (1994) pp. 31–47.

Wellmer, Albrecht. *Critical Theory of Society*. Translated by John Cumming. New York: Herder and Herder, 1971.

————. *The Persistence of Modernity: Essays on Aesthetics, Ethics, and Postmodernism*. Translated by David Midgley. Cambridge, Mass.: The MIT Press, 1991.

Wiggershaus, Rolf. *The Frankfurt School: Its History, Theory and Political Significance*. Translated by Michael Robertson. Cambridge, Mass.: The MIT Press, 1994.

Williams, Raymond. *Culture and Society: 1780–1950*. Harmondsworth, Middlesex: Penguin Books, 1963.

————. *Television: Technology and Cultural Form*. New York: Schocken Books, 1975.

Zuidervaart, Lambert. *Adorno's Aesthetic Theory: The Redemption of Illusion*. Cambridge, Mass.: The MIT Press, 1991.

Index

Adler, Alfred, 154n21
Adorno, Theodor W., "The Actuality
of Philosophy," 159n7; *Aesthetic
Theory*, 101, 126; "Aldous Huxley
and Utopia," 146n72, 155n35;
"Anmerkungen zum sozialen
Konflikt heute," 156n43; *The
Authoritarian Personality*, 17, 18,
19, 20, 21, 143n48, 144n59;
"Beitrag zur Ideologienlehre,"
151n57, 160n17; "Cultural
Criticism and Society," 81,
160n22; "Culture Industry
Reconsidered," 33, 68, 70,
149n41; *Dialectic of
Enlightenment*, 5, 10–11, 31, 32
35, 39, 40, 44, 45, 48, 54, 55, 64,
69, 70, 74, 83, 85, 88, 91, 92, 93
107, 111, 122, 126, 156n37,
160n15; "Fernsehen als
Ideologie," 44, 45, 68, 85, 90, 116;
"Fortschritt," 153n2; "Free
Time," 3, 67, 68, 90; "Freudian
Theory and the Pattern of Fascist
Propaganda," 15, 20, 57, 71, 72,
99, 122; "How to Look at
Television," 45, 88, 116, 151n57;
The Jargon of Authenticity,
145n69, 166n37; "Kann das
Publikum Wollen?" 70, 90; "Late

Capitalism or Industrial Society?"
11, 62, 63, 140n14; "Letters to
Walter Benjamin," 105, 149n41;
Minima Moralia, 11, 20, 21, 72,
81, 85, 127, 143n44; "Music and
Technique," 149n41; *Negative
Dialectics*, 72, 77, 82, 84, 92, 94,
98, 101, 117, 137; "On the Fetish
Character in Music and the
Regression of Listening," 31, 49,
105; "On Popular Music," 39, 60,
68, 70, 90, 117; "On the Social
Situation of Music," 3, 105,
162n2; *The Positivist Dispute in
German Sociology*, 78, 99;
"Prolog zum Fernsehen," 59, 60,
70, 160n17; "The Psychological
Technique of Martin Luther
Thomas' Radio Addresses," 57;
"Reflexionen zur Klassentheorie,"
6, 153n4; "Die Revidierte
Psychoanalyse," 20, 25, 145n60;
"The Schema of Mass Culture,"
44–45, 127, 150n56, 151n57;
"Sociology and Psychology," 20,
56, 58, 60, 62, 63; "Subject and
Object," 77; "Theory of Pseudo-
Culture," 71, 72, 99, 122;
"Thesen über Bedürfnis"
("Theses on Need"), 25, 34, 62,

185

entertainment, 32, 69, 127, 131
epistemology, 78, 159n9
essentialism, 43–44
Ewen, Stuart, ix
exchange, principle, 27, 29, 114, 122,
 123, 124, 125; value, 28–33, 113
existentialism, 153n2

family, 5, 7, 8, 10, 16, 18, 19, 20, 54,
 57, 74, 153n4
fascism. *See* nazism
father, 4–5, 7, 14–18, 57, 58
fetish, 29, 30, 50, 111, 114, 115, 125
film, 17, 28, 38, 45, 48, 49, 58, 60, 68,
 105, 106, 113, 126
Fiske, John, 35, 152n1, 157n46
formatting (format), 38, 44, 103
Foucault, Michel, 73
freedom, 42, 54, 64, 66, 80, 81, 82,
 88, 89, 90, 92, 93, 95, 96, 97, 98,
 104, 105, 107, 123, 133, 137
Frenkel-Brunswik, Else, 18
Freud, Anna, 59–60
Freud, Sigmund, x, xiii, 4, 9, 21, 25,
 27, 132; and defense mechanisms,
 59; and the ego, 56; and group
 psychology, 13, 17, 153n4; and
 instinct theory, 1–2, 22–23, 140n8;
 and internalization, 54, 154n16;
 and narcissism, xiii, 13–14, 15, 23;
 and the superego, 19, 54
Fromm, Eric, 1, 20, 21, 144n59,
 154n21
Führer. See Hitler, Adolf

Garnham, Nicholas, 36, 37, 49–50,
 112, 126
Gendron, Bernard, 40–41, 43–44
Gesamtkunstwerk, 126
Giner, Salvador, 12
"Godfather, The," 58
gratification. *See* needs, gratification
 of

group psychology, xiii, 13, 15, 16, 17,
 51, 71, 154n4. *See also* mass
 psychology
Grunberger, Béla, 15

Habermas, Jürgen, ix, 4, 9–10, 24, 79,
 92, 93–96, 98, 135, 136, 142n32,
 157n55
Hacker Foundation, ix, 151n57
Hansen, Miriam, 46, 58, 70, 157n48
Haug, Wolfgang, 30, 31, 32, 48
Hegel, G. W. F., 78, 80, 96, 99, 158n3
Held, David, 78
Hilferding, Rudolf, 7
history, of art, 107; of culture
 industry, 33–34, 107
Hitler, Adolf, 2, 22, 100
Hohendahl, Peter, 136
Hollywood, 60, 160n23
Honneth, Axel, 53–54, 55, 63, 65,
 67–68, 73–74, 152n1
Horkheimer, Max, 5, 10, 20, 31, 35,
 39, 49, 55, 69, 86, 91, 93–94, 107,
 111, 124, 127, 143n48, 151n57
Horney, Karen, 1, 154n21
Hoy, David Couzens, 91, 92, 159n9
Hullot-Kentor, Robert, 153n2
Huyssen, Andreas, 50, 70, 74–75, 91,
 106, 110, 111, 117
Hyman, Herbert, and Sheatsley, Paul,
 20

id, 18, 25, 55, 56, 59, 109
identity, 47, 78–79, 80–81, 87–88,
 90, 98, 125. *See also* ideology,
 positivist
ideology, liberal, 72–73, 74, 81, 89,
 96, 124, 133, 134; positivist, 82,
 84–88, 90, 104, 106, 121, 122,
 125, 169n9
ideology critique, 81, 87–88, 90,
 95–98, 99, 100
identification, 14, 15, 19, 54–55,
 154n16

About the Author

Deborah Cook completed her B.A. and M.A. at the University of Ottawa. She received her doctoral degree in philosophy from the Université de Paris I-Panthéon-Sorbonne. Currently, she is Associate Professor of Philosophy at the University of Windsor. Her work has appeared in the *Journal for the Theory of Social Behaviour, British Journal of Aesthetics, Philosophy and Literature,* and *Telos,* among other publications. Her first book is entitled *The Subject Finds a Voice: Foucault's Turn Toward Subjectivity.*

DATE DUE

DEC 1 1 REC'D			
MAY 14 '99 FA			
JAN 1 6 REC'D			
ILL			
5 6 4 747			
JUN 2 8 REC'D			
JUL 0 7 REC'D MAY 1 7 2004 MAY 1 5 REC'D			
DEC 2 3 2005 DEC 1 3 REC'D APR 1 8 2006			
MAR 3 0 REC'D			
NOV 0 8 20 DEC 1 5 2010			